BARRY GOLDWATER

Portrait of an Arizonan

BARRY GOLDWATER

Portrait of an Arizonan

by

EDWIN McDOWELL

HENRY REGNERY COMPANY
CHICAGO 1964

Second Printing, August, 1964
Third Printing, September, 1964

Copyright © 1964 by Henry Regnery Company
Manufactured in the United States of America
Library of Congress Catalog Card Number 64-14594

Dedicated to

CAROLE

SUSIE

and PRUFROCK

Acknowledgments

For their assistance in the preparation of this book I would like to thank: Fritz Marquardt . . . Jack Williams . . . Charles McDowell . . . Robert Early . . . Morrie Ryskind . . . Jim Campaigne . . . James L. Wick . . . Elaine Riker & crew . . . Ivan Mashek & crew . . . and Eleanor Fidler. A special note of thanks is due Bert Fireman, who probably knows more about the Goldwater lineage than any living man.

Whatever merit is reflected in the following pages is due in large measure to the combined efforts of each of the above named. But they are in no manner to be held accountable for any shortcomings in the book. Nor, because each occupies a different point on today's political compass, should it be assumed that they necessarily agree with all or any of the judgments expressed herewithin.

Credit is due Wide World Photo, Inc., for several of the photographs; and I would like especially to thank Herb McLaughlin of Arizona Photographic Associates, Inc., who supplied the bulk of the pictures used.

Contents

CHAPTER 1

The Conservative

*"There is a tide in the affairs
of men
Which, taken at the flood,
leads on to fortune."*
—SHAKESPEARE

THE crowd was on its feet applauding, whistling, and cheering as the convertible entered the stadium from right field. Slowly it circled first base, home plate, third base, and left field, before turning and heading once more toward the infield. Soon thousands of voices were chanting in unison, "We want Barry! We want Barry!"

It was still a long ten months until the Republican National Convention at San Francisco in July, 1964. But to the 42,317 faithful who turned out in Los Angeles' Chavez Ravine for the liveliest Republican rally in southern California political history, there was no doubt about who deserved the GOP presidential nomination: the erect, bronzed figure slowly making his way from the car to the podium near second base, Arizona's Sen. Barry Morris Goldwater.

Barry Goldwater long had been the almost-unanimous choice of both Republican and Democratic conservatives for the presidency. Now suddenly, toward the end of the summer of 1963, it was apparent—from public opinion polls, from polls of political pros, and especially from the indications of deep, enthusiastic support that the Goldwater name had generated

1

from one end of the nation to the other—that Mr. Conservative's widening political appeal was winning him the backing
of voters who only short months before were content to accept
the popular description of conservatives as political anachron-
isms—reactionaries descended from the dodo and the Tyrannosaurus Rex.

The rally in Chavez Ravine was final, irrefutable proof that
Goldwater, as a serious candidate for the GOP nomination,
had indeed arrived. For few major political rallies ever faced
such seemingly-insurmountable odds: For one thing, it was a
Monday evening on a soft September night. But, more important to Los Angeles' sports-mad millions, tonight was Showdown Night for their beloved Dodgers.

Some two weeks earlier the Dodgers, in first place with a
seemingly unbeatable seven game lead, were ready to claim the
National League pennant. But the St. Louis Cardinals won 19
of their next 20 games, extended their longest winning streak in
11 years to 10 games, and pulled within one game and .008 percentage points of Los Angeles. With 12 games remaining in
the regular season, the Dodgers limped into St. Louis' Busch
Stadium for a crucial three-game series, which was to be televised back to Los Angeles. And the opening game coincided
with the Goldwater rally.

But the crowd in Chavez Ravine, although worried about
the Busch Stadium proceedings (the priest who delivered the
invocation ended his prayer with a fervent, "Bless the
Dodgers"), appeared more worried about the future of the
American republic. They cheered mightily when the outfield
scoreboard announced the news that the Dodgers scored two
runs in the ninth inning to win the series opener. But they
cheered even more lustily, and longer, when, just a split second
after the announcement, the Goldwater auto entered the
stadium.

"America needs a change. Freedom needs a chance," Goldwater began, peering out into the blaze of lights from television

cameras trained on him. "Holding the line, preserving the status quo isn't enough. Big talk and little actions aren't enough. A frontier full of ox-cart philosophies isn't enough. This is 20th century America, not the old deal America of the 1930's."

As he talked he warmed up to his subject quickly. This was Goldwater at his best—earnest, convincing, just as his admirers remembered him from previous speeches during the eleven years he had criss-crossed the nation in his self-appointed role as a salesman for conservatism.

Fidgeting with his dark-rimmed glasses, he spoke in a restrained voice, even as he indicted the Democratic administration: "The change we need desperately is a Republican President and a Republican Congress in 1964. We need an administration to serve all the people and not just the big political machines. We need an administration to stand up for America all over the world—to work for freedom all over the world. We need a Republican administration to draw together the real will and the real needs of this nation.

"Pie in the sky for a few isn't enough. Self-respect and opportunity here and now are what Americans want. Not promises, but performances. Not handouts, but jobs. Not a government that takes and takes, but a government that works and works—*with* the people, not *over* the people. We consent to be governed in this great nation. We do not elect to be ruled."

As always, he managed to slip in a plug for conservatism, which he identified with the GOP. "The Republican Party," he remarked, his voice rising ever so slightly, "believes that government is the servant, not the master. That the job you have and hold, that the money you earn and save or spend is the first order of business—and that government's job is to preserve those things, not take them over.

"The Republican Party believes that this is a nation of 50 great states, united in dedication to one great Constitution.

The Republican Party believes that the representatives of those great states, in the Congress, are the key to freedom, not a barrier to it. The Republican Party believes in an executive branch that is an equal partner, not a ruthless boss; in a judicial branch that also is equal and independent, that interprets laws but does not make them."

This speech—interrupted with applause 48 times, according to *Newsweek*'s count—was not just another routine speech for Goldwater; no opportunity to deliver his message is ever routine to the trim, silver-haired, jet-age Senator from America's true frontierland. Since he arrived on the national political scene following an upset victory in 1952, on what he unabashedly claims were Dwight Eisenhower's coattails, the 55-year-old Goldwater has never deviated from his self-imposed mission to "make the word conservative a respectable word."

Few have ever worked harder in behalf of any cause. During the past half-dozen years Barry Goldwater tirelessly has traveled from Atlantic to Pacific, from the Mexican to the Canadian border, delivering his message—sometimes speaking on both coasts the same day. By commercial airplane or flying his own twin-engine Beechcraft Bonanza, by rented auto or in his Corvette Sting-Ray, he has traveled to massive rallies in New York's Madison Square Garden and Detroit's Masonic Temple, to informal coffee sessions in Maine and Nebraska, and to all-Democratic gatherings in the heartland of Dixie, where since Reconstruction no Republican official dared set foot.

Once, when commercial airliners were grounded in El Paso because of high winds and bad weather, Goldwater himself flew a plane to Phoenix in time to keep a scheduled appearance at a Press Club forum and then, a few hours later, to address a graduating class at Phoenix Indian School. On another occasion, after waiting 45 minutes in a rainstorm at a desolate airport at Bagdad, Ariz., he hiked miles down a rocky, muddy road to town—while his welcoming committee huddled in the banquet hall, thinking the Senator was scheduled to arrive by auto.

In each of his more than 400 speeches a year, Barry Goldwater has sought constantly to refurbish the conservative image which became tarnished from decades of partisan attacks and conservative ineptitude. Time and again, just when it seemed that conservatism in the 1950's would finally die of political anemia—particularly after the death of Sen. Robert A. Taft and after the disastrous congressional elections of 1958—it was Goldwater who breathed new life into its moribund body. The Arizona senator, friend and foe alike agree, was the midwife of contemporary conservatism; because of him, what had been only an embattled, abstract theory a decade ago is today a viable political force.

Each day for the past three years has seen Goldwater's Phoenix and Washington offices flooded with letters, telegrams, and phone calls begging the Senator to speak at Oregon Rotary luncheons, before New Jersey businessmen's groups, to Wisconsin women's socials or to South Carolina conservative study groups. And no speaker in America has been more in demand on college campuses during these years.

His thrice-weekly newspaper column, "How Do You Stand, Sir?" appeared in more than 200 newspapers coast to coast. His political credo, *The Conscience of a Conservative* (required reading for history 169b at Harvard University in 1961) has, almost unbelievably, sold more than a million copies (and has been described—probably accurately—as the best-selling book of political philosophy of our century). And Goldwater himself, in what he describes as "the best experience I ever had at a college," spent four days at Yale in 1962 under sponsorship of the Chubb Fellowship (which brings prominent persons in public life to the campus), explaining his beloved conservative philosophy.*

---

* Goldwater's worst experience with a college occurred late in 1962 when the campus newspaper of the University of Colorado carried an article by a student who labeled Goldwater "a fool, a mountebank, a murderer, no better than a common criminal." This was the same university where, seven months earlier, the Young People's Socialist League

Undeniably, the Goldwater charisma has attracted sizeable numbers of converts to conservatism. In an informal poll conducted by M. Stanton Evans, editor of the *Indianapolis News*, students—asked to name the individuals or publications that were most effective in crystallizing their political views—pointed to Barry Goldwater and his book. By summer of 1963, Goldwater, according to the Gallup Poll, commanded a higher proportion of pre-convention votes among Republicans than any conservative candidate in modern political history. And among Independents, those voters whose political views generally fall somewhere outside those of Democrats and Republicans, he more than doubled the mark set by Senator Taft eleven years earlier.

Widespread popular support for Goldwater, which began to be heard a few short weeks before the 1960 GOP nominating convention, can be seen on auto bumper stickers across the land: "Au H_2O_4-64," "Don't Tarry—Back Barry," "We Need a Space Age Candidate—Go Goldwater in '64." In Chicago, enterprising merchants are selling "Gold Water—A Cologne for Americans" at a dollar an ounce. During Labor Day races at Daytona Beach, one of the competing sports cars was decked out with bold "Goldwater in '64" strips on both sides. A Georgia youngster carrying a Goldwater sign picketed the White House . . . with a pet monkey perched on his shoulder. And in Miami, a strip teaser, caught up in the spirit of the times, plied her ecdysiastic trade under the name of Garry Boldwater.

---

and its faculty admirers subjected the Arizonan to worse discourtesy and outright hostility than at any of the more than 250 other colleges he had visited. The university discipline committee termed the libelous tirade "a philosophical point of view," ruling that it "could not be considered a political attack." Ultimately, the university president fired the newspaper editor (although, as the Dean of the University's School of Journalism pointed out, Goldwater did not demand the editor's removal). And the firing subsequently was upheld by a student body vote of better than 2 to 1.

Goldwater backers on California and Indiana campuses sported sweatshirts with a picture of their political hero.* Shapely Arizona and Colorado coeds wore Western-style vests featuring Goldwater's picture and proudly proclaiming "I'm one of Barry's Girls." New York dowagers and Kansas truck drivers arrived at political rallies wearing buttons declaring their support for the Arizonan.

In Amarillo, Tex., copies of special savings account deposit receipts, earmarked for Goldwater once he won the nomination, poured into the post office box of an organization called "Millions of Americans for Goldwater." In Omaha, a pretty 35-year-old mother of three temporarily abandoned the Junior League and other outside activities to form a similar "Gold for Goldwater" organization which quickly spread across country. Under this plan, Goldwater supporters sent checks postdated after the close of the GOP National Convention. The checks were to be held in escrow by a bank, and if the Arizonan were nominated they were to be cashed and sent to his campaign headquarters. Otherwise they were to be burned. A similar trust fund was established in Rockford, Ill.

Enthusiasm for Goldwater, which began as a slight breeze and now seems to be a powerful gale, has engendered a fear psychosis among those who see in the Arizona conservative a nefarious Pied Piper threatening to lead America away from what Goldwater terms liberalism, and all that it has represented —or, in his view, misrepresented—these past three decades. But

---

* One Indianapolis manufacturer ran an ad proclaiming, "You'll delight in watching liberals recoil in terror when they see you in your Barry Goldwater Sweatshirt . . . made in genuine sweat shops." An "anonymous steel company executive" was quoted as saying, "I dreamed I was allowed to make a profit in my Barry Goldwater Sweatshirt." A "Madison Ave. advertising executive" called it "a thinking man's sweatshirt," a "Harvard professor" said he dreamed he was sent to Washington in his. The only hitch, the ad said, was that customers would have to order immediately before the administration forced it to lower its profitable prices.

little of the opposition is as psychotic as *Pravda's* warning that "Goldwater will end up in a pine box," as hysterical as *Tass'* description of him as the leader of America's "wild men," as vicious as the cartoons by the Washington *Post's* "Herblock" (Where Goldwater is labeled "Senator Goldweasel" and, in time-honored Herblock tradition, made to appear a denizen of the underworld), or as outraged as Walter Lippmann's animadversion that Goldwater "is a roaring reactionary" whose possible candidacy "strikes at the heart of the American party system."

Surprisingly, much of the opposition has been downright humorous. For example: Sen. Hubert Humphrey's quip that Goldwater is so handsome that 18th Century Fox wanted him for a screen test. Or the description, during the "doll game" fad, of the Goldwater doll which, when wound, walks backwards. Or the claim that Goldwater's watch goes "tock-tick." Or that the Goldwater bird flies only on the right wing.

Some critics accuse Goldwater of wanting to repeal the 20th century. Others display bumper stickers proclaiming: "Goldwater in 1864," "Bury Goldwater," or "FeS$_2$" (the formula for iron pyrites, known as "fools' gold"). And, until the Goldwater family sold the Arizona specialty stores almost two years ago, a favorite anti-Goldwater bumper sticker read, "Back to the store in '64."

Liberal Republican Sen. Jacob Javits commented that Goldwater "satisfies the American longing for the five cent cigar." Sen. Wayne Morse asked that Goldwater be nominated "so the people could have a clear choice between progress and Neanderthalism." And bumper stickers inspired by a Herblock cartoon (which *Time* described as one of the lowest blows of his editorial cartooning career) feature a scowling Goldwater saying, "If you had any initiative you'd go out and inherit a department store."

In the face of these and other less humorous attacks, Barry Goldwater adopted an impregnable defense: He merely laughed at himself as quickly and as loudly as did his enemies. He thought it uproariously funny when Washington newsmen lampooned him at the 1961 Gridiron Club dinner with the following song (to the tune of "There's Gonna Be a Great Day"):

"Let's move to the right
I'm here to lead your fight,
There's gonna be a great day.

"Put away your fears,
Watch me roll back the years,
Then it will be a great day."

In February of 1963, he saw the "Dime a Dozen" show at Julius Monk's Plaza 9 in New York, listened to a satirical rendition of "Barry's Boys," then went backstage afterwards to congratulate the cast and speak of an America where performers can make fun of the President or a Senator without fear of reprisals. ("The show was funny as could be," he remembered. "It was refreshing to see young people with a new idea.")

The following month he led the laughter at the 78th annual dinner of the Washington Gridiron Club in the Statler-Hilton when the performers, depicting Goldwater and New York Gov. Nelson Rockefeller, sang the following duet:

"Could I run with you?
Could you run with me
Could we run with two
Different as we?
We're a ticket they would care for
We're a slate they'd say a prayer for.

"You are on the right
On the left I'd be
With the two of us

Hopes bright would be.
Robert Welch will surely love you
Liberals will go for me."

And the following month he joined an overflow crowd in laughing at the needle-sharp ribbing dished out to him by the Washington P. T. Barnum tent of the Circus Saints and Sinners Club. He was especially amused when a clown wandered through the large luncheon room depicting Goldwater as a "major general in the Colonial Army."

It was something new in Washington—a politician who not only could dish it out but could take it as well . . . and could make himself the brunt of jokes. During a speech to Washington's Alpha Club, the audience was delighted by his lambent wit when he proclaimed: "I think I'm in the American tradition. I was born in a log cabin, which I had moved to Phoenix, and except for some air conditioning, a swimming pool, a bowling alley, a bar, a shooting range, and a golf course, it remains the simple log cabin it always was." Even those who dismiss Goldwater's views as "quaint," or "ante-deluvian," are impressed with his refusal to take himself too seriously.

In fact, Goldwater has been able to obtain a hearing even from those critics whose disagreement with his political views runs from mild to almost pathological. William S. White wrote in *Harper's*, "Here in Goldwater is an absolutely *honest* politician." James Reston, writing in the *New York Times*, said of Goldwater: "He is an honest conservative. He is attractive personally." The *Washington Post*'s Jules Duscha praised Goldwater's "pleasant personality," and added: "He is quick with a quip, as bright a conservative as Robert A. Taft was ponderous." William E. Bohn, writing in *The New Leader*, said, "No one who falls within the circle of the Senator's warm personality can resist being personally impressed by him." Syndicated liberal columnist Max Freedman observed: "A political figure is entitled to respect when he speaks his convictions without an eye on the Gallup Poll and without servile fear of popu-

lar prejudice. Senator Goldwater certainly passes that test."
And NBC's Chet Huntley praised Goldwater before a Phoenix
audience, saying, "Barry Goldwater has said some things which
no slick politician would dream of saying."

Most surprising of all, perhaps, was the assessment of Goldwater by Karl E. Meyer, editorial writer for the strongly anti-
Goldwater *Washington Post*. Writing in *The Progressive*
almost three years ago, Meyer spoke of the "stoutness and general decency of his character." Goldwater, Meyer said, "*cares*
about principles . . . fights cleanly and has usually shown a
scrupulous regard for the rules of the game." He is "a decent,
upright and thoroughly attractive politician."

But it is not solely because Goldwater is a politician, or even a
principled politician, that he has successfully taken the conservatism of Burke, or Madison, or Jefferson, and made it come
to life in thousands of cities and towns across the United States
. . . breeding conservatism out of the dead political landscape.
Nor is it because of his favorable character traits that those who
see in conservatism the negation of all the works and days of
liberal hands have been content to snipe from the sidelines,
rather than wheel up the big artillery and stalk him as though
he were the Hound of Hell.

It is principally because in the past critics could afford to
tolerate the Arizona anomaly, for there seemed little or no
chance that his philosophy ever would appeal to more than an
insignificant few in either party. However, now that Goldwater
has, almost singlehandedly, shifted the Republican Party to
the terrain of the right, after it aimlessly drifted during eight
years of Eisenhower Modern Republicanism, his supporters
think it unlikely that the critics will remain as tolerant.

In one sense, however, the critics may be too late. Whereas
for years there was little organized opposition in Congress to
liberal ideology, and then only to occasional, specific bills, today there is a strong core of conservative thought, especially in
the House of Representatives. Here some two dozen unabashedly conservative "Young Turks" ("Goldwater conservatives"

is the way some of them bill themselves) are fighting an effective delaying action, awaiting reinforcements from other "Goldwater conservatives" who are entering public life in increasing numbers. And these "Young Turks" are philosophical conservatives—not the stereotyped "Southern conservative" who too often rubberstamps every liberal spending proposal in sight and is "conservative" only when it comes to denying Negroes civil or political rights or blindly opposing labor unions.

Above all, it is the Goldwater personality, the Goldwater dynamism—in short, the Goldwater *image* (a word that makes him uncomfortable)—that has focused the nation's attention on Mr. Conservative, making him perhaps the only genuine grass roots presidential candidate of this century. As much as rock-ribbed conservatives may not like to admit it (naturally preferring to think that conservative ideas rather than a conservative personality accounts for conservative catechumens), it is the man himself who has managed to cut across political party lines in his constant appeal to the nation to check the power of centralized government.

It is the man himself who has proved the emptiness of charges that conservatives are troglodytes and reactionaries, by whizzing cross country faster than the speed of sound, by driving gadget-loaded sports cars, by being acclaimed Phoenix's "Man of the Year" (1949), by being named the best-dressed man in public life by the Fashion Foundation of America (1962), and by winning the Distinguished Service Medallion of the Phoenix Regional Board of the National Conference of Christians and Jews (1962).

In short, it is Barry Morris Goldwater who has demonstrated that conservatism is not synonymous with high-button shoes, Model T's. or the starched collar. And it is he, more than any of his contemporaries, who has convinced independent voters that the conservative idea of Elysium does not nostalgically envision Calvin Coolidge as President, Mark Hanna as Secretary of State, and Jay Gould as Secretary of the Treasury.

CHAPTER 2

The Candidate

---

*"No army can withstand the strength
of an idea whose time has come."*
—VICTOR HUGO

E ARLY in the fall of 1963 the loquacious Cassius Marcellus Clay journeyed to Detroit to recite poetry at a rock-'n-roll show. At that time the Louisville Lip was riding high. He had just cut a record—long play, naturally—of his more notable poems. The *Yale Literary Magazine*, not long before, had bestowed upon him the Ephraim Barnard Gates award for having done the most for poetry during the past year or two. And Clay, who modestly dubbed himself "the double greatest, the handsomest boxer of them all," was at that time undefeated in XIX professional fights, XVI of which he won by knockouts. Furthermore, this Bard of Boxing had demonstrated an uncanny ability to call the round in which his opponents would land on Dream Street.

There may have been room for debate as to whether this pugilist (how the sensitive ear of a poet would blanch at the word "boxer"!) really did more for poetry than, say, T. S. Eliot, the late William Carlos Williams and Robert Frost, or Randall Jarrell. Or even Allen Ginsberg! But there was absolutely no doubt but what Clay was the idol of the Common Man everywhere.

It is easy, then, to imagine the fear that passed through Goldwater supporters when a reporter cornered Clay in George Romney's home state and asked, "What do you think of Barry Goldwater's chances?" Clay, for once, was silent. Then, forsaking dithyrambs, heptameter, and iambic pentameter, he replied in his finest prose style, "I never heard of him."

When the reporter persisted, Clay admitted that he knew little about politics, that his interests were purely poetic and pugilistic. Only then did stunned Goldwater hopefuls revive, dismissing Clay's answer as mere poetic license.

Yet if Cassius Clay, as late as the fall of 1963, had not heard of Barry Goldwater—and there is reason to believe he was being deliberately evasive, wisely preferring not to mix eclogue and elections—he was one of the few who hadn't. Months earlier the Gallup Poll showed that 58 per cent of Americans interviewed knew of the Arizona Senator. And during the intervening months the Goldwater name had become as much a household word as . . . as even Cassius Clay's.

Goldwater supporters, now anticipating his candidacy for the GOP presidential nomination, were distributing pro-Goldwater bumper stickers, pens, imitation straw hats, and handkerchiefs at an ever-increasing pace. An enterprising Texan had dreamed up Draft Goldwater auto license frames, and a bridge set of playing cards, complete with Goldwater's picture on the back, was selling briskly for $2.50. But Goldwater remained indifferent to efforts to force him to declare his candidacy. And he continued to joke about his conservatism. "Many predict I might make our finest Civil War President," he told a group of cartoonists on one occasion. On another, he graciously accepted the mock-nomination bestowed on him by the Alfalfa Club of Washington, adding that "When I'm sworn in . . . Earl Warren . . . will no doubt regard this act as a violation of his oath of office. . . ."

When, on January 3, Goldwater finally announced his decision to seek the Republican presidential nomination, he did so only after considerable soul-searching. In fact, it is probably accurate to say that no serious candidate ever was more reluctant to declare for the presidency.

This is not to suggest that Goldwater doubted that he would like to be President, or even a serious contender for the presidency. As he said during a news conference in Hartford, Conn. last October, "Any man would be a damned liar if he said he wouldn't accept the Republican nomination if it were offered by the convention." But in Goldwater's case two major obstacles loomed. The first, and most apparent, was underscored by Stewart Alsop, who wrote in *The Saturday Evening Post*:

"Let us try to imagine a politician with no chance whatever of becoming President of the United States.

"First, let us suppose that our man is a junior Senator from a small state with a mere five electoral votes, and that he is half Jewish. No such politician has ever been nominated for the Presidency, much less elected.

"Then, just to make sure that our man hasn't a prayer, let us suppose that he has consistently taken positions nicely calculated to alienate *all* the major voting blocs in the country—labor, the aged, the teachers, the Negroes, the subsidized farmers, all the beneficiaries of the welfare state, the liberal-minded independent voters, and finally, just to make doubly sure, the inhabitants of the entire East Coast."

Except for the fact that Goldwater's positions were not "calculated" to alienate anyone or any vote bloc—the essence of Goldwater's domestic program is a common sense appeal to *all* Americans as Americans, regardless of their status as a minority—the statement accurately pointed out the odds facing Goldwater. Until it became apparent that the groundswell for Goldwater *was* deep and *did* cut across bloc lines, the Arizona maverick could not afford to let himself be carried away by the tumult and the shouting. "Nobody from a state as small as Arizona is ever going to get the nomination," he said early last year. "I just don't think it's in the political cards."

For, political realist that he is, Goldwater was well aware
of Taft's charge, after his defeat at the 1952 nominating convention, that, "Every Republican candidate for President since
1936 has been nominated by the Chase Bank." Taft, of course,
was speaking metaphorically, although his meaning was unmis-
takable. Yet the realization that chairman of the board of the
Chase Manhattan Bank was David Rockefeller, brother of the
liberal New York Governor who also had his eye on the GOP
nomination, could scarcely be expected to comfort the Goldwater camp.

The second major obstacle facing Goldwater was, in fact, a
series of considerations involving conservatism. In replying to
a Gallup Poll last fall, respondents—asked to identify themselves as either liberal or conservative—were just about evenly
divided (51 to 49 per cent, in favor of the conservatives). But
as Goldwater readily understood, it is one thing to designate
oneself conservative, and quite another to vote for a conservative candidate. Especially when the dividing line on major issues is often so easily obscured during an election campaign.

Therefore, a major Goldwater consideration was what effect
his candidacy would have on conservatism. "If I were nominated and got the living hell beat out of me," he said, "it might
end the conservative movement in this country, or at least
retard it seriously." What he had to decide, Goldwater said,
was whether he could win or at least run a close enough race
to bring into Congress a sufficient number of conservatives to
"slow down the liberal express train."

It seemed, then, as though Goldwater was one of the few
persons in the country who harbored doubts about his political
appeal. As early as last summer it became apparent that the
Democrats had singled him out as the leading Republican presidential candidate. In an analysis written last July, the *Washington Post*'s Edward T. Folliard reported that the administration was giving serious attention to the presidential boom for
Goldwater. "Some of the top New Frontiersmen say that the

Arizona conservative could win the Republican nomination for President in 1964," Folliard reported. "They also say they would expect a 'tough fight' if Goldwater is chosen."

A more dependable tip-off, at least as far as Democratic sources were concerned, came later that month when Sen. William Fulbright, columnist Walter Lippmann, and the AFL-CIO's Committee on Political Education (COPE), simultaneously launched a free-swinging assault on Goldwater. Lippmann, as *Time* observed, "practically excommunicated Goldwater from the GOP as one whose 'philosophy is radically opposed to the central traditions of the Republican Party.' " He warned that if Goldwater "were to win the election, which is conceivable but unlikely, we should face dangerous days of reaction at home and jingoism abroad."

COPE devoted most of its four-page biweekly newsletters to the identical theme, and sought also to link the head of the National Draft Goldwater Committee to the right-wing John Birch Society.

Senator Fulbright, in a speech dripping with sarcasm, attempted to associate Goldwater with the anti-coexistence policies of Red China: "I am confident that no fair-minded American will misinterpret the interesting parallel between the Senator's views . . . and those of the Chinese Communists. The Senator, without doubt, is a loyal and patriotic American."

But the Arkansas Democrat skipped hurriedly over Goldwater's loyalty and patriotism, charging instead that the Arizonan "has stated unequivocally that he favors boldness and courage and determination over craven coexistence. These words, of course, are a bit vague and the Senator has not yet seen fit to translate them into specific proposals for a bold and courageous foreign policy.* But perhaps we can speculate. Both the United States and the Soviet Union possess hydrogen bombs and intercontinental missiles with which to destroy each

---

* Goldwater was to "spell out" his specific foreign policy the following January in *Life* magazine.

other's societies. Neither has the means of preventing the other from doing so. Under these circumstances the only alternative to coexistence is mutual destruction. This, perhaps, is the key to the foreign policy by the Senator from Arizona, a bold, courageous, and determined policy of co-annihilation."

This attempt to link Goldwater with far right extremists and to paint him as a reckless man bent on plunging the globe into nuclear war, was, of course, all part of the developing Democratic strategy for the 1964 campaign—a strategy *Life* was aware of when it editorialized, "Goldwater is neither an isolationist nor a warmonger and should not have to answer to either charge." And Ohio's conservative Representative John M. Ashbrook was also aware of that strategy when he introduced into the Congressional Record the following parody, written by a group of Young Republicans:

Mine ears have heard the horrors of the militant extreme,
I've been told about their tennis shoes and eyes that madly gleam.
They are armed and more fanatical than you would ever dream,
I'll track down every one.

CHORUS

Glory be, there goes another. Glory be, there goes another,
Glory be, there goes another. I'll track down every one.

Extremists are the people to the right of Chester Bowles,
For they don't believe in giving in to socialism's goals.
They don't even favor foreign aid to Yugoslavs or Poles,
I'll track down every one.

(Repeat chorus)

I've found them underneath my bed, I've seen them near and far,
I have spotted them at caucuses and seen them in the bar.
They control the Y.A.F. and they control the C.Y.R.
I'll track down every one.

(Repeat chorus)

They are hiding in my closet, they are always in my way,
They are lurking in the hallways—I saw 54 today.
They are spying on our meetings til my hair is turning gray,
I'll track down every one.

(Repeat chorus)

I am not afraid of Commies, for their numbers are so small,
But extremists come in millions, and each one is 10 feet tall.
Yes, extremists total millions, and are patriotic, all,
I'll track down every one.

(Repeat chorus)

Exposing them in public was a brilliant thing to do,
Now the *People's World* adores me, and the *Nation* loves me, too.
But extremists have to get their praise from *National Review*,
I'll track down every one.

(Repeat chorus)

It was obvious that Goldwater was causing restless nights in the Democratic camp. At a meeting of some 300 Western state Democratic leaders in Salt Lake City in September, Idaho's Sen. Frank Church, keynote speaker at the 1960 nominating convention, told assembled delegates, "You may wonder why I have chosen to discuss the candidacy of Sen. Barry Goldwater, a man with whom I differ politically, but who is personally my friend. The reason is simple enough. It is the Goldwater brand of Republicanism against which we Democrats must prepare to wage the coming campaign."

Shortly afterward, in what was billed as a five-day, 10,000-mile non-political conservation tour through eleven Western states, President Kennedy, two months before his assassination, finally acknowledged the Goldwater ascending star. In a speech in the Mormon Tabernacle in Salt Lake City, the President conveniently forgot the problems of conservation and tore into critics of his foreign policy, especially—the press agreed almost unanimously—critic Goldwater. From then on the eyes of the nation increasingly turned toward Goldwater, the implausible candidate from a politically insignificant state. Before long every major magazine and most major newspapers had reporters crawling all over the Arizona landscape, seeking clues to the sudden emergence of a politician who had seemingly defied every rule in the political handbook, and yet despite—or perhaps because of—this was attracting a deep nationwide following.

If non-conservatives had difficulty understanding the sudden rise in Goldwater's political fortunes ("The Goldwater balloon is going up so fast that it is almost out of sight of this fog-bound capital," wrote Marquis Childs last September), their bewilderment was not shared by Goldwater partisans. To them the wonder was that it had taken so long for the rest of the nation to discover the Arizona Senator. During a speech in Chicago last summer he drew the state's top GOP brass, including all three candidates for Governor. (Among them was Charles Percy, youthful president of Bell & Howell, who was generally credited—or blamed—with having played a decisive role in affixing a liberal seal to the 1960 GOP party platform.) Pennsylvania's Sen. Hugh Scott, long known as a liberal, warmly praised his Arizona colleague during a party fund-raising rally in Hershey, Pa. New Hampshire's Sen. Norris Cotton, the state's foremost Republican (and a man who supported Dwight D. Eisenhower against Senator Taft in his state's 1952 presidential primary), spurned Nelson Rockefeller's request for endorsement and chose Goldwater, saying: "He has fought courageously and unceasingly for a philosophy of government and a way of life to which this nation was dedicated and to which it must return if it is to endure."

On the 4th of July, while Parade Marshal Goldwater (dressed in Levis, a faded blue shirt, and a gray cowboy hat, and sitting atop a Palomino) was cheered by some 20,000 persons lining the streets of Prescott, Arizona during the 76th annual Frontier Days celebration, conservatives arrived in Washington, D.C., by special trains, planes, and buses. An estimated 9,000 of them packed the Washington National Armory for a National Draft Goldwater Independence Day Rally. Among those on hand to boost his candidacy were Arizona Gov. Paul Fannin, Nebraska Sen. Carl T. Curtis, Texas Sen. John Tower, Ohio Rep. John Ashbrook, and celebrities Walter Brennan, Chill Wills, William Lundigan, and Efrem Zimbalist, Jr. As the crowd lustily cheered every mention of the Goldwater name, scores of young "Goldwater Girls," dressed in red, white, and blue, passed among the throng collecting funds for the National Draft Goldwater Committee.

Earlier that same week, delegates to the biennial convention of the Young Republican National Federation elected as president an avowed Goldwater supporter, and they cheered the Arizona Senator so long and so fervently at the completion of his speech that the organist was forced to play "God Bless America" to quiet the crowd. (Drew Pearson, who in his columns regularly has sounded the death knell of conservatism these many years, was so upset by the pro-Goldwater sentiment that he warned ominously about "Fascist tactics used by Goldwaterites" at the convention.)

Last May 9, Goldwater's Republican colleagues gave a $1,000-a-plate dinner in his honor, in appreciation of his three two-year terms as chairman of the Republican Senatorial Campaign Committee—in which capacity he raised millions of dollars (the testimonial dinner alone netted the Party $357,000) and campaigned tirelessly for both liberal and conservative GOP Senate candidates.

A year later, in March, 1962, more than 18,000 persons had paid their way into Madison Square Garden for a rally sponsored by the conservative political organization Young Americans for Freedom. When Goldwater was introduced, the crowd gave him a five minute standing ovation; red, white, and blue balloons were released from overhead, Goldwater banners were unfurled, and the audience sang two choruses of the "Battle

Hymn of the Republic" (which were notable more for their gusto than their euphony). Not all rallies for Goldwater were as well organized or well attended, of course. Yet ever since the summer of 1960, when he put aside his personal disappointment with the Republican platform to work for the Nixon-Lodge ticket, Goldwater has been second in demand only to Presidents Kennedy and Johnson as a speaker and fund raiser.

If any one date can be said to mark the turning point in the political fortunes of Goldwater, that date almost surely would have to be July 27, 1960. For it was on that night, while the cameras of all three television networks were trained on Chicago's Convention Hall, that Arizona Gov. Paul Fannin rose to address the delegates assembled for the GOP National Convention. Near the conclusion of his brief remarks he said the action he was about to take "was contrary to the wishes of a man who has been my friend since boyhood." Then he added: "There are moments in history when power is given to a man to do what is right for his fellow men. . . . Mr. Chairman, I place in nomination for the office of President of the United States a man with the courage of heroes, United States Senator Barry Goldwater of Arizona."

For the next eleven minutes, while the cameras alternately focused on snake-dancing delegates and on Goldwater's wife and 16-year-old daughter, both weeping unashamed tears of pride while viewing the scene from their box seats above the convention floor, the auditorium was a bedlam of Goldwater placards, of ear-splitting shouts and cheers for the Arizonan. The demonstration had not subsided perceptibly when George Murphy, producer of the convention, ruled that time was running out.

Time, in fact, had run out on that Goldwater boom, even before the Senator entered Convention Hall. Earlier in the day Goldwater invited to his hotel room the Arizona delegates and those Arizonans who had journeyed to Chicago to demonstrate their fealty to their favorite son. He spoke of the pride and happiness he felt for the thousands of telegrams and phone calls that had been sent urging his candidacy. But he added: "I don't want to hoodwink you. We can't win this one on rumors or 3,000 telegrams. Those aren't delegate votes. So far, I've got enough rumors to be elected king. But it's my neck and the neck of the conservative cause. I'm not going to stick out either of them unless I'm assured of support from at least 300 delegates."

"Furthermore," he said, "we can't expect to change these delegates in three days. It can't be done. But if we work hard between now and 1964, maybe we can do something then."

Goldwater, without any organization except the zeal of his politically inexperienced partisans, and bereft of funds, knew that the well-organized Nixon machine would roll over him in record time, even if he could depend on the 280 first ballot votes that had been pledged to him. And he realized that the defeat would reflect badly on conservatism. As he told the press afterwards, "I'll be damned if I was going to let the liberal columnists crow over Goldwater's handful of votes."

Moreover, when he journeyed to Chicago, Goldwater entertained no illusions about wresting the nomination from Nixon, who in effect had clinched it eight years earlier. Nor did he envision himself a serious Vice-Presidential candidate—even though a poll released three months earlier by *Human Events* disclosed that Republican county chairmen preferred him for the Vice-Presidency over Henry Cabot Lodge, and even though a poll of Young Republicans disclosed that Goldwater was strongly favored over Rockefeller for the Vice-Presidency.

His purpose in going to Chicago was simply to exert conservative influence on those responsible for drafting the party platform. More than 18 months before the convention Goldwater warned a Republican National Committee meeting in Des Moines, "Let the Republican Party quit copying the New Deal, seeking only for votes, and remember that a two-party system needs two philosophies, not just one." The party platform Goldwater proposed offered a philosophy decidedly at odds with that embraced by the Democrats. When he submitted it to the Republican Platform Committee on July 19, he commented that in recent years platforms had become a catch-all of detailed but ambiguous promises, designed to please everyone and offend no one. They are loosely worded in order not to bind the party to any definite course of action, he said. Furthermore, no successful political party, even when in control of the Presidency and Congress, ever even attempted to pass all the legislation suggested by the platform promises.

The result, in Goldwater's view, was that the American people had become either cynical or indifferent with respect to the platforms. He felt the GOP would do well to eliminate platforms similar to those issued in the past: "I suggest the American people will be far more eager to place their destiny in the hands of a man who announces his beliefs and his principles," he said, "than in the hands of a man who promises and promises and promises."

Goldwater's "Suggested Declaration of Republican Principles" rejected the notion of a planned stalemate in the war against Communism and declared, "victory must be our goal." It proposed that the party condemn deficit financing and work toward a sound and balanced budget. It condemned "30 years of federal tinkering and interference in the lives of the American farmers." It affirmed the principle of voluntary unionism, while concomitantly condemning "the concentration of power in the hands of a few unconscionable men . . . those self-seekers who have sought to distort the legitimate labor union movement in this country and create an instrument of political and economic power—to be directed against the consumers, producers, and the public."

It concluded:

"We believe that any government or political system which seeks to level all men to a common standard of achievement by penalizing ability, initiative and thrift, is guilty of opposing

God's will and our expressed recognition of the source of our freedoms.

"We believe any society which proposes to relieve its citizens of all responsibility—and thus condemn them to a state of perpetual childhood—is acting contrary to the best purposes for mankind.

"We believe every man is entitled to an equal position on the starting line in the race for personal achievement. But no man is to be guaranteed a preferred position at the finish line. . . .

"We believe that to tell men cynically they can get something for nothing is wrong, that to buy votes by legislating benefits for some at the expense of others is wrong, that to incite the envy of one group of citizens for another is wrong, that downgrading those virtues of thrift, honesty, self-reliance and reverence for the wisdom of tradition is to court disaster.

"Our aim is to achieve justice for all men, to require responsible citizen participation in the affairs of government; to support voluntarism rather than compulsion; pluralism rather than centralization; and freedom rather than a controlled, falsely paternalistic government."

Goldwater was wise enough to realize the platform would not be adopted *in toto*. Nevertheless, he felt that if the Party adopted enough of it to give the GOP a decidedly conservative tone, in contrast to the Democratic platform (which lifetime Democrat James F. Byrnes, a former governor and secretary of state, described as "the most dangerous program adopted by a political party"), it would appeal to millions of non-voters who Goldwater believed were basically conservative but stayed away from the polls because they discerned so little difference between the two parties that they saw no point in voting. But on the morning of the convention, while the platform committee was busy hammering out what Goldwater had reason to expect would be a platform satisfactory to conservatives, he was told that Nixon had made a secretive convention-eve visit to the New York apartment of Nelson Rockefeller.

Goldwater was stunned . . . and infuriated. He knew the trip could have only one purpose—to enlist Rockefeller's support in exchange for a party platform oriented toward his brand of liberalism. No other interpretation made sense. For up until then, Rockefeller deliberately had withheld endorsement of Nixon as the presidential nominee; furthermore he had hinted that he would force a floor fight unless the platform was liberalized—"modified" is the term he used—to his satisfaction. Thus, when he heard about Nixon's trip, Goldwater understood that whatever hopes he had for even a moderately conservative platform now depended solely on the extent of the Nixon-Rockefeller rapprochement.

Nixon's furtive action, Goldwater said, constituted a "surrender." Rockefeller, he charged, "is out to destroy the Republican Party." When newsmen pressed him further he labeled the meeting "a Munich," saying that the trip "can be interpreted in no other way than as a bid to appease the Republican left."

Goldwater's disappointment was understandable, yet while he refused on principle to second Nixon's nomination, he realized that the vague Nixon-Rockefeller platform was closer to his philosophy than was the Democratic platform. Therefore, as his nomination was being seconded by Texas' Bruce Alger, South Carolina's Greg Shorey, South Dakota's L. R. Houck, and his own state's Rep. John J. Rhodes, Goldwater glanced hurriedly through his prepared remarks. Then, as the television cameras prepared to carry his message into millions of homes, he strode quickly to the microphones and said emphatically: "Mr. Chairman, delegates to the convention, and fellow Republicans: I respectfully ask the chairman to withdraw my name from nomination."

When Goldwater supporters in the Convention Hall remonstrated, he held up a hand to quiet them. "Please," he said, "I release my delegation from their pledge to me and while I'm not a delegate I would suggest that they give these votes to Richard Nixon."

Many of his more enthusiastic supporters felt betrayed. But, staring into the cameras, Goldwater appealed directly to conservatives by pointing out what he was to say again and again during the next few months: namely, that although the Republican platform left much to be desired, it was infinitely better than the platform adopted by the Democrats.

"We've had our chance, and I think the conservatives have made a splendid showing at this convention," he said. "We've had our chance. We've fought our battle. Now let's put our shoulders to the wheels of Dick Nixon and push him across the line. Let's not stand back. This country is too important for anyone's feelings: this country in its majesty is too great for any man, be he conservative or liberal, to stay home and not work just because he doesn't wholly agree. Let's grow up conservatives. Let's, if we want to, take this party back—and I think we can someday. Let's get to work."

And get to work he did. He wrote articles telling conservatives why they should support Nixon. He went on radio and television to drum up support for a ticket whose leader had disappointed him deeply by journeying to New York. And he raised large sums of money from conservatives who were reluctant to contribute to what they considered a liberal Republican Party. Between the convention and election day the supererogatory Goldwater made 126 speeches in 26 states on behalf of Nixon-Lodge. As the *Wall Street Journal* noted, he criss-crossed the country in hectic 18-hour and 20-hour days. He spoke in shopping centers and ball parks, before 20,000 at an ox roast in Portland, Ore. and before 50 business leaders at a fund-raising dinner arranged by Nelson Rockefeller.

And when it was over, although Nixon and Lodge lost the election, the Republican Party had uncovered a rutilant, new political personality—a crusading conservative from a sleepy southwestern state.

CHAPTER 3

The Pioneers

"Conquering, holding, daring, venturing
as we go the unknown ways,
Pioneers! O pioneers!"
—WALT WHITMAN

IN 1851, Horace Greeley advised in his *New York Tribune*, "Go West, young man." No one doubts the prescience of Greeley, at that time the most influential editor in America. But the West he had in mind was Erie, Pennsylvania, some 440 miles west of Manhattan. (It was later discovered that he was merely repeating what John Babsone Lane Soule had expressed earlier that year in the *Terre Haute* (Ind.) *Express*.) To thousands of Americans, however, it seemed like sound advice—and had seemed so for some time. For already an innumerable caravan was rolling westward—not just to Erie, but as far west as that wild and largely uninhabited land of California.

And no wonder. For just three years earlier James Marshall, a carpenter employed to construct a sawmill not far from a fort belonging to John A. Sutter—a German immigrant who embraced Mexican citizenship and then acquired vast land holdings in the Sacramento Valley—discovered flakes of gold in the millrace. Sutter, who had endeared himself to weary travelers stumbling into his fort after the perilous trip across the Sierra Nevadas, did his best to keep the news secret. For he knew an army of prospectors would soon invade his property and upset his dream of building an independent state called New Helvetia. But news of the discovery leaked out, and within months people all over the world were repeating tales of how the golden nuggets were just waiting to be picked out of California stream beds. President Polk, in his annual message to Congress, confirmed the news . . . and the lure of gold touched men, women, and children from every corner of the earth.

Sailors jumped ship in San Francisco Bay to join the gold rush. Soldiers deserted army posts. Farmers mortgaged their farms, pioneers deserted their clearings, and clerks swapped their desks for a pick, a shovel, a wash-pan, and a bedroll.

Many (45,000 in 1849 alone) came overland by covered wagon along the "trail of the moldering ox"—so named because the gold-obsessed settlers didn't tarry long enough even to bury oxen and other animals that died along the way. Others made the eight-month sea voyage around Cape Horn. (In 1851 the new, trim clipper "Flying Cloud" sailed from New York to San Francisco via Cape Horn in a record 89 days, eight hours, but its performance was a notable exception.) Thousands of others, undaunted by the twin threats of yellow fever and malaria, sailed to Panama, paid as high as five dollars for the privilege of walking the 50 miles across the Isthmian jungle in the relative safety of the uncompleted Panama Railroad Co. right-of-way, then boarded another ship which would carry them to California for the completion of their two-month journey.

As the '49ers pushed westward, Congress, on March 3, 1849, authorized the coinage of gold dollars. Bayard Taylor, an adventurous Pennsylvania Quaker on the staff of Greeley's *Tribune*, journeyed to California and wrote two volumes about the gold fever, which he titled *El Dorado*—a name (from the Spanish, meaning "the gilded") perhaps inspired by Edgar Allan Poe's poem of the same name a year earlier. And Sutter, as he had feared, was victimized by newcomers who claimed that his land claim papers were defective. He died a pauper in Washington, trying to reclaim his former holdings.

In one three-month period in 1849, some 1,200 adventurers were said to have sailed from the East for California. San Francisco, which in 1840 had only 500 inhabitants, had some 35,000 by the end of 1850. Law and order were almost non-existent. A fire in December, 1849—one of six fires in San Francisco within 18 months—destroyed more than a million dollars' worth of property, mostly tents and shanties housing the new-comers. And a group of Australian ex-convicts, known as the "Sidney Ducks," roamed the streets robbing and killing. (In the early '50's there were nearly 1,000 murders and only one conviction, despite the formation in 1851 of the San Francisco Vigilance Committee, organized to preserve order.)

Prices skyrocketed almost out of sight. Eggs sold for ten dollars a dozen. A shot of whiskey cost a pinch of gold dust, a bottle sold for $100. Coffee sold for four dollars a pound, flour cost $400 a barrel. In this frontier melting pot, according to historians Morison and Commager, Englishmen and Frenchmen, Yankees and Hoosiers, Georgia crackers and Missouri pikers rubbed shoulders with Indians, Mexicans, and the "heathen Chinee" (who first arrived in California in 1848). Fortunes were made in the gold-diggings, only to be lost in a night at a 'Frisco faro palace; much more was made by speculation in goods and land.

Still the adventurers flocked westward. In 1848, California had fewer than 15,000 white inhabitants; ten years later the population was a half-million, and growing. And, as they made their way to what they hoped would be El Dorado, the pioneers sang "Nelly Bly" and an updated version of "Oh! Susanna"—

> "Oh! California,
> That's the land for me;
> I'm off for Sacramento
> With a washbowl on my knee."

The London newspapers, like newspapers everywhere, were filled with stories of the gold bonanza. Michel Goldwasser had read about the discovery and, if only briefly, had given some thought to the new land across the Atlantic. Who hadn't? But he already had two children by that time and was reasonably well established as a tailor. Besides, he was tired of traveling. In the four years since he had left his native Konin, in the province of Poznan after the third partition of Poland, he had been to Paris (where he mastered the tailor's trade before the French Revolution sent him sailing across the English Channel) and then to London. Here he married Sarah Nathan. And here on his marriage certificate appears, for the first time, the name of Goldwater.

No one knows why Michel left Konin. It may merely have been wanderlust, or it may have been that life was difficult for the supposed 22 children of Hirsch Goldwasser. Or it may have been anti-Semitism, that constant companion of eastern European Jews, which drove him toward the large cities, where he felt he could overcome the restrictions of ghetto and discrimination. One can only guess, for little is known about the Goldwassers of Konin. Family records, even now being added to by searches in Poland on behalf of the Arizona Historical Foundation, are insufficient to establish the truth about the 22 children. But a Jewish community is known to have existed in Konin as early as 1412. In 1765 there were 133 Jewish taxpayers. In 1856 there were 2,006 Jews and 3,141 Christians. And the census of 1897 shows a Jewish population of 2,502 out of a total population of 8,522.

Hirsch Goldwasser was a publican, a loose term generally used to describe one who was both an innkeeper and a storekeeper. Little else is known about him, other than the fact that he could not write. At that time Yiddish, Polish, and Russian were all acceptable on official documents. Yet Hirsch Goldwasser merely affixed an "X" to a circumcision certificate. The origin of his name is likewise unclear, although at this time in the environs of Konin there was a popular drink called Danziger Goldwasser, a sort of native brandy of Poland which contained small flecks of a gold-like substance. It is not unlikely that the family name was adopted from the drink.

Mike left Konin in 1848 and not long after he arrived in London he married Sarah, a dressmaker whose well-to-do father had imported furs from Russia and then bequeathed the business to her upon his death. A portrait painted about the time of her marriage shows that Sarah was a fastidious dresser given to wearing fancy clothes. It was obvious that she lived a privileged life. One can imagine her reaction, then, when not long after her marriage, her husband's adventuresome brother Joe showed up in London and began begging Mike to go with him to America. No one knows what resplendant pictures of wealth, and prosperity Joe painted. But somehow his importunity struck a responsive chord in the older brother, and in 1852 the two of them sailed for America. Family tradition says that they landed at New York. But an examination of official lists reveals no Goldwaters among the passengers, so it is probable that they landed elsewhere—perhaps at Philadelphia, Baltimore, or Boston.

The earliest evidence of the Goldwaters in the new world dates from the early summer of 1854, when Mike was operating a general merchandise establishment in Sonora, near Stockton, California. But it is thought the brothers reached California two years earlier, via the Isthmus of Panama. In July of 1854, Mike journeyed to San Francisco to welcome to the new world his wife and children, who had earlier landed in the East before taking a steamer to Nicaragua, crossing to the west coast, and boarding the steamer *Sierra Nevada* to sail to San Francisco. With Sarah was her sister, Esther Tash, and Esther's son Marcus.

A few days before Mike left to meet Sarah, he was joined in Sonora by Joe. Sometime during the next four years Joe became a partner and the brothers joined "under the name and style" of J. Goldwater & Co. The store did reasonably well until the late 1850's. Then, with the failure of the Adams & Co. Express (a company which rivaled Wells Fargo, but was, in addition, a banking business), and with the virtual exhaustion of the mines around Sonora, depression came to the southern mines. Like many other businesses in the area, J. Goldwater & Co. failed.

In 1857, Joe journeyed south to Los Angeles, a town which was just then awakening. He established a tobacco and "Yankee Notions" store in the Bella Union, the largest, most important hotel in the city. Located directly across Main St., from what is now the Los Angeles City Hall, the Bella Union was the terminus for stage lines from intermediate points and for the stage line from San Francisco to Los Angeles. When the Butterfield Line began a few years later, carrying passengers on a 25-day, 2,759-mile trip from Tipton, Mo. to San Francisco, it too stopped at the Bella Union.

Mike and his family followed Joe to Los Angeles. Together the brothers enlarged the shop, and added a billiard parlor and saloon. In a few years they opened two other stores, one in the building next door, one on a nearby corner, and were handling a wide selection of merchandise. In about 1860, Mike bought a spring wagon and 4-mule team and began peddling from community to community in southern California. It is believed that at this time he also may have wandered into what is now Arizona. For, especially along the southern wagon route to the goldfields, people were constructing tiny settlements in the territory acquired from Mexico by the Gadsden Purchase of 1853.

The peddler was a familiar sight on the frontier and, as Harry Golden wrote in his book, *Forgotten Pioneer*, "always he followed the Western movement and was often its co-traveler. When the first schoolteacher arrived at the new settlement of homesteaders, or at the new mining town, she already found the peddler with his stock of underwear, needles and thread, men's and women's stockings, a bolt or two of yard goods, rib-

bons for the children, and dozens of notions, geegaws that
brightened the drab monotony of the isolated Western town
or Southern farm community."

For an immigrant, Golden noted, it was the quickest way to
get started in the new world. It offered him an opportunity to
learn the language and the ways of America, while concomitantly earning a living—and he could start earning the day after
he got off the boat. Peddling, Golden commented, was the
"preparatory school" of America. Mike Goldwater had been off
the boat for some time by then. But his experience as a peddler
did indeed serve as an ersatz prep school, which later was to
prove to be of inestimable value.

In 1862 bad luck again struck the Goldwaters, and thousands
of other southern Californians. A drought caused crops to fail
and cattle to die. Then a flood drowned thousands of the remaining cattle. And the Civil War, then in its second year, cut
off California's developing trade. The Goldwaters, like many
Los Angeles businessmen of the day, had purchased goods from
San Francisco on an open note. But the creditor panicked because of general business conditions, and when he demanded
immediate payment the brothers were forced into receivership.
Once more they were forced to start anew.

In January of 1862, gold had been discovered in La Paz,
Arizona, on the Colorado River. Thousands of Californians
joined a trek to the Arizona wilderness, where the Indian population far outnumbered all others and where Cochise, chief
of the Chiricahua Apache, was still on the warpath. Leaving his
family in Los Angeles, Mike Goldwater joined the eastward
migration to La Paz. One of the first and most prosperous businesses in the Arizona boom town was a general merchandise
store owned by one Bernard Cohn, who had been a jeweler
and pawn shop owner in Los Angeles, not far from the Bella
Union. Mike joined him as an employee, later became a part-

ner, and five years later bought him out. Then he sent for Joe, who had returned to San Francisco from Los Angeles, and once more "J. Goldwater & Co." was back in business.

By then Mike had branched out into other ventures. With Cohn he had invested in mines and had undertaken contracts to haul supplies—chiefly grain—from La Paz to military posts in the interior of Arizona (which was proclaimed a Territory by President Lincoln on Feb. 24, 1863). To these profitable sidelines he added the freighting business, in which he became a partner with Dr. W. W. Jones, a graduate of the University of Maryland who served for a while as Los Angeles County Recorder before becoming interested in mining after journeying to Arizona in 1858.

Aboard ship traveling from London, the Goldwaters had struck up a friendship with the Drachman brothers, Philip and Sam, who were eventually bound for Philadelphia. And in 1863, Philip Drachman showed up in La Paz and renewed his friendship with the Goldwaters. Joe and Mike advanced the brothers merchandise on credit for a business they had established in Tucson. (Mike's ledger reveals that in 1867 the Drachmans owed J. Goldwater & Co. $9,203.59.) The Drachmans not only became successful merchants, but Philip was elected to the legislature in 1867 and is credited with playing a major role in having the territorial capital moved from Prescott to Tucson, where it remained until 1877. (Even today the Drachmans are a successful Tucson family. Philip Drachman's granddaughter, Rosemary Taylor, is the author of *Chicken Every Sunday*.)

La Paz soon became so important that California newspapers —especially the *San Francisco Bulletin*, the *Los Angeles News*, and the *Alta California*—carried regular correspondence describing life in the "Colorado mines." But by 1867 the gold placers along the Colorado were just about exhausted. The few remaining deposits were in dry washes and gullies, as far as eight miles from the river. As a result, the future of La Paz gradually shifted from mining to that of a supply port for towns—Florence, Prescott, Wickenburg—developing in the interior.

In time the Goldwater businesses prospered, and the brothers began being sought out for advice or financial help. East of La Paz, along a road known as the Trail of Graves (because so many travelers were killed by Indians or died from lack of water), Henry Wickenburg discovered the Vulture Mine, one of the richest of early Arizona. But production was spasmodic, dependent on the whims of an *arrastra*, a crude Mexican device using a horse or mule which walked in a circle around a spindle. A group of businessmen had hoped to construct an efficient mill to crush the ore so the metallic content could be separated from waste rock. So they came to Mike, who by then was the leading wholesaler on the upper Colorado River, and he agreed to put up $35,000. When the group ran into difficulty, Mike was asked to operate the mill until it became profitable enough for the loan to be repayed.

In 1868 the Colorado changed course, leaving La Paz high and dry, too isolated to be a port. So the brothers moved six miles downstream and built a large store and warehouse on the water's edge. They named it Ehrenberg, after a friend, Herman Ehrenberg, who had been murdered in 1866 at Dos Palmas station, near the eastern shore of the Salton Sea. The station keeper said he had been killed by Indians who came in to rob the station. But the belief persists that the station keeper himself murdered Ehrenberg, a German-born mining engineer who, among other accomplishments, had mapped San Francisco in 1849.

The town of La Paz followed the Goldwaters to Ehrenberg. In their new surroundings Mike had Joe appointed postmaster on Sept. 20, 1869. And Joe also became a member of the first school board, which brought education to the remote community within a short time after territorially supported schools opened in Arizona. According to legend, when the first school teacher arrived by river boat and the welcoming crowd gathered at the dock, a desert breeze wafted her wide-brimmed hat into the Colorado. Joe returned to the store, selected a new hat for her, and made a gallant presentation as she stepped ashore.

The grain hauling business expanded steadily, but Indian attacks upon the wagon trains caused inconvenience and considerable financial loss. Ever since the Civil War had broken communication lines in the Southwest, Arizona was at the mercy of Indian raids. In fact, lack of military protection in Arizona was the decisive factor in the refusal of the Butterfield Line—seized by Confederate troops in 1861—to resume operations. After one Indian attack on their wagons, Joe Goldwater spent three weeks at a make-shift hospital at Camp Date Creek, an Army outpost near Prescott, recovering from a bullet wound. After the bullet was removed, he wore it on a watchfob for the remainder of his life. But the Indian raids—which didn't end until the banishment of Geronimo in 1886—were not sufficient to shut down the grain hauling operation. They *were* troublesome enough, however, to cause the dispatch of scout Kit Carson to help subdue the Navajos, and to cause the Goldwaters to search for a supply source closer to the interior towns and military posts. Finally they decided to open a branch store in Phoenix, an expanding city which, together with the entire Salt River Valley, was becoming an important breadbasket for the growing Arizona territory.

The first Goldwater store in Phoenix opened in 1872, the year President Ulysses S. Grant rolled up the largest majority vote ever polled by a presidential candidate up to that time. Manager of the new establishment was Mike's 20-year-old son Morris, who had come to Arizona soon after completing school in San Francisco (the city Sarah adopted as her permanent home about the time Mike and Joe moved to Ehrenberg). This too was a general merchandise store. But its principal function was to serve as a base of operation for an association of farmers who would supply the grain necessary for the Goldwater hauling business.

Morris, an ambitious, friendly youth, quickly demonstrated the ubiquity which stamped his character throughout his life. As he was to do from then on, he took an active part in community affairs. When he learned that a telegraph line to Prescott was scheduled to bypass Phoenix, he donated a section of the Goldwater store for use as a telegraph office and offered—without pay—his services as telegraph operator. Thus he was instrumental in routing the line through Phoenix. And he was instrumental in introducing into the territory the first automatic telegraph recording instrument—a device that received perforated messages on paper tape. Inevitably, competitors complained that telegraph operator Goldwater was in a position to receive inside information about grain needs at military bases, and they exerted political pressure sufficient to have the office removed from the store. But their fears appear to have been groundless. For official records do not reveal any unusual contracts during this period, nor do they offer any hint that Morris used the telegraph line to the advantage of the Goldwater enterprises.

During his stay in Phoenix, Morris served as deputy county recorder, ventured into farming (at one time he owned what is now Fraternity Row at Arizona State University in nearby Tempe), and ran for the legislature on the Democratic ticket. He and his opponent tied. But when it seemed certain that he would be defeated in the runoff, Morris withdrew in favor of a man who had been a former Arizona delegate to the Confederate Congress, and the alternate candidate won an easy victory.

Despite Morris' indefatigability and managerial talents, the Phoenix store didn't live up to Mike's expectations. Furthermore, Mike was convinced that the center of Arizona trade was swinging north toward Prescott. So the brothers closed the Phoenix store in 1875 and the following year they opened their first Prescott store in a 2-story building erected for them by a blacksmith-carpenter named James Howey, who several years earlier had worked for Mike at Vulture Mill.

The Prescott store was an immediate success. And it was a cut above the other Goldwater stores in the quality of its merchandise. On their intermittent journeys to San Francisco to visit their families, Mike and Joe (who, with another of Mike's sons, Henry, continued managing the Ehrenberg store) ordered many of the latest fashions and a wider stock of general merchandise: soft goods, hardwares, food, mining supplies, powder, and farming implements. But their reputation spread largely because they sold flour, the staff of life for most frontiersmen, at wholesale prices. For, although the $400 a barrel charged by San Francisco merchants during the height of the gold rush was admittedly high, and an isolated occurrence, many settlers still felt they had been gouged on the price of flour by early merchants.

It took time for merchants to dispel the hostile memories of the frontiersmen. And the Goldwaters were no exception. When they finally did, however, their business prospered. Within a few years the Prescott store became too small for the expanding enterprises, so a warehouse was added. Not long afterwards it became necessary to move again, so the brothers purchased property a block away from the store and began construction of a larger two-story brick building. Principally through the efforts of Morris, who became manager in 1879, the new store began catering to the ladies. Home furniture, furnishings, and fancy goods now were considered as important as wholesale liquors and tobaccos.

For some inexplicable reason, Joe seemed not to be in harmony with the expansion plans. There is speculation that his disagreement may have sprung from an inability to get along with Mike's wife, even though Sarah lived almost a thousand miles away. When his own wife died in 1877, leaving him with three small children, Sarah, as far as can be determined, made no offer to take the children into her household. Perhaps it was because at the time she had three youngsters of her own to care for. At any rate, although members of his wife's family looked after the children, in 1880 Joe sold his share of the business to his brother.

A year or so later Joe went into business with José Miguel Castañeda in Bisbee, Arizona. Here occurred the Bisbee Massacre, an event second only to the Gunfight at O.K. Corral in the annals of Arizona gunfighting lore. A gang robbed more than $1,000 in gold and $200 in silver from the store, and killed four citizens before riding out of town—ten minutes before an $18,000 payroll, for employes of the Copper Queen Mine, arrived aboard the stagecoach. One of the bandits had taken an old Spanish coin marked with the initials of Sr. Castañeda, and it was found in his possession when he was captured. He and three companions were hanged in Tombstone (the city made famous by the exploits of Wyatt Earp and the imagination of television script writers) after a legal trial. Another gunman was not so fortunate; he wound up on the business end of a rope belonging to an angry lynch mob.

After Joe left, Mike decided that the completion of the Southern Pacific Railroad lines across Arizona had made river travel—and with it, the value of Ehrenberg—relatively unimportant. So he sold the store to an old friend and former customer, Abraham Frank.

Morris, meanwhile, had proven to be a valuable addition to the business. In addition, the short, dapper son of Mike Goldwater, sporting a handlebar moustache and replete with wise saws and sage sayings, proved to be a leader in the growing Prescott community. He believed strongly that prosperous businesses depended on a strong, stable community. And he believed just as strongly that it was the moral duty of successful people to repay, by whatever means, the communities which helped make possible their success.

These beliefs were not held lightly. Morris and his father

were the first to pledge to buy $5,000 in bonds for a railroad into Prescott; and he and two partners later organized a bank which financed the construction of a railroad running to Phoenix. He aided in developing mines and real estate throughout the unsettled territory. And he served for many years as secretary of the Prescott Rifles, a local militia company organized to protect the populace from possible Indian attacks. (The head of the Prescott Rifles, Capt. F. C. Ainsworth, later became adjutant general of the U.S. Today the war records office in the National Archives is known as the Ainsworth Room.)

In 1880 a fire broke out in Miss Givens' dress shop near the Goldwater store, and rapidly leaped from rooftop to rooftop. Through uncommon effort and cooperation, the fire was finally extinguished, without—surprisingly—having caused too much damage. But Morris was concerned that there was no firefighting system in Prescott, or even any effective firefighting apparatus. So he organized the first of four volunteer fire companies in the city. These companies—one composed primarily of businessmen, another of saloon keepers, a third of artisans, and the last of liverymen—doubled as quasi-social organizations which held holiday races and competitions. One of their significant contributions was in digging wells at the corners of Prescott's streets, and equipping them with pumps. (In honor of Morris' contribution, the city later named the water reservoir in the surrounding mountains "Lake Goldwater".)

His work in behalf of fire protection soon led Morris into politics. He helped organize the Arizona Democratic Party at a time when Arizona Territory was under the control of a Republican administration. He helped send Granville Oury to Washington as one of Arizona's early Democratic territorial delegates. He served as Vice-President of the 1910 Constitutional Convention and as President of the Twentieth Territorial Council. He acted as official and unofficial spokesman for the conservative Jeffersonian Democrats. And he served as Mayor of Prescott for 22 years.

All his life Morris had assumed responsibility, familial as well as political. All his life he subjugated his personal interests for the family welfare. For years, whenever he returned to San Francisco, his mother—in keeping with an old European custom—had a nice Jewish girl lined up for him to meet, in the hope that he might marry. But he had been too busy helping to build a business and helping to mould a community. Therefore, it wasn't until after his parents' death, when he was 55, that he married Sarah Shivers Fisher, a widow from an old pioneer family.

After Morris' first term as Mayor, his father complained that he was devoting too much time to politics and to community activities. So Morris talked—or perhaps shamed—Mike into running for Mayor, and he too won. But whereas Morris was easy-going and personable, his father—who had spent a lifetime conquering strange languages, strange customs, marauding Indians, and countless other hazards—was undiplomatic and politically gauche.

Once he initiated a program of putting crosswalks at the main intersections of town so the ladies wouldn't get mud on their dresses. This proved to be so popular that an ordinance was passed requiring all property owners to put board sidewalks outside their property. But some owners objected, and with good reason. They were mostly absentee owners who had bought the property for the sake of helping to develop the town, not for any profit motive. They were, in essence, benefactors paying taxes without hope of ever making a profit. Yet suddenly here came an ordinance warning that if they didn't install the sidewalks, the city would do it for them and then assess them the cost. And in many cases, Mike discovered, the cost would have been more than the value of the property. So the Mayor then found himself in the difficult position of refusing to enforce an ordinance for which he was in part responsible.

Another time he became embroiled in a fight over the collection of dog fees. This degenerated into a name-calling episode with the town constable, prompting Mike to introduce in the City Council a resolution fining the constable $100. The council supported him at first, but then had second thoughts about the $100 misunderstanding—especially when it was noted that the constable's salary was only $150 per month. But Mike, out of wounded pride, insisted that the fine be levied; and when he didn't receive unanimous backing he resigned as Mayor. A blacksmith finished out the remaining three months of the one-year term. But by then Mike had his fill of politics. And by then he knew enough never again to criticize Morris for his participation.

After his disastrous experience as Mayor, Mike become somewhat disenchanted with his role as a leading citizen. Furthermore, he was growing old and his wife, who had visited Arizona only once during all these years, was still patiently waiting in San Francisco, a city that was enough like London—with its fine clothes and its active Jewish community—to make her life in America tolerable. So he sold his remaining business interests to Morris, with the understanding that Morris would care for his parents as long as they lived, and he left Arizona to be reunited with Sarah.

It is inaccurate to say that Mike Goldwater, the hardy pioneer and peddler, retired to San Francisco, for he continued to do some buying for the Goldwater stores. But most of his time was devoted to religious and charitable work on behalf of Congregation Sherith Israel, a conservative congregation comprised largely of Polish Jews. He took charge of resettling an old cemetery; he was a founder of the Eureka Benevolent Society (a Jewish charitable organization); and he generally kept active in those Jewish activities that had been inaccesible to him during his years in the wild Arizona territory.

By the time Mike had returned to San Francisco, his eight children had long since reached adulthood and—with the exception of Elizabeth, a spinster who stayed with Sarah—had gone their many ways. Morris was now in charge of the Goldwater enterprises in Arizona. Another son, Ben, was a traveling salesman for B. Blumenthal & Co. of San Francisco. He was very often in poor health, and later died of tuberculosis. Sam, another son, came to Arizona to work in the stores. But his penchant for gambling and his itinerant ways kept him always on the fringes of the Goldwater enterprises. And he too died of tuberculosis, shortly after the ailing Ben came to live with him.

Henry was another Goldwater who suffered from wanderlust. He served as postmaster of three Arizona towns. He established a freight forwarding business in northern Arizona. He worked as an accountant in Los Angeles and owned a furniture factory in Richmond, Calif. And for about 10 years he was a full partner in the Goldwater stores. But his quixotic visions soon sent him wandering from place to place in search of El Dorado. And until he died in 1931, he was always sure that prosperity—the kind that dominated his dreams—was just around the corner.

Caroline Goldwater married Philip Aronson, who proved on numerous occasions to be a savior of the Goldwater businesses. He was a sound businessman who served as advisor and often advanced money to the Goldwaters for expansion and for paying off creditors. And he represented the Goldwaters in San Francisco as a buying agent. When he moved east after the earthquake of 1906, he negotiated loans from eastern banks. And over a 40-year period his name continually appears as a financier and silent partner, but one who declined to share in the company's profits.

When young Baron completed school, he spent a year with a jewelry firm in San Francisco and then came to Arizona in 1882. He was put to work as a clerk in the Prescott store, and he was expected to learn every phase of the business—while he stocked shelves and swept floors. In his spare time, and on his own initiative, he canvassed the neighborhood taking orders for pianos (records show that one year he sold a dozen) and he obtained an interest in a local express company. After a decade of apprenticeship his brothers thought enough of his business acumen to reward him with a full partnership. More than that, however, they thought enough of him to bestow upon him the responsibility for doing what the Goldwaters had failed to do 18 years earlier—make a success of a store in Phoenix.

Family tradition holds that Baron Goldwater was chosen to come to Phoenix after playing a showdown hand of casino with brother Morris. The tale is colorful, and not entirely out of character for the unorthodox Goldwaters. But undoubtedly it is more fanciful than factual. The reasons which led the brothers to decide to open a Phoenix store were twofold: the fact that the capital, which had been retrieved from Tucson by Prescott in 1877, was permanently located in Phoenix in 1889; and the fact that in 1895 the Sante Fe, Prescott, and Phoenix Railroad connected the northern cross-country route with the southern route, making Phoenix a hub of Arizona transportation.

There is an amusing story connected with the arrival of the first locomotive in Tucson, in March, 1880. Citizens of the Old Pueblo were understandably ecstatic over this modern link with the outside world, and city officials sent effusive telegrams to the President, the Governor, and officials of several large cities. One message, dated March 17, read:

"To His Holiness, the Pope of Rome, Italy. The mayor of Tucson begs the honor of reminding Your Holiness that this ancient and honorable pueblo was founded by the Spaniards under the sanction of the Church more than three centuries ago, and to inform Your Holiness that a railroad from San Francisco, California, now connects us with the Christian world. R. N. Leatherwood, mayor. Asking your benediction, J. B. Salpointe, Vic. Ap."

However, upon learning of the telegram, three Tucsonians bribed the telegraph operator to withhold the message. And that evening, in the midst of a celebration banquet, the following "reply" was read:

"His Holiness the Pope acknowledges with appreciation re-

ceipt of your telegram informing him that the ancient city of
Tucson at last has been connected by rail with the outside
world and sends his benediction, but for his own satisfaction
would ask, where in hell is Tucson?

[Signed] Antonelli."

The mayor and his celebrants, it is said, were somewhat
chagrined that the Pope hadn't heard of Tucson. But they
never thought to question the authenticity of the telegram.

Once the decision was made to open a store in Phoenix, for
the first time since the beginning of the Goldwater enterprises
an outsider was allowed to join. He was E. J. Bennitt, a civil
engineer who worked with the Goldwaters on mine surveys
when they first arrived in Prescott, and who at one point was
employed by them briefly while he was temporarily out of
work. In the intervening years Bennitt had moved to Phoenix
where he became one of the first bankers in the Territory, and
by 1895 he had become a wealthy man. When the Phoenix
store was opened in a rented building in 1896, E. J. Bennitt
was a non-working partner with Morris, Henry, and Baron
Goldwater. He later joined both Morris and Baron separately
in various real estate transactions in Phoenix and Los Angeles.
But when Baron Goldwater, a somewhat reserved, fastidious
man, journeyed to Phoenix, he cared little about real estate
transactions—or about anything other than making a success
of the Goldwater name in the capital. His determination was
quickly rewarded; within a few years the store was forced to
move to larger quarters, and in 1908 it was forced to move once
again.

Twelve years after his arrival, Baron Goldwater married
Josephine Williams, a spunky Chicago nurse who struck out
for Arizona when doctors told her she had tuberculosis and
might live only a short time. The doctors were wrong. "But I
didn't know it then," Josephine Goldwater recalls, "so I bought
a ticket on the Sante Fe and headed West." The ticket took
her as far as Ash Fork, Arizona. "I watched the train pull out,"

she said, "then started walking down the tracks until I spotted an old freight. One of the men waved me to the caboose and I sat there until it pulled out, destination Phoenix."

Josephine Williams and Baron Goldwater married on New Year's Day, 1907. Two years later, to the day, Barry Morris Goldwater was born . . . three years before the Arizona Territory became the 48th state. A Phoenix newspaperman wrote that the new arrival "promises to add luster to a family name already distinguished in the annals of Arizona."

CHAPTER 4

The Early Days

---

*"How beautiful is youth! how
bright it gleams
With its illusions, aspirations,
dreams!"*
—LONGFELLOW

THE phoenix, according to Greek mythology, was an eagle-sized bird with brilliant gold and reddish-purple feathers. And it had a sweet voice not unlike that of the nymphs who tempted Ulysses as he sailed by the coast of the Sirens. When he reached the age of 500, the phoenix built a funeral pyre of twigs and spice trees, lighted it by fanning his wings, and stood in its midst until he was consumed by the flames. Before long a young phoenix would rise from the ashes, carry the remains of its father to the altar of the sun god in the Egyptian city of Heliopolis (City of the Sun), then live out its five-century life in the Arabian desert.

There are numerous variations to the myth. But most accounts which have come down to us agree that the phoenix, with its dramatic rebirth from its own ashes, was a symbol of spiritual rejuvenation and immortality—a bird about whom it also could be said, as Keats said about the nightingale:

*"Thou wast not born for death, immortal Bird!
No hungry generations tread thee down."*

48

When Darrell Duppa—an English adventurer, inebriate, and reputed scion of nobility—deliberated over a name for the Arizona valley upon which he gazed, he was mindful of the remains of prehistoric mounds and canals, evidence of the ancient Hohokam ("people who have gone"). And, remembering his Greek (which he is said to have read in the original), he exclaimed: "Let's call it Phoenix, for here upon the old a new and more beautiful city will rise, phoenix-like, from these ashes of the past."

When Barry Goldwater was born in 1909, Phoenix was a typical Southwestern town, unhurried and undiscovered by the outside world. It's 3.2 square miles were not many by big city standards, but were enough to afford its 11,000 residents elbow room. Statehood was still three years away for the Arizona Territory, but everyone knew it was only a matter of time. Things had been relatively quiet in Phoenix and in the interior ever since the Chiricahua Apaches had surrendered 25 years earlier, but memories of the frontier remained vivid; and only a month after the first child of Baron and Josephine Goldwater was born, a fearful reminder of frontier days, Geronimo—the legendary Apache chief who led his warriors on raids throughout Arizona and New Mexico—died in a military prison at Ft. Sill, Oklahoma.

"The earliest thing I can remember is mother taking the flag down and sewing two new stars on it for New Mexico and Arizona," Barry Goldwater wrote in 1940, "and I would like to know where that flag went because it would be a curiosity now. The flag was always on the flagpole in front of the house on the days that it should be. My mother was very religious in seeing that this was carried out. . . .

"I remember Central Ave. [today, as then, the main street in Phoenix, on which the Goldwater residence was situated] as Center Street and its being unpaved, with ditches on either side. On the banks of these ditches grew the beautiful ash trees that once lined Central Avenue and made it, to my memory, the most beautiful street I have ever seen. I remember that the old ash in front of our house formed a perfect canopy over the walk to the house."

Paving of Phoenix's city streets and sidewalks began in 1910. But it wasn't until four years later that most of the sidewalks and streets were fully paved. Still, the city had come a long way during the less than half-century since Jack Swilling, a Georgia native who had participated with Confederate troops in Arizona's lone Civil War battle, stumbled upon its Indian ruins after journeying the 53 miles from Wickenburg. Swilling saw the traces of some 300 miles of hand-dug canals which had been used by an earlier civilization to divert water for the irrigation of more than 250,000 acres of land. And when he returned to Wickenburg he organized the Swilling Irrigation Canal Co. (which included "Lord" Duppa), for the purpose of digging a new canal through the parched land. This canal was less than three miles long, but when it was finished, and when a stream had been diverted from the Salt River, it became possible to grow crops. Life could be sustained on the desert. A new and more beautiful Phoenix was preparing to rise, if not from the ashes of the past, at least from a barren and desolate land.

On March 5, 1872, a correspondent wrote in the *San Diego Union* about Phoenix: "This is a smart town which had its first house completed about a year ago. Now it contains many houses, also stores, work shops, hotels, butcher shop, bakery, courthouse, jail, and an excellent school which has been in operation for months. Lately hundreds of ornamental trees have been set out which in a few years will give the town the appearance of a forest city and will add to its beauty and comfort. . . . The Salt River Valley will be the garden of the Pacific Slope, and Phoenix the most important inland town."

There was legitimate cause to be optimistic about Phoenix's future growth, as two major events soon would prove. The first was the arrival of the Southern Pacific Railroad in 1887, which meant that merchandise could flow into the city by train instead of being hauled by cart. And it meant that Phoenix would be able to send her products by rail to outlying markets. The second major event occurred in 1902 when President Theodore Roosevelt signed a bill making it possible to erect dams on western streams for reclamation purposes. In 1906 work was started on the largest masonry dam in the world, 80 miles northeast of Phoenix up the Apache Trail. When, in 1911, Roosevelt dedicated the dam named in his honor, it opened a new era in farming for the entire Phoenix area.

The day that Arizona was admitted to the Union, Feb. 14, 1912, was a big day in the life of three-year old Barry Goldwater. He was ring-bearer at a wedding. The *Arizona Gazette* reported the next day: "Master Cupid was indeed present and gallantly guided the bridal party toward the altar, this office being performed by a tiny white-clad figure bearing the name of Master Barry Goldwater . . . who carried in his arms a bow and quiver of arrows." The *Arizona Republican* was equally descriptive: "Master Barry Goldwater carried two callalilies and the rings. . . . He was wearing a chaplet of silver leaves and pink rosebuds."

It seems that Barry was not the only Goldwater child to play Cupid. Recalling his days in kindergarten, Goldwater wrote: "I remember that my brother was supposed to be Cupid, and they made him come out practically naked, which embarrassed him nearly to death. Today nothing embarrasses him!"

The Goldwater children—Barry, Bob (19 months Barry's junior) and Carolyn (born in 1912)—led normal, active lives. The boys organized the North Central Athletic Club, with headquarters atop the garage of the Goldwater home. Together with the neighborhood kids, the Goldwater boys played football, basketball, baseball, and boxed. A special boyhood companion was John Henry Lewis, a Negro who went on to become world light-heavyweight boxing champion from 1935 to 1939.

"John Henry's father had a gym and he taught us all how
to box," Goldwater remembered. "We all used to run around
together. We even boxed John Henry but he got too good in a
great big hurry, so we soon scratched him. He's blind now—the
fight with Louis set it off. I was told he was in Oakland and I
had Bill Knowland try to find him, but we haven't yet been
able to."

When light heavyweight champion Archie Moore came to
Phoenix several years ago he mentioned to a local sportswriter
that Goldwater had all the necessary abilities to become an outstanding boxer. This, Moore said, he learned firsthand—from
John Henry Lewis' father, in Moore's opinion one of the finest
boxing teachers of all time. The thing that discouraged Goldwater, the elder Lewis felt, was the constant thumping he
received from John Henry, who even then showed signs of
becoming a professional boxer.

Goldwater laughs off his boxing potential, and cites the time
he and Paul Fannin, now governor of Arizona, decided to go a
round with a professional fighter. When Fannin finished his
round in good shape, Goldwater thought the match wouldn't
be too difficult. So when his turn came he began flailing away
and somehow caught his opponent with a sharp overhand right.
It proved to be the only punch he landed, and for the rest of
the round the humiliated and irate pro knocked the insolent
amateur from one corner to the other.

Barry, always searching for new outlets for his unbridled
energy, soon discovered an exciting new invention—radio.
"When radio was first gaining national prominence my father
bought me a receiving set," he remembered. "This was in 1921
or 1922. To my knowledge this was the first factory-made radio
set in Arizona. Where it is now the Lord only knows, but I have
my second one, which is no spring-chicken itself. I became a
radio operator in 1922, and operated amateur station 6BPl for
two years."

He entered Phoenix Union High School in 1923. "After school," he said, "I used to work for Earl Neilsen, who ran the first radio store in Phoenix and who made the first radio sets ever built and sold in Arizona. I did odd jobs—selling, helping with the silver-plating that was done in the back room when re-silvering automobile headlights was a prosperous business, and helping in the workshop wherever I could. I worked a whole year without pay, and at Christmas I remember he gave me a set of head phones. I was the proudest thing in six counties."

The gang around Neilsen's built the first broadcasting station in Arizona, and operated it from the rear of the building. "It wasn't the first station authorized by the government to broadcast, but nevertheless we operated it as 6BBH, which is now KOY [a 5,000-watt station]. And on a good, cold clear night the music from our phonograph records could be heard in Mesa [a city 16 miles east of Phoenix]."

In April 1962, after a 40-year short-wave silence, Goldwater rejoined ham radio operator ranks with call letters K7UGA. He has put a Michigan serviceman's parents in contact with a ham operator in England with a message about their boy. Other contacts have reached Argentina, the Bahamas, and Venezuela. Last fall, while operating his ham set from Washington, a Scottsdale, Arizona woman answered his broadcast long enough to extend an invitation for him to attend a fashion show for the benefit of a hospital auxiliary. This past November, Goldwater spoke from his Washington apartment via a two-way radio hookup to a 10th grade world history class in New York State. "He is continually sending out cards to people both in this country and other countries to whom he has talked on the radio," said Arizona State University coed Marylin Fullerton, who spent the summer of 1963 working in the Senator's Washington office.

Last October, Goldwater and Peace Corps director Sargent Shriver worked out plans for forming a committee to provide amateur radio equipment and educational electronic kits for the peoples of the world, especially in underdeveloped areas where the Peace Corps is working.

Little of the indefatigable Goldwater energy during his formative years was devoted to studies. His father, therefore, decided not to allow him to return to Phoenix Union, where he had served as president of the freshman class, but where he also came dangerously close to failing. "All the various means of hazing were used on me at Phoenix Union," Goldwater remembered, "and on all the other freshman too—such things as being thrown in the town ditch, which ran through the back of the old campus, having my hair clipped, head painted, and so on." Baron Goldwater decided to enroll his son in Staunton (Va.) Military Academy, where he felt the rigorous physical and academic discipline would straighten out Barry's wayward ways. "I imagine I was getting a little hard to handle," Goldwater said, "and I was also getting a hankering to go into the army via West Point."

The four years at Staunton added little to his love of formal schooling, but it wasn't without its rewards. He captained the swimming team, which in 1927 won the Virginia state championship. He decided against making a career of the military. When he was graduated in 1928 he was awarded the Kable Medal as the outstanding all-around cadet.

The following fall Goldwater journeyed to Tucson, 120 miles southeast of his Phoenix home, to enroll at the University of Arizona. Sporting a 1925 Chrysler roadster, he began making the same name for himself on the Tucson campus that he had made at Phoenix Union and at Staunton. He was first-string center on the freshman football team. He pledged Sigma Chi fraternity. (Thirty-one years later, he was to write to his son: "A fraternity is a wonderful institution, but it can also be a rather dreary institution if the concepts and basic beliefs expressed in the initiation rites are not followed. It is the reiteration of basic philosophy in the rites of all fraternities that I think makes them important, because they impress upon the individual the need for participation. So it is with life in this country. The country gives you nothing but you give the country everything.") He was elected class president for the second semester, and became chairman of the freshman Stadium Fund committee, in which capacity he directed his fund-raising talents towards raising money for construction of a University football stadium.

Life was generally good to college students of that era. The Kellogg-Briand Pact, outlawing war and agreeing that the settlement of international disputes "shall never be sought except by pacific means," had been signed in Paris the previous summer and ratified by Congress on Jan. 25, 1929. Newly inaugurated President Herbert Hoover was presiding over a tranquil and relatively prosperous nation. Cornelius McGillicuddy (more familiarly known to baseball fans as Connie Mack, manager of the Philadelphia Athletics) had been awarded the Edward W. Bok prize for distinguished service to Philadelphia—an honor previously bestowed on educators, artists, scientists, and philanthropists.

A young Ernest Hemingway had just published A Farewell to Arms. James Thurber and E. B. White lampooned the nation's morals and manners in a gentle spoof entitled, Is Sex Necessary? Everyone seemed to be discussing William Faulkner's The Sound and the Fury and Erich Maria Remarque's All Quiet on the Western Front, and many of those who appeared most conversant with the books actually took time to read them. Even out in Arizona, which was far more distant than forty-five minutes from Broadway, people—like people everywhere in America—who couldn't recall the name of the Secretary of State knew who George M. Cohan and Al Jolson were; people who knew nothing about the Teapot Dome scandals knew all about George White's Scandals—thanks to a wonderful invention called radio.

Like most college kids of his day, Barry Goldwater partied

his way through "Sweet Sue—Just You," "Making Whoopee!" "Crazy Rhythm," "Button Up Your Overcoat," and "I Can't Give You Anything But Love." Then one March evening in 1929 the bottom fell out of the fun-loving freshman's pleasurable life: Baron Goldwater had died of a heart attack shortly after returning home from a party marking the opening of Wrigley's plush Arizona Biltmore Hotel, designed by family friend Frank Lloyd Wright. Suddenly, at age 20, Barry was now the man of the Goldwater household. He could no longer enjoy the luxury of college.

Barry never really had become well acquainted with his father. Baron had little patience with the noise or antics of the youngsters, and in those days he was very busy establishing a successful business. When the business had become solidly established, Barry was away at school. Yet Baron Goldwater, for all his fastidiousness and reserve, was not an unfriendly person. One of Barry's earliest memories was of visitors dropping in on his father. "I can see these men yet," he reminisced, "as they walked past our house on their way to work. I can remember them coming home from work in the evening; they stopped in the house to have a drink with my father before going home. Some of them did not even bother to knock because they knew they were always welcome. They knew where the bottle was and just went in and helped themselves, whether anyone was around or not."

Josephine Goldwater was the disciplinarian, and the parent from whom the children acquired their sense of individualism. Often she drove the children to Phoenix Indian School (at that time on the outskirts of the city, today well within city limits) to view the nightly flag-lowering ceremony. She took her children camping and taught them how to shoot. She drove them from one end of the state to the other, and across the desert to California on wooden roads that, in Barry's words, "caused a flat tire every hour or so." She smoked in public when it was considered unladylike to do so. And she wore knickers on the golf course when, in her late 30's, she took up golf (and went on to win the Arizona Women's Amateur Championship).

In 1961, the Arizona town of Show Low dedicated the Josephine Goldwater Hospital, named as a tribute to that former nurse who donated $25,000 after being inspired by the zeal of townspeople who raised money for the hospital by promoting dances, suppers, bazaars, rodeos, and similar events, and who spent numerous nights, weekends, and vacations building the structure.

"Even modern psychologists might blanch at her permissive methods," said a close friend of the Goldwaters. "But when the kids went too far she would deprive them of their liberties and privileges. And all three of the kids learned from her that you pay the price of misbehaving with loss of liberty. They learned that the degree of freedom they had was up to them as individuals."

The Goldwater children were baptized and raised in the Episcopalian faith. Like brother Morris, Baron never renounced his faith. (In fact, Morris, who died in 1939, stipulated in his will that he should rightly be given a Jewish burial, but that since there were no rabbis available he wanted a Masonic burial.) There was little organized Jewish religion in the early days of Arizona, and Baron simply followed the Jewish custom of allowing his children to be raised in the faith of their mother. It never occurred to the children that being half-Jewish made them "different" in the eyes of bigots. "I just never thought about it," said Goldwater. When he received the award of the National Conference of Christians and Jews in 1962, he said, "I had to go back East to discover that there was supposed to be a difference between Christians and Jews, and that we should treat our Negro friends differently."

Barry Goldwater did not step immediately into his father's well-polished shoes in the family store, the oldest retail mercantile company in Arizona. Like Baron, he also started as a

clerk. "He's one boss's son who really worked in every department in the store," confided Mrs. Sugar Burlingham, a Goldwater employee for almost 40 years. "He was always one of us;
you'd never know he was the boss's son." Gene Warren, who
has been with the Goldwater organization more than 42 years,
recalled that "Barry was always a good salesman. And he was
always a good worker, no matter what department he was in. I
remember when we were delivery boys together. One time we
delivered a COD package to a house in Gold Alley, the Negro
red light district. We were paid off with 88 silver dollars and
we had to cart them back to the store. I thought Barry would
be mad about it, but he thought it was a big joke."

Barry went off to New York, to the store's buying office, to
spend a year learning the finer points of merchandising. When
he returned he began experimenting with new merchandising
ideas. In 1937, the year 28-year-old Barry became president of
the stores, Goldwater's introduced to the nation, by way of
national advertising in the *New Yorker*, the Branding Iron
design for dresses, and for men's and women's sport shirts. Ten
years later Barry dreamed up and had designed the famous
"antsy pants," men's shorts with designs of red ants on them.
No less than Gen. Harry Vaughn, Harry Truman's confidant,
wrote to the store requesting six pairs to be sent to him at the
White House. He said he had seen another general wearing
them. Barry thoughtfully enclosed an extra pair for the President with the note, "We don't think the Republicans can do
this to you, but just in case there is a chance, you should get
used to having ants in your pants."*

* In June 1963, during a speech in Tucson, Goldwater criticized the
Kennedy administration for its lack of a forthright policy. This was not
the case during the Truman administration, he said, adding, "The more I
think about it, the more I think Harry Truman will go down in history as
one of our greater Presidents." Truman responded: "That's awfully nice
of him. I never had any argument with Goldwater. I think he is honestly
trying to do a good job, and I thought that before he said those nice
things about me. . . ."

The Goldwater stores had always been pace-setters in Arizona and the Phoenix store was no exception. It boasted the first telephone switchboard in the city, the first tube carrier for money, the first store passenger elevator, and the first electronic-eye doors. Under Barry's leadership, the stores in 1945 introduced a generous profit sharing plan open to everyone from top executives to the lowliest workers. The Goldwaters hosted an annual breakfast, presided over by Barry, in which employees were given a rundown of the store's financial status. The store was one of the first businesses in the state to provide life insurance, and hospital and surgical policies for employees. Employees were paid when they were sick, and they enjoyed liberal discounts. "Under Barry, the stores had the most liberal, progressive labor relations of any store anywhere in the state," said former Phoenix Mayor Jack Williams. "They were far and away the best."

An example of this was the farm the Goldwater stores—"they're *specialty* stores," Goldwater insists, "not department stores"—established during the war for employees. "This enterprising store," commented *Retail Management*, a national trade publication, "has set an excellent example of labor-management cooperation in the retail field and in the community." In an effort to afford recreation for employees, and to help them obtain fresh vegetables, meat, milk, and other scarce items, the stores acquired a 25-acre farm some eight miles from the Goldwater store in Phoenix.

It was known as the Jack Thornton Farm, in memory of the employee who had been with Goldwater's longest. And it was equipped with a picnic area amid numerous cottonwood trees, a barbecue pit, swimming pool, an air conditioned clubhouse, and an outdoor dance floor. Free kiddie rides were available. The store furnished free nursing service for mothers who worked in the store, transporting the children to the farm for the day and returning them in the evening. And employees who wanted to raise their own food—and many did, inasmuch as

Victory Gardens occupied three acres of the farm—were permitted to leave work any afternoon an hour and a half before the store's regular closing time.

The entire operation of the farm, including distribution of the produce, was left to committees elected by the workers. After the war the Goldwaters donated the site to the Phoenix Technical School for use as an agricultural training center.

Just after the war, when flying was popular, Barry bought an airplane for employees, formed a flying club, and provided free airplane lessons. Before the club disbanded because of lack of interest, 24 pilots were graduated. Another time, he bought a large cabin at Queen Creek, near Prescott, so employees could spend vacations and weekends amid Arizona's cool pines. And when the store in 1951 initiated a 5-day work week for all employees, Goldwater—who often is accused of being heartless toward the working man—said, "The tempo of today's working and living makes a 5-day week imperative to maintain human rights." During the stores' annual party in May 1960, some 600 employees presented the Goldwater family with a plaque commemorating "their great understanding of the principles of humanitarianism."

"Barry was one of the best-loved men there was," said Kathleen Wuersch, who recently retired after 37 years with the store. "Even as a young boy he inspired people. There was just something about him. Oftentimes girls came to Arizona with sick husbands, went to work in the store, and when Barry heard about their troubles he helped them out with their doctor bills. He was that kind of a person—one in a million."

William E. Saufley, former vice-president and director of Goldwater's Phoenix store, remembers once when Barry walked through the store and fell into a conversation with a saleslady in the notions department. When he learned of her ill health he told her to go home, that she shouldn't be working, and that she would receive a check each month for as long as she lived. "This was before our retirement plan," Saufley said, "and she received a check regularly for her many remaining years." Another time an employee in the display section was worried about his ill wife and children. "He had doctor bills piled on doctor bills," Saufley remembered. "So at Barry's direction, his bills were paid and I was instructed to tell him he owed nothing because it had been arranged through a civic agency."

Saufley was himself the beneficiary of Goldwater's generosity. "When my house was being built," he said, "Barry came by one day and learned that the costs had made it necessary for me to do without a cooling system. He immediately told the foreman to hold up work, and the next day a central cooling unit was delivered—compliments of Barry."

The Goldwater stores were sold to Associated Dry Goods Corp. of New York in 1962. Barry is now chairman of the board and brother Bob remains president—a position he assumed in 1953 when Barry left for Washington.

Late in 1932, Barry was introduced to Margaret ("Peggy") Johnson, a Muncie, Ind. girl whose father was a founder and vice-president of Borg-Warner Corporation and whose parents had maintained a residence in Phoenix since 1927. She had attended Elmhurst girls school in Indiana and graduated from Mount Vernon Seminary in Washington (a junior college where daughter Peggy currently attends, and where, on the day Nelson Rockefeller opened his New Hampshire primary campaign, the Goldwaters dedicated an art gallery which they donated to the school). Later she attended Grand Central Art School in Manhattan, and was courted by G. Mennen Williams, afterwards to become Governor of Michigan and currently State Department Assistant Secretary for African Affairs. But the Arizona businessman was persistent. And after what he describes as "a cross-country courtship" which took him to Michigan, Washington, and Indiana, he proposed on New Year's Eve—in a phone booth. They were married on September 22, 1934 in Grace Episcopal Church in Muncie amid the good wishes of relatives and friends . . . including one G. Mennen Williams, who attended both the wedding and reception.

A few years before his marriage, Goldwater decided to take flying lessons. Flying was still a relatively risky business in those days, but the challenge was irresistible to the adventuresome young man. "I was up at 5 o'clock those mornings," he recalled. "I'd beat it out to the field, take my lessons and get back to the store in time for work. Mun [his nickname for his mother] never asked me what I was doing up that hour and I didn't tell her. I found out later she thought I was visiting a woman—as if I would do such a thing!"

Goldwater learned to fly in a Great Lakes trainer under Jack Thornberg, now a California rancher. "I soloed for the first time under Irving Kravitz," he said. "He's a captain for TWA today, but I didn't know it until a couple of years ago. I got on a plane in Chicago and I saw the sign saying Captain Kravitz, or I. Kravitz, or something similar. So I asked the stewardess, 'Is that Irving Kravitz?' Well, the stewardess loved it because they never could find out his first name, so they kept calling him 'Oiving,' the rest of the trip. When I got off he said, 'Damn you. I didn't want that name known.' "

Since his first solo flight, Goldwater has piloted more than 75 different aircraft, including 16 jets. And airplanes continue to hold a strange fascination for him. Last year, while sightseeing aboard the carrier *Enterprise* off the North Carolina coast, he borrowed a Navy flight suit and rode as a passenger in an F-4B Phantom during a catapult take-off.

At the time he was learning to fly, Goldwater also became seriously interested in photography, and in a few years he became an excellent photographer. During the 1930's his photographs of Arizona were exhibited in salons all over the world and throughout the U.S.A. He was elected to associate membership in the Royal Photographic Society of London. Today, there is scarcely an Arizona mountain, prehistoric ruin, or town that he has not photographed. He has a collection of some 8,000 slides and photographs of Arizona—its people, its color, its natural landmarks—and has put together two volumes of striking photographs titled *Arizona Portraits*. One entire wall of Arizona Congressman John J. Rhodes' Washington office is covered with photos taken by friend and fellow legislator, Barry Goldwater. And late last year, in an effort to raise funds for Goldwater's 1964 Senate or presidential campaign, Arizona Republicans selected 50 photographs from his collection, bound them in a 14x18 inch volume titled *The Faces of Arizona*, and sold a limited number of autographed copies for $1,500 each.

Another Goldwater interest is music. He taught himself to play the saxaphone, clarinet and mandolin, and was for many years a member of the AFL musicians union in Tucson and Phoenix. He still retains his musical interest, especially in Dixieland or uptempo music. When they have time, both he and wife Peggy like to watch singer Maggie Peterson, an exuberant bundle of energy whose nightclub performances throughout the country often bring her to neighboring Scottsdale. "We think that cute little gal is the best singer around," he said. "She can belt out those old songs—'Mississippi Mud,' 'Bill Bailey,' 'Alabamy Bound'—better than any singer I've ever heard." He stopped, then added smilingly, "Well, I guess maybe those critics who accuse me of longing wistfully for the past are right—if they're talking about that kind of music."

"Whenever Senator and Mrs. Goldwater are in the audience," said the sprightly singer (who is also an accomplished television actress), "we always know to perform 'My Cutie's Due at Two-to-Two.' One night we were doing 'Crazy Words, Crazy Tune,' and I didn't know the Goldwaters were in the audience. So when I came to the line that goes, 'You all heard yesterday, what did President Coolidge say?' I improvised a little and substituted the words 'Barry Goldwater' for 'Presi-

dent Coolidge.' After the show he and Mrs. Goldwater told me
how much they enjoyed it, so now whenever we perform in
Arizona I always use his name."

Goldwater's interest in sports remains strong, although he
finds little time for them anymore. "I still get to play a round
of golf once in a while," he said, "but not enough to sharpen
my game. And I'm no match for my brother." Bob Goldwater,
known as "Mr. Golf of Arizona," has won the state amateur
title three times, the Southwestern three times, the Phoenix
Invitational seven times, the Broadmoor (Colo.) Invitational,
and was runner-up in the Western Amateur. Barry had to settle for just one golfing title—the amateur half of the pro-
amateur crown he won in 1940 when he teamed with golf great
Sammy Snead. "And I damn near didn't win that one because
Snead wasn't sure he wanted to play with me when I waltzed
out on the course wearing Army shoes, Levis, and a T-shirt,
looking like a middleclass beatnik. But he stuck it out and now
I play with him at Greenbrier once every spring." That same
year, during the Western Open golf tournament, Goldwater
and some friends planted a microphone under the 18th hole.
"Then we sat in the bleachers with a mike," Goldwater recalled, "and the minute a golfer bent over to pick up his ball, a
voice coming from the cup would say, 'Thanks for coming—
come again next year.' They were some of the most surprised
golfers I've ever seen."

Playing early last year at Pine Valley, N.J. with Gen. Nathan
Twining and Michigan Rep. Gerald Ford, Goldwater scored a
hole-in-one on a 175-yard shot. Yet his card showed a three.
Goldwater's first tee shot landed in a lake. So after taking a
one-stroke penalty he tried a second time and popped it into
the cup.

When Barry came into the Goldwater organization full
time, his uncle Morris was still its president. And it was he,
above all others, who was instrumental in helping shape Barry's

views. "Morris had the greatest political influence on me," Barry admits. "I was always struck by his basic honesty, his sense of humility—of caring not whether people were Democrats or Republicans, but whether they were right or wrong. When he'd visit us in Phoenix or I'd go to Prescott he would talk to me for hours about the importance of abiding by your convictions."

When he was still in his teens, nephew Barry acted as chauffeur for Uncle Morris and his Republican debating opponent. "I was young then, but I'd listen to them argue publicly as though they were mortal enemies," he said. "Then the three of us would pile in the car and they'd have their arms around one another and be drinking a bottle of hootch. I'd drive off to where I thought we could collect another crowd and then I'd honk the car horn until a crowd gathered and they'd go at it again, just giving the devil to one another."

From Morris, too, the young Barry first acquired an idea of the family's role in Arizona history, and the role of all those pioneers who had fought and died facing fearful odds—if not, as Macaulay put it, for the ashes of their fathers and the temples of their Gods, at least for the opportunity to live, and die if need be, as men in search of freedom. Together with Morris he made a nostalgic journey to Ehrenberg to visit the once-prosperous store of his grandfather, and his interest in Arizona was heightened when he unearthed an old ledger and papers that had belonged to Mike Goldwater.

During the speech in Prescott which officially kicked off his 1952 senatorial campaign, Goldwater spoke of "those pioneers who came westward in their Conestoga wagons . . . those trappers and traders who traveled the mountain wilderness . . . those prospectors of the Walker party who first found paydirt in the hills of Yavapai . . . those stalwart Mormon pioneers who came south from Utah fortified with thrift, industry, and faith. These men and women, by individual initiative, by energy and hard labor, and by sheer grit and courage brought civilization ın a wilderness, established a well-ordered society in a lawless land, and laid the foundation for all that is good and great and worthwhile in Arizona today."

That could very well have been Morris Goldwater speaking.

As a result of his conversations with Uncle Morris, Barry Goldwater for the first time began thinking seriously about politics, about economic problems not directly connected with the operation of the Goldwater stores. He began reading those books of political theory he had neglected during his school years: Burke, Jefferson, Plato, Madison, Locke, Hamilton— their words now took on new meaning. He discovered that the history of the United States was inextricably related to the history of the Western frontier, and that there is an important historical thread which connects Appomatox and Arizona, Phoenix and the Philadelphia Constitutional Convention. He read and thought about the foundations of American constitutionalism, about the historical antecedents of the Declaration of Independence, about natural rights philosophy. And, perhaps because as the late Prof. Carl Becker phrased it, "Generally speaking, men are influenced by books which clarify their own thought, which express their own notions well, or which suggest to them ideas which their minds are already predisposed to accept," Goldwater was deeply impressed—so impressed that the one-time carefree playboy wrote a "guest editorial" in the *Phoenix Gazette* in the late 1930's, criticizing the New Deal for what he felt were its profligate spending tendencies.

A few months before America's official entry into war, when many Americans knew it would be only a matter of time before their sons would be fighting on foreign soil, 31-year-old reserve officer Goldwater signed up for a year's active duty with the Army Air Corps and was assigned to nearby Luke Field. He suffered at that time from astigmatism and from knees badly battered from his days playing semi-pro basketball. But he was valuable enough to the quickening defense effort to teach pilots the art of aerial gunnery and to co-author the Air Corps manual on fixed gunnery.

"I used to lecture quite a bit in those days and you know how guys are in the military," he said. "They'd be tired from being out the night before, or from their rigorous schedules, and I'd be showing them slides on gunnery and on aviation and about half the guys in the room would begin nodding their heads and some of them would go to sleep. So I sneaked in a few sildes of nudes one day and they almost hit the deck. I'd do it every once in a while and I never had trouble again with anyone dropping off to sleep during lectures."

But Goldwater wanted to fly military planes. And before long he hit on a workable scheme: Riding as a passenger in the rear cockpit of the training planes, he used his talents as a photographer to take pictures of pilots as they flew by in other planes. Instead of selling the pictures, he traded them for flight instruction . . . and became so proficient that when he later demanded an opportunity to qualify for service pilot wings he passed without difficulty. Soon thereafter he passed the test for a full pilot's rating.

In 1942, Captain Goldwater volunteered for the lone flight of single-engine fighter planes (P-47's) across the North Atlantic—a hazardous journey even under peaceful conditions. Later he flew cargo from India across the Hump to China. When the war ended, Lieutenant Colonel Goldwater remained in the reserve, becoming the first federally recognized officer in the Arizona Air National Guard when it was organized in 1946. Two years later he was awarded a trophy as the outstanding officer of the squadron, and was awarded a silver "loving cup" by the popular vote of 60 flight and administrative officers of the squadron. After his election to the Senate, Goldwater became commanding officer of the 9999th Combined Air Force Reserve Squadron, comprised of congressmen and congressional staff members.

But while Goldwater's Air Reserve duty permitted him to

combine his love for flying with his respect for the military (culminating in his promotion in 1962 to the rank of Major General), the Arizonan was soon to make his most enduring mark elsewhere—in the political arena, from where, in 1912, that colorful combatant Theodore Roosevelt (a frequent visitor to Arizona during his Rough Rider days) had defiantly proclaimed: "My hat's in the ring. The fight is on and I'm stripped to the buff."

CHAPTER 5

Goldwater's Arizona

"He speaks, and the words emerge in a soft, sepulchral baritone. They undulate in measured phrases, expire in breathless wisps. He fills his lungs and blows word-rings like smoke. The sentences curl upward. They chase each other around the room in dreamy images of Steamboat Gothic. Now he conjures moods of mirth, now of sorrow. He rolls his bright eyes heavenward. In funereal tones, he paraphrases the Bible . . . and church bells peal. 'Motherhood,' he whispers, and grown men weep. 'The Flag!' he bugles, and everybody salutes."

—TIME

IT Was obvious to readers of *Time's* cover story on Everett McKinley Dirksen, the subject of the ornate lines quoted above, that the writer—whose literary skill even John Lyly would have envied—enjoyed this euphuistic portrait. And with good reason. For if Dirksen had not existed, it would have been necessary for some imaginative writer to invent the euphonic orator whose florid phrases and resplendent responses have enabled him to become a Senate institution during his lifetime—and have led colleagues to suggest that perhaps Homer had anticipated the Illinois Republican when, more than twenty centuries ago, he wrote:

> "But when he speaks, what elocution
> flows!

> Soft as the fleeces of descending snows
> The copious accents fall, with easy art;
> Melting they fall, and sink into the
>   heart."

As eloquent as Everett McKinley Dirksen is, however, in the opinion of Arizonans his oratory could not compare with the grandeur, the flamboyance, the grandiloquence of their late, beloved Henry Fountain Ashurst.

"Five Syllable Henry," as Ashurst referred to himself, was born in Nevada but presented himself to Arizona when he was a year old. "I developed my passion for big words when studying Blackstone's Commentaries," he used to brag. "I practiced hurling five-syllable words across the desert. At the end of the second year I would throw 56-pound words clear across the Grand Canyon. As a matter of course I went into politics." But not before finishing college and law school. Shortly afterwards he was elected to the Territorial House of Representatives, then the Territorial Senate, and finally—when Arizona was admitted to the Union—to the U.S. Senate, where he served for 29 years.

Dressed in a black-braided cutaway coat, striped trousers, winged collar, and twirling silk-ribboned eye glasses, Ashurst was an unforgettable figure on Capitol Hill. "What marked him out in Washington," noted the *New York Times* after his death on May 31, 1962, "was not the dust of the far West, but his courtliness, his irresistible tendency to quote Shakespeare and other respected writers, and his passion for polysyllabic words." The *Washington Post*, in its obituary, called him "the last of the Senate's swashbuckling orators, who wielded words like a duelling sword. . . ."

When it was pointed out that the Arizonan twice voted for and twice voted against a soldier's bonus, Ashurst, in fine fustian style, and choosing the proper sesquipedalian words, told his colleagues, "My faults are obvious. There can be no doubt I have my full share. I suffer from *cacoethes loquendi*, a mania, or itch, for talking; from vanity, morbidity and, as is plain to everyone who knows me, from an inborn, inveterate flair for histrionics. But there never has been superadded to these vices of mine the withering, embalming vice of consistency. . . . Never have I let what I say yesterday bind me today. No Senator can change his mind quicker than I."

When Barry Goldwater arrived in Congress, Ashurst had been gone from the Senate for more than a decade. Shortly after he was defeated for reelection in 1940 he told his fellow senators, "When my present colleagues are here worrying about patronage, worrying about committee assignments, and about the scorching demands of constituents, I shall possibly be enjoying the ecstasy of the starry stillness of an Arizona desert night, or viewing the scarlet glory of her blossoming cactus, and possibly I may be wandering through the petrified forest in Arizona, a forest which lived its green milleniums and put on immortality 7 million years ago." But Ashurst had been too long in Washington by then and "Potomac fever," as well as the lure of other government jobs, proved a more powerful attraction than his remembrance of things past. He never returned to Arizona to live.

Still, he had served Arizona long and faithfully in the Senate, and his constituents long had admired him. "I knew him all my life," Goldwater recalled. "He was a close friend of my Uncle Morris." Therefore, in 1953, Goldwater decided to sort the many Ashurst speeches and select 14—one for each of Arizona's counties—which he believed indicated Ashurst's classic command of the English language and his range of subjects. "When he learned that I had published his speeches he was flattered," Goldwater said. "But when he heard that the collection was limited to 14, he said, 'Fourteen? My boy, I've made over 5,000 speeches!'"

And so he had, each one more sententious than the next. "There either is or there isn't a hereafter," he once said. "If there is, I'll be there. If there isn't, I'll never know it. But if

there is an eternity, don't think God will say, 'Henry Fountain
. . . you've cavorted and raised Hell and broken my Commandments . . . so you'll have to stay out.' No, I don't think
He'd want to run a Heaven that would keep Henry Fountain
Ashurst out."

"Communism," he said on another occasion, "is a fanatical
delusion that has no regard for the sacredness of human life nor
the value of human liberty; it would deprive labor of its wage,
ambition of its stimulus, excellence of its supremacy, and character of its respect. Many, if not most Communists, are persons who will remain obscure unless they become obnoxious,
and unhappily they choose the latter."

Another time he confessed, "The welfare of the United
States, and the happiness of our people, does not hang on the
presence of Henry Fountain Ashurst in the Senate. When that
realization first came to me I was overwhelmed by the horror
of it, but now it is a source of infinite comfort."

Before he died, at 87, Henry Fountain Ashurst had become
a movie actor—playing the part of a dozing Senator in the film
of the best-seller *Advise and Consent.* Seeing him on the screen,
none could doubt his serenity. And just a few years earlier,
when he turned 80, he had discoursed:

"When a man has reached the age of 80 years he should
have learned many things; he should have learned to make
peace with the Lord; with mankind; with himself, and to make
his will. When he has reached 80 years he has atoned, or tried
to atone, for the wrongs he has committed and has forgotten
the wrongs, if any, against himself.

"He finds that life runs in sort of a cycle: he is born without
teeth or hair, and in old age he is usually bereft of teeth and
hair. In early childhood days one's steps are short and uncertain
—in old age one's strides will be short and uncertain. He has
learned that as one grows old, one either develops the childish
intolerance of hardened arteries, or slides gracefully into a beautiful senility.

"He has learned that fame and riches may take wings, but that cultural and spiritual resources abide with him. He has learned that happiness may not be captured as a general would capture a city or as a hunter would capture a wild beast; he has probably learned the lessons taught by the prophets of ancient Palestine and the sages of ancient Athens: that happiness always eludes those who seek it for themselves, alone, but wells up like a loving tide around those who seek to give happiness to others."

(Undoubtedly the Arizona orator was confident that the same God who wouldn't want to run a Heaven without Henry Fountain Ashurst, just because he "cavorted, raised Hell, and broke Commandments," also wouldn't exclude him just because now and then he plagiarized from Shakespeare, among others.)

When Ashurst died, probably no one was more upset than Barry Goldwater, who, in addition to publishing the Ashurst speech sampler, also wrote an appreciation of the Southwest anachronism in *A Many Colored Toga: The Diary of Henry Fountain Ashurst*. The sorrow was genuine. For Ashurst, in addition to having been a personal friend and a link with Uncle Morris, had also been a link with that Arizona past which so captivated Goldwater.

Perhaps no public figure has been more influenced by his environment than Barry Goldwater. Few men ever have taken more from, or given as much in return to, their native states. A decade before he ran for public office, he wrote: "Arizona is a state of mind, some say. To others, it is a state of reality—but to all people it is a state of Beauty in all its many facets. Sometimes hers is the beauty of dark clouds and rain. Sometimes the beauty of her people and her history. Then again the light touch of moonlight adds softness to the contrasted brilliance of her sun."

Those are not the saccharine sentiments of a professional politician, one who expresses such statements for the record—

invariably the *Congressional Record*—and then mails copies of the remarks to constituents, in hopes they will be impressed that he has not forgotten them. They are the words of one who has been carrying on a life-long, deep love affair with his state.

Goldwater owns the world's largest—and perhaps only complete—collection of Kachina dolls (images of the Hopi and Zuni Gods), some 400 of which are exhibited in the Phoenix store. "John Rinker Kibby, an architect, started collecting the Kachinas about 1910," Goldwater said. "He acquired some of them for twenty-five cents, or an old razor blade, or anything the Hopis thought was a bargain. When he married, his wife wouldn't let them in the house. She didn't want them cluttering up her home. I was in the service at the time and I heard that the Belgian government was bidding for them so I phoned Kibby and said, 'I'll give you every cent I have in my savings account.' He asked me how much that was, and I replied, 'Twelve hundred dollars.' And he said, 'Sold.' Peggy picked up a few more for me, some I collected on my own, and together with Kibby's 300 the collection is now valued at $50,000 or more."

It was Kibby who escorted young Barry Goldwater on his first trip to the Indian reservation, somewhere between 1916 and 1918—a trip Goldwater was to repeat time and again. His affection for Arizona's Indians (83,387 of them, from 14 tribes, representing the greatest concentration of Indians in America) was acquired during these boyhood years, long before his entry into politics. From 1948 until 1950 he served on the Interior Department's advisory committee on Indian affairs. The Goldwater stores have long cleaned and repaired used childrens' shoes and given them to Indian children. And the first bill sponsored by freshman Senator Goldwater was, characteristically, aimed at benefiting the Papago Indians.

A few years ago, Maurice McCabe, Executive Secretary to

the Navajos, said that more legislation favorable to the development of the Navajo country was passed during the congressional session of 1958 than ever before in history. And he added, "We are pleased that Goldwater was the author or cosponsor of every one of these bills." The following year, Goldwater was named to serve on the board of Arrow, Inc., a nonprofit organization aimed at promoting Indian self-help projects, and developing educational and training programs for Indian youth.

Goldwater for many years has been a silent partner in a trading post backed against the Utah border on Arizona's sprawling Indian reservation. And, until it burned down in 1951, he owned Rainbow Lodge, adjacent to the trading post. The lodge accommodated 500 guests, and provided tours on mule-back to the spectacular Rainbow Bridge, to Indian cliff ruins, and to Navajo Mountain. And it boasted a 2,000-ft. runway strip, cleared primarily for Goldwater's frequent flights in and out. After the lodge burned, Goldwater never bothered replacing it. "I want to keep the property, though," he said, recently. "It's 18 miles from the nearest telephone, 70 miles to the nearest post office, and there's no mail service. Maybe someday I'll talk Peggy into having it rebuilt just for us."

The trading post remains in business, and still sells canned foods, shoes, clothing, hats, gasoline, tires, tubes—anything the Navajos need. "They do business on credit, which they call 'pawn,' " Goldwater explained. "They want to buy something, so they leave a necklace or belt, or something of value. They're very honest people—they always pay. It may take them forever, but they always pay."

Jack Williams, former Phoenix Mayor, recounted the time when he and Goldwater flew to the Navajo Reservation in Goldwater's private plane. "The reservation missionaries were giving a party to celebrate Christmas," Williams said, "and Barry thought it would be a good thing to take some gifts. So he loaded the plane with toys, trinkets, and presents and we flew up there, dropped off the gifts, and flew back the same day."

On another occasion Goldwater gave Mayor Williams a copy of *Dineh Bizad*, a Navajo-English dictionary. Over the years, however, he lost the copy he had purchased for himself. Williams, therefore, delighted in writing him letters in Navajo, knowing he couldn't translate them completely. Once, after Williams wrote a lengthy letter in Navajo to Goldwater's Washington office, Goldwater replied: "I don't know of any book I have given anyone that has produced as much hilarity and as much culture as has the gift of *Dineh Bizad* to you. Someday I'm going to give you an English dictionary and it should help as much as the Navajo one has."

Goldwater is a member of the Smoki Clan, a group of Arizona business and professional men who banded together in 1921 in an effort to reproduce artistically the age-old Indian ceremonials endemic to the Southwest Indians. Each August in Prescott, the Smoki Clan performs native dances in Indian costumes (the rituals were authenticated by study of the U.S. Bureau of Ethnology reports to the Smithsonian Institution). The only spurious note is that during the Snake Dance—a prayer for abundant rain and successful crops—the Smokis grip harmless bull snakes between their teeth, rather than the deadly rattlers used by the Hopis. Last August, Goldwater, who has performed in the ritual a half-dozen times (and has four dots tatooed on the fleshy part of his left hand as proof of membership in the Smokis), returned from Washington to narrate the ceremonies. In keeping with Smoki tradition no one, other than the Smokis themselves, knew he was scheduled to appear there; and there was no prior publicity and no announcement of Goldwater's appearance, either during or after the ceremony.

Goldwater's concern for the Indians reflects his affection for Arizona and its southwestern heritage. For years he has lectured extensively on Arizona's history and on her Indians. He has written frequently on the Southwest for *Desert* magazine and was at one time a heavy contributor to *Arizona Highways*. "When the pros started selling their pictures," he said, "I got out; it wasn't right for me to deprive a man of his livelihood." In 1959, he presented the art department of nearby Arizona State University with a collection of 78 prints, taken, between 1903-26, by the late Edward S. Curtis, the internationally known historian and photographer of North American Indians.

Two years ago, in the midst of a very busy congressional session, he took time to narrate and display 100 hand-colored slides of Arizona and New Mexico Indians, for members and guests of Phoenix's Heard Museum of Anthropology and Primitive Art. (Afterwards he donated some 900 slides from the famous Maude and Barto collection to the museum.) A few months later he journeyed to Tucson to sketch Arizona's history for members of the National Conference of Editorial Writers. And last December, a capacity audience at the annual membership meeting of the Arizona Historical Foundation listened as Goldwater described "The Colorado River: Mainstream of Arizona History."

Shortly after the war Goldwater installed in the Phoenix store an Electra-Map which he designed. Customers, by pushing a button, could light up any of 75 color views (which Goldwater photographed, often from the air) of Arizona landmarks, national parks, missions, or scenic spots. At the same time, a light flashed on the map, showing the geographical location of the lighted picture and telling which highways led to any given site.

Even the Goldwater house (named "Be Nun I Kin," meaning "House on the Hill" in Navajo) reflects his love of the Southwest. Viewed from the air, the house—situated on a hill overlooking surrounding Paradise Valley and Phoenix—is shaped like an arrow and Indian craftsmanship is woven throughout the interiors. The green slate for the floors was brought from the Navajo reservation and the massive front door is made of birch inset with mahogany in Indian designs. Shelves along the entry way are bordered with Navajo wood designs, inset panels of ceramic executed by Hopis are beneath the built-in ovens in the kitchen, the fireplace and andirons are of Hopi design, and Goldwater's desk carving is of Indian design.

Even the 150 tons of sandstone which went into the home were hauled by truck from the Navajo Indian Reservation some 300 miles away (after "Barry Sun Dust," as he is called by many Indians, obtained special permission of the Navajo Tribal Council). "The sandstone cost me $1 a ton," Goldwater remembered, "and it cost me $19 a ton to have it transported. I found it while I was riding up there during my boyhood. I had University of Arizona geologists analyze it and they say it's about 130 million years old."

The house also reflects its owner's life-long fixation for gadgets. Just outside the door is a small, abused pistol target. Not far from that is a flagpole hooked to a motor with a photoelectric cell. The motor raises the flag from a canister at sunrise and lowers it into the canister at sundown. Inside the home are motor-operated bar doors; a remote-control command post in the headboard of the master bed which operates a concealed TV set; a VHF radio next to his desk in the study, which gives the weather and permits him to monitor Phoenix's Sky Harbor Airport tower; a darkroom; a movie screen which automatically lowers out of the ceiling; and a home intercom system.

Each of these gadgets was installed by Barry Goldwater, usually with the aid of at least one of his sons.

Goldwater's fascination for Arizona has led him to undertake more than a half-dozen journeys down parts of the mighty Colorado River. On one occasion he guided a group of Boy Scouts (including his own son) down part of the river. And in 1939 he escorted Bob Ripley. "Ripley was doing his 'Believe It or Not' broadcasts at that time," said Goldwater. "He knew I knew something about the Colorado, so he phoned and asked whether I'd handle the microphone on the Grand Canyon portion of the show. Emery Kolb [a veteran explorer] and I went down to Phantom Ranch and Ripley gave Emery $25 to get a boat. Naturally the boat was of poor quality. According to the agreement, we were supposed to come down the river in it. Then Ripley told me he wanted us to come down at night, with me describing the trip as we came.

"I agreed. And everything went okay until I decided I'd have a little fun. Ripley had everything timed to the second, including the length of time I was to talk. So when I still had about a minute of airtime I announced, 'I have to leave the broadcast, the boat is sinking.' Ripley was all shook up and I never have discovered what he said to fill in that extra time. We set the boat adrift so some damned fool wouldn't try a trip down the river in it. And about a year later, at Tuna Falls, we found it crushed and wrapped around a rock 20 feet above water."

One of Goldwater's ambitions had always been to undertake a lengthy trip down the Colorado. Thus, early in July 1940, he began what was to prove to be a 700-mile, six-week journey. And, at the suggestion of Bill Saufley, he kept a day-by-day journal, 300 copies of which he later published in a private edition titled, *A Journey Down the Green and Colorado Rivers*. If the journal "merely serves the purpose of recording a delightful journey," Goldwater wrote in the Foreword, "I will feel repaid for the efforts expended. If anyone but myself should ever refer to it, I will be surprised."

The first evening, Tuesday, July 9, he wrote: "Here I was starting out to do something that has held a fascination for me ever since I first heard of the Colorado—the Powells—the Dellenbaughs—the Kolbs—and the other men who have tried their hands at running this strange river—this same river that intrigued my forefathers eighty years ago—this same river on which their successes and their failures came as often as this fickle river changed its course. Yes, here I was going to have my little whirl at it, to get it done and out of my system—then probably sit back on my haunches and wonder why."

The group, which kept scientific records of botanical, mineralogical, and natural life phenomena, consisted of three women and six men in three boats which had been constructed the previous winter by one of the members of the group, Norman Nevills. The boats were patterned after one Nevills used in making a similar trip two years earlier. They weighed 600 pounds, were 16 feet long, and approximately six feet wide at the center. They were constructed of half-inch plywood and contained two waterproof spaces, one forward and one aft, each equipped with hatch covers. And they were flat-bottomed, in order to avoid sandbars and rocks.

After guiding two boats through Hermit Falls on August 13, Goldwater noted in his journal: "I may be wrong but it seems to me that if one keeps one's eyes open and exercises caution, these rapids are nothing more than a little fast work plus a good dunking. Of course, the water is at an extremely low level and the rapids are undoubtedly less of a problem than they normally are, but I have come to believe that if one forgets the ominous roar of these rapids and the fact that people have built a halo of awesomeness around them, that they present nothing but a physical problem that can be easily overcome."

The rapids did not bother Goldwater, perhaps, but other things did. "Last night was one of those nights when God just makes up his mind He is going to be mean about it," he noted on July 23. "First of all, there were millions of those damned May flies. They live only 24 hours but that is too long. They squish when you swat them, and you have to swat them because they just roost on you and won't leave. Why we have May flies in July, the Lord only knows. A breeze came up and blew them away; then the breeze turned into a gale, and before you could wink, we were nearly blown away. Sand came in too copious quantities, and my ears, mouth, and eyes were soon filled. All this stopped in the early morning hours, however, and sleep finally came well past midnight."

Two days before the end of the exhausting journey Goldwater noted: "Sleeping in the open under God's own sky is one of the most overrated of all the acts of man or woman. It takes the finest of indoor sports and removes therefrom glint, glamour, and original intent. Forty nights of huffing and puffing my lungs into the deep recesses of a rubber void known as an air mattress have convinced me that an inner spring has ten thousand advantages. If one isn't tired when bedtime comes, one is in a complete state of collapse after spending many minutes blowing into one of these things.

"Another distinct advantage my bedroom has over God's big chamber is the one of sand and bugs. To begin with, at home nary a grain of sand ever enters my dreams. Out here where men are men, my dreams are born in sand, spend their early childhood in the sand, and spring at me in blasts of cutting, biting, itching, penetrating, everlasting emissaries of hell.

"Bugs—while I have on occasion entertained minor members of the clan between the sheets at home—are here ever with me. They falleth on the place beneath me and I am twice bitten—once before and once aft. Bugs of all shapes and sizes have promenaded over my body from top to bottom. Bugs with only a cursory interest have wandered over me and with no more than a 'humph' have let me be. Others, carrying knives, sabers, and broken bottles, have passed my way and left a divers collection of such tools of torture firmly implanted in my being. I have, as a result of their nocturnal visits, as fine a collection of bumps and itches as man ever sported. The lovely thing about these bites is that they never itch until one is almost asleep."

Goldwater's love and respect for nature, however, is stamped on almost every page as he knowingly describes the many canyons, rapids, and rivers encountered during the journey, outlines the history of different regions, and explains Spanish and Mexican influences along the way. Early in the trip he ends his daily insertion by noting that "all that remains to close this day, and allow us to go to our bed of sand, is for night to draw her blankets over the tops of the canyon that towers nearly 1,000 ft. over us. She is doing that very rapidly, so I'll say good night."

After a particularly fruitful conversation one night he noted: "These talks I have had with different people on the trip at night, lying under the stars, constitute one of its most enjoyable phases. This night in its full moon glory has been no exception. A mind is improved only when it is taken out once in a while and kneaded on the boards of discussion. Now it is time to close our camera shutters and also a good time to close the shutters of our eyes although I consider it sacrilege to blot from view such a glorious Arizona night. However, in this instance Brother Morpheus has more to say than have I, so good night."

Throughout the journey, Goldwater expressed his appreciation toward his fellow journeymen. "This Sabbath will be our last on the river," he wrote, "and while I will not use such a holy day for a prayer that such a trip be repeated, still I will thank the Lord for the friends I have had the honor to travel with these six weeks past."

Again he noted: "As we lay under a large willow this afternoon, we suddenly realized that day after tomorrow will be our last together. I can't say any of us is sorry enough to be bothered, but there will be some sadness in leaving good friends. One cannot eat, live and sleep with people for 42 days without some attachment growing therefrom. The nucleus for a splendid trip was presented by those present and a lot of our fun and interest has been of our own manufacture."

At the end of the journey he wrote: "I cannot express my happiness at seeing not only my wife standing on the boat but also my beloved daughter, Joanne. Weeks of lonesomeness were wiped away in an instant—weeks that had seemed years became moments. I know that every member of our party who had a loved one on that boat felt as I felt. Nothing in God's world gives one such an appreciation of home and family as does a prolonged absence. . . . We have landed. Our journey is over. The Colorado River has shown nine more people its closely guarded beauties and nine people are tonight happy for having been along, and happy that it is over."

As Goldwater predicted at the outset, the journey did not turn up anything of earth-shaking interest. Rather, it was the culmination of his desire to undertake an arduous and potentially risky trip through what up until then had been virtually undiscovered land. But a subsequent expedition of Goldwater's did turn up something unique—a natural bridge.

During a flight over the eastern end of the Grand Canyon in 1951, on his way to view the charred remains of Rainbow Lodge, Goldwater glanced from his airplane and noted the shadow of what appeared to be a bridge. "I had never heard of a bridge of this seeming magnitude being located in this part of the Canyon," he wrote in *Arizona Highways* in 1955. "So I circled at great length and . . . verified the fact that the sun's rays going through an opening in the cliff indicated the existence of a bridge." That afternoon, flying over the identical spot, the bridge was nowhere to be seen.

About a year later, on a trip over the Canyon to Utah, Goldwater again spotted the bridge in the morning but could not find it when he returned in the afternoon. Some months later he reported his findings to a group preparing to embark on a journey down the Colorado, and he gave them instructions. But the group was unable to locate the bridge in either of two surrounding canyons.

Goldwater planned a boat trip to the site in 1953 and again in 1954. But by then he was in the Senate and both times long congressional sessions interfered with his plans, even though during the Christmas holiday in 1953 he completed an aerial reconnaissance of the area and photographed the bridge from his plane. Discussions with officials of the Department of the Interior and with the park naturalist of the Grand Canyon convinced him that it was an undiscovered bridge.

Goldwater then arranged with Bob Gilbreath, a helicopter pilot with Arizona Heli Dusters, to land in Nankoweap Canyon, which he was sure would be within walking distance. The hike proved to be far more difficult than either had envisioned, and it wasn't until hours later that they came upon the 200-foot-high bridge.

"By then I was exhausted and every muscle in my body ached," Goldwater wrote, "but a great peace and calmness came over me as I realized that here at the end of this arduous trail was that which I had been seeking. I sat there and wondered if any other white man had ever looked upon this thing from such a close vantage point. I suspected that Indians in the past had travelled up here because we found pottery down below and because we know that Indians at one time lived at the mouth of Nankoweap. None of the usual evidence of man's visits, however—tin cans, empty cartons, and the like —disturbed the cool calmness of this bit of God's handiwork. . . . Hundreds of feet above it is the start of a waterfall that must be spectacular when the Winter snows are melting and water comes over the redness of that sheer rock. The water would fall behind this bridge and I imagine fill it with spray as it gushed out to fill the dry stream bed in which we were standing."

Goldwater photographed the bridge from every possible angle. On Nov. 22, 1954, the National Park Service confirmed his discovery. "That was the toughest walking I ever did in my life," he recalled. "Bob [Gilbreath] said that he'll never do another trip like that again. He says if he ever hears of me again he's going to run."

Goldwater long has been interested in the pronounced Spanish and Mexican influence in Arizona. During a vacation in Spain in 1955, he decided to pursue his personal research of the history of early Spanish explorations of what is now Arizona. Through the cooperation of the Spanish government he tracked down several items from old parchment records in Madrid's naval museum, then photographed and microfilmed the material. When the project is finished, after Goldwater forsakes politics, he intends to make copies available to libraries and historical societies throughout the state.

One such society is the Arizona Historical Foundation, which Goldwater endowed and helped finance through proceeds from his newspaper column and from money donated by organizations which otherwise would have paid Goldwater a fee for his speeches. This non-profit foundation seeks to stimulate the study of Arizona history in the state's schools and colleges, and it publishes books and collects information about Arizona from out-of-state sources.

Although Arizona's Spanish-speaking community (which comprises approximately 15 per cent of the state's population) is 90 per cent Democratic, it has rallied strongly behind Goldwater in his two previous elections. Last summer a group of Spanish-Americans formed a statewide Goldwater-for-President group, Arriba Con Barry ("Up With Barry"), similar to the Latinos Con Goldwater organization of Spanish-speaking Americans throughout the Southwest (headed by the 1960 national co-chairman of the Viva Kennedy clubs).

Goldwater gained the support of the Spanish-American community for his successful efforts on behalf of a World War II veteran whom the Immigration Service sought to deport for illegal entry, for his long-time life membership in the American Legion Thunderbird Post #41 (Comprised of Spanish-Americans), for organizing and flying relief missions carrying medical supplies and food to areas of northern Mexico which suffered a disastrous flood shortly after the war, and for being able to speak the language. "Peggy and I went to Mexico City

right before the 1952 campaign," Goldwater said, "and I
wanted to brush up on my Spanish but I had a devilish time.
Everybody I ran into wanted to brush up on his English.
Finally I found a janitor in the hotel who said he'd help me
out. So I got up early each morning and beat it downstairs to
converse with him."

There is no mistaking Goldwater's pride in Arizona, a state
whose rugged beauty and sharp contrasts, whose sparse desert
and majestic Grand Canyon, have enthralled visitor and native
alike. "It is a land of never-ending wonder and beauty—a land
of both age and youth, of antiquity and newness," Goldwater
wrote. "There must be many places here still unexplored by
man, such as that cool, quiet place high up in a side canyon of
Nankoweap, where Bob [Gilbreath] and I sat in peace and saw
the bridge for the first time. More of us should seek the
hallowed, untainted grandeur which God has tucked away beyond the sunswept highways of our beautiful State."

Typical denizen of the Arizona desert in the late 1800's.

An ore train leaving the Silver King (Ariz.) mine, c. 1890.

The first Goldwater store at Prescott (1876-80). This was the fourth store, following previous establishments at La Paz, Ehrenberg and Phoenix.

Members of the Arizona Rangers, at the turn of the century.

Central Avenue in Phoenix, 1911.

Mike Goldwater

Morris Goldwater

Two-year-old Barry Goldwater

Baron Goldwater

Josephine Goldwater

Bob, Barry, and Carolyn Goldwater in 1920.

Phoenix Union High School, attended by Barry Goldwater in 1923, as elected president of the freshman class.

Football center Goldwater at the University of Arizona, 1928.

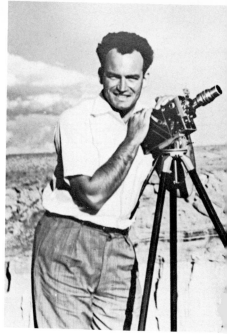

Motion picture filming in the Grand Canyon, late 1930's.

Barry Goldwater (front-center) as Captain of Company C, Staunton Military Academy, 1927.

Captain Goldwater,
instructor at
Luke Air Force Base, 1942.

Wedding of Barry and
Peggy Goldwater, Muncie,
Indiana, 1934.

Major Goldwater,
China-Burma-India theater, 1944.

Bob and Barry Goldwater in
store office, late 1940's. On
wall is painting of Morris
Goldwater.

Barry Goldwater and sons Mike (left) and Barry, Jr. (right) on camping trip, 1950.

Bob "Believe It or Not" Ripley and Barry Goldwater, on trip into Grand Canyon.

Barry Goldwater (standing, right) with Neville Colorado River expedition.

Goldwater and victorious Phoenix City Council reformers, 1951.

Campaign manager Goldwater and Republican Arizona gubernatorial candidate Howard Pyle, 1950.

Senator Goldwater campaigning for re-election in 1958, with Phoenix rancher John M. Jacobs.

Senatorial candidate Goldwater and presidential hopeful Eisenhower, at political rally in 1952.

Swearing-in of Senator-elect Goldwater in 1953. At right is Vice-President Barkley; center is Senator Frank Barrett (Wyo.).

Jet pilot Goldwater in 1955.

Be Nun I Kin, House on the Hill—the Goldwater home in Paradise Valley. A thousand yards distant is Camelback Mountain.

Goldwater in Senate office with part of 500-piece Hopi Kachina collection, 1958.

Rear: son Mike, daughter Joanne and son-in-law Dr. Thomas Ross. Center: daughter Margaret ("Peggy, Jr."), wife Peggy and Barry Goldwater. Kneeling is Barry, Jr. Photo taken at Newport Beach, Calif. vacation in 1962.

Goldwater and his bulldog, Cyclone. Hopi design inset on front door of Goldwater home.

Goldwater and Vice-President Nixon at Republican National Convention in 1960.

Goldwater speaking to Republican Convention in 1960. At left is Senator Thruston Morton, Convention chairman.

Barry Goldwater with Democrat friends: above left, Senator and Mrs. Goldwater at the home of Senator Harry Byrd; above right, Goldwater and ex-President Truman; below, Goldwater and President Kennedy share a joke in front of the White House.

(Left) Goldwater at a Hershey, Pa. rally in 1963; (right) Goldwater after speech to 13th biennial Young Republican convention at San Francisco.

Senator and Mrs. Goldwater scan the 18,000-plus crowd at Madison Square Garden rally of political youth organization, Young Americans for Freedom, in 1962.

Parade marshal Goldwater at Prescott (Ariz.) 76th annual Frontier Day celebration, July 4, 1963.

Major General Goldwater in cockpit of Convair F-106B Delta Dart fighter, after flight at twice the speed of sound over California desert.

Barry Goldwater, following his January, 1964 announcement that he would seek the Republican nomination for the Presidency. On crutches following foot surgery, Goldwater stands with daughters Joanne (left) and Margaret, and Mrs. Goldwater.

(Below left) Barry Goldwater at the White House in 1963; (below right) Barry Goldwater campaigning in New Hampshire for that state's presidential primary, January, 1964.

CHAPTER 6

Politics

"Organization is man's solution to his sense of guilt. The very fact of organization attenuates personal moral responsibility; and, as organization becomes more elaborate and comprehensive, it becomes increasingly the instrumentality thru which moral man indulges his natural desire to commit immoral deeds. A crime which would press heavily on the conscience of one man, becomes quite endurable when divided among many."
—ARTHUR SCHLESINGER, JR.

AFTER the war, Barry Goldwater returned to his family and to the store. Much had changed during the interim. By now there were four children—Joanne, Barry Jr., Michael, and Peggy—with whom he had to become re-acquainted. And he also would have to adjust to the different pace of civilian life.

Before long the ex-pilot had resumed his favorite civilian activities. He took the children on camping and hunting trips to every corner of the state. He resumed his talks and lectures on Arizona history. And he added to his photographic and slide collection. But the older, more mature businessman also developed other interests, and he soon experienced his first brush with public life. Arizona, in 1946, became the third state to pass a right-to-work law, and Goldwater led the retailers' portion of the campaign. "I volunteered to help," he said. "Actually, I didn't do much. I wrote a few letters and gave a few speeches, but that was all. Even at that time, most Arizonans agreed on the fairness of not requiring a worker to join a labor union, or any other organization, against his will."

The following year Goldwater became general chairman of the Community Chest Campaign, which raised the largest sum ever collected to that date on behalf of the city's chest activities. He served on the Arizona Interstate Stream Commission and as a member of the Interior Department's advisory commission on Indian affairs. Through it all, however, he managed to stay aloof from actual partisan politics. So did most of the other leading citizens of Phoenix, with the result that the city fell into a state of social decay.

By the late 1940's, widespread prostitution and gambling flourished in Phoenix, openly and in defiance of city ordinances and state laws. A city manager, told by the police chief that no organized prostitution existed, discovered the town's brothels for himself. But when he demanded that the City Council crack down, both he and the police chief were replaced. In October of 1949, the American Social Hygiene Association surveyed the city (so that the military would know of vice conditions in areas next to its Arizona establishments) and reported that as many as 15 brothels were in operation, that members of the city police vice squad secretly ordered the bordellos to turn off their lights at night and limit their operation to only one girl per house just before impending city elections, that city officials were being paid off by prostitutes, and that taxi drivers were equipped with a "preferred list" of brothels.

The city was plagued with other ills. Under its weak city manager-commission form of government, the city manager could be replaced at the whim of a majority on the commission. (In the 35 years prior to 1950, the city changed managers 31 times, the average tenure being about 14 months.) Near the end of the 1940's, deficits loomed everywhere in the city's finances. Capital funds and even bond funds had been diverted to meet current bills and city purchases were based to a large extent on favoritism. Cronyism was rampant.

In 1947, the decent citizens of Phoenix decided they had had enough. The Mayor appointed a committee of 40 prominent Phoenicans to study possible revisions in the 34-year-old city charter. This group demanded that the City Council call a special election on a proposed charter amendment to establish a strong, qualified, and experienced city manager, responsible for city administration but also secure from the caprice of the Council. The amendment also proposed enlarging the Council from five to seven at-large members, eliminating staggered terms, and investing in the Council all authority to adopt ordinances, establish policy and remove the manager.

The changes were approved the following year. But the administration of the city changed little, for the majority bloc of the Council merely appointed persons of like mind to fill the newly-created Council seats. So, another citizens committee was formed; this one, independent of the city administration, was composed of more than 100 prominent people. The aim of the Charter Government Committee, as it came to be known, was to elect a Council which would live up to the city charter, especially the amendment which called for a strong, qualified and experienced city manager.

The Committee approached Goldwater, Phoenix's Man of the Year, and asked whether he would run for a seat on the Council. He declined, pointing to his political inexperience and his involvement in the family business. But when a candidate withdrew a few days before the deadline for filing, long-time friend Harry Rosenzweig, former North Central Athletic Club member, inveigled Goldwater into accepting a place on the nonpartisan Charter Ticket. But not before Goldwater thought long and hard about Uncle Morris' belief that it was a moral obligation for successful businesses and businessmen to repay, by whatever means, the communities which helped make possible their success. When he reached his decision, and was unable to contact brother Bob (to this day a registered Democrat; "Barry's the honest one in the family," the younger Goldwater says) and Phoenix store manager Bill Saufley, both of whom were out of town, he wrote them the following letter:

"You both will probably think me seven kinds of a dirty bastard when you hear that I have decided to run for councilman along with Harry. . . . I don't think a man can live with himself when he asks others to do his dirty work for him. I couldn't criticize the government of this city when I myself refused to help. I don't know if we can win but if we do then I know Phoenix will have two years of damned good government that I hope will set a pattern for the coming years and the coming generations. There has always been one and sometimes two Goldwaters damned fools enough to get into politics and they always did it with service in their minds, which is the way I approach this thing. My unbounded confidence in the organization of this firm gives me assurance of its being well run no matter who is around and that helps a lot. I do however look forward to an unusual amount of time to give this business as well as the city. The city needs help more than any of our governments. Maybe we can give it to them. Maybe we will suffer doing it, but in our minds we will be doing what Americans should always be doing. Helping each other.

"Don't cuss me too much. It ain't for life and it may be fun."

In November of 1949 the highest percentage of registered voters in a city election for the period between 1947 and 1961 went to the polls. When the results were in the 40-year-old businessman not only led the ticket, carrying every precinct, but he polled three times as many votes as his nearest rival in pacing the Charter Government's sweep of city hall. The following month, Goldwater was elected vice-chairman of the new City Council.

The surgery performed on Phoenix by the new administration was sure and swift. Three months after the Charter group took office, and six months after the initial American Social

Hygiene Association report deplored the extent of vice in Phoenix, the association issued a new report, saying, "Phoenix is a changed city. It is no longer a vice center." It quoted a madam as saying, in the wake of the crackdown on prostitution following the Charter Government victory, "It looks as though it [her brothel] will stay closed for the next two years, until a new election can be held." In 1950 Phoenix was presented with an All-America City Award, given by the National Municipal League and *Look* magazine.

The refurbishing of Phoenix's image continued along other fronts. When the reform group took office in January of 1950, revenue projections showed that the city would spend itself $400,000 into the red on the budget prepared by the preceding administration. But, as the result of revised spending and a series of economy moves, the city actually ended the fiscal year with a $277,000 surplus. Modern budgetary control procedures were established. Duplications were eliminated and contracts were awarded on the basis of competitive bidding. The police department was reorganized along lines suggested by the Northwestern University Traffic Institute. The city property tax rate declined from $2.28 per $100 of assessed valuation in fiscal 1949-50 to $1.87 the following year, declined two more cents the following year, and in 1955 dropped to $1.75, where it remains today.

But more important than any set of weighty statistics was the fact that the reform movement, of which Goldwater was an integral part, brought order out of chaos, drove crime back underground, and allowed law abiding citizens once again to hold up their heads.

"Barry was the same then as he is now when it came to spending tax money," recalled Jack Williams, who served on the Council with Goldwater. "He just raised Cain at budget hearings whenever he thought we were spending too much. And he always disliked contingency funds, which he pretended not to understand. I didn't know until later that he thought it was excess money that should be returned to the taxpayers. He argued that the availability of such funds was a temptation that should be removed."

At one Council meeting, Goldwater, whom some critics accuse of being subservient to big business, assailed Southern Pacific because the railroad stood in the way of expansion of the Phoenix city limits in a southeasterly direction. He wanted the carrier to bring its yards and roundhouse inside the city and improve them. On another occasion he told downtown merchants that the city had no intention of providing public parking lots. "He told the merchants that if they wanted parking lots, they would have to build them themselves," Williams said. "They were rather unhappy with Barry, but they knew he meant business."

The year after his election to City Council, Goldwater was approached by Howard Pyle, a popular Arizona radio announcer who today is head of the National Safety Council. Pyle, a Republican, had been impressed with the increasing number of Republicans in the state and he decided it was time for someone to challenge the strong Democratic tradition. If he ran, would Barry manage his campaign? Goldwater agreed, on the stipulation that the race not be used merely as a barometer to record GOP sentiment; he would manage it only if Pyle were sincere about waging a tough, round-the-clock campaign. Pyle agreed, and subsequently announced his choice of Goldwater to serve as campaign manager. On May 28, 1950, *The Arizona Republic* editorialized:

"The choice of Barry Goldwater as campaign manager for Howard Pyle, Republican candidate for Governor of Arizona, is a particularly fortunate one. He is a young man, full of enthusiasm as well as sound ideas, and should add a great deal of strength to the already formidable movement to give new life to the party in Arizona. . . .

"One of the hopeful and refreshing aspects of the appointment of Barry Goldwater to work with Howard Pyle is the fact that neither is a saddle-galled politician who has spent his life at the public trough. Both are young businessmen, with . . . progressive ideas. For this reason, they should contribute much to a revival of the party and add greatly to its strength."

If ever a party was in need of strengthening, it was the moribund Arizona GOP. Despite the stirring at the grass roots, Democrats in 1950 still outnumbered Republicans by 5-1. Only twice had Republicans controlled the state house. The situation was even worse in the county government. But Pyle had made a promise to run scared, and Goldwater intended to see that he kept it. All during that summer, candidate and campaign manager hopped, skipped, and jumped from city to town in Goldwater's red, white, and blue Beechcraft, running up more than 22,000 miles together. When the vote was in, Pyle had won by almost 3,000 votes—a tribute to his pleasant personality, the fact that overconfident Arizona Democrats had nominated a female to oppose Pyle, and to the tireless campaign mapped and waged by Pyle's indefatigable campaign manager. Almost overnight, the Republican Party of Arizona found itself alive and kicking.

When Goldwater resigned from the City Council (to which he had been re-elected in 1951) to run for the U.S. Senate, the odds were more heavily against him than they had been against Howard Pyle. The Democrats had learned the penalty of complacency: the Republican challenger would be facing the party's strongest candidate—the incumbent Ernest McFarland —a rustic, slow-spoken gladhander who not only was extremely popular in Arizona but also held the prestigious post of Majority Leader of the U.S. Senate. Furthermore, the national Democratic Party, in an effort to stymie Arizona's drift toward Republicanism, unleashed its big guns—Senators Lister Hill (Ala.) and Robert S. Kerr (Okla.); Speaker Sam Rayburn (Tex.) and Vice-President Alben Barkley (who made TV plugs)—in support of McFarland.

McFarland, who had proved his political appeal when he defeated the popular Henry Fountain Ashurst in the 1940 state Democratic primary, appeared little concerned with Goldwater. His strategy seemed to be to ignore the upstart businessman as though he were some kind of temporary aberration on the Arizona political scene.

But Goldwater had no intention of being ignored, or of ignoring McFarland. Even before he opened his formal general election campaign for the Senate on Sept. 18, 1952, he was busy lashing out at McFarland. In a speech that March, Goldwater said that McFarland was "a clean, honest American." But he added that he had succumbed to political pressures and condoned dishonesty in government. Referring to the Majority Leader's staunch loyalty to President Truman, Goldwater asked, "How can Senator McFarland defend the President when Harry Vaughn [Truman's military aide, whose name figured prominently in White House influence-peddling and deep freeze scandals] sits in his lap?"

When, two months later, the publisher of the *Arizona Daily Star*, a Tucson newspaper, asked editorially, "What Kind of a Republican Are You, Mr. Goldwater?" Goldwater quickly answered:

"I am not a 'me too' Republican. I am not a Fair Deal Republican. I am a Republican who believes that all Republicans and all Democrats must practice in their personal and business lives those principles of honesty, integrity, devotion, and thrift which all of us long to see re-established in our national government. I am a Republican opposed to the super-state, gigantic bureaucratic centralized authority, whether it be administered by Democrats or Republicans.

"I am a Republican who is opposed to appeasement, who is shocked and saddened at the failure of our 'now do nothing— now do anything' State Department, whose vacillating policies have resulted in a deterioration of world affairs and the loss of prestige and respect for the flag which I hold dear.

"I am a Republican who is opposed to Communism, and particularly to the Communist-inclined sympathizer and the Communist-inclined policymakers and their companion wishful thinkers. They have exercised far too much influence upon our stand in world concerns. I am a Republican who gives more than lip service to a balanced budget. I believe individuals and individual local government, city councils, county supervisors and state legislatures must reassert their independence and their responsibility, that we the free people of this nation must demand an end to government subsidies, deficit financing and living beyond our income. . . . I am a Republican who believes we must practice economy in regard to our own projects, and I am a Republican who believes that economy can and must be had in respect to the present national budget."

Fittingly enough, Goldwater chose Prescott—home of his pioneer forebears—for the formal kickoff of his campaign. Addressing a crowd of some 700 plus a statewide radio audience, from the steps of historic Yavapai County Courthouse, Goldwater sighted in on McFarland and the Democrats. The principal issue of the campaign was a simple one, he said: "The Truman Fair Deal, after seven years of expanding governmental bureaucracy, of increasing central authority, of economic tinkering, of government-created inflation, of pyramiding confusion on crisis, and crisis on confusion . . . seven years of the highest taxes ever extracted from the American citizen . . . seven years of the greatest spending program . . . seven years which have brought us from a peak of power and respect in the world to a position where we must now get down on our kneees and pay ransom for the release of an American citizen . . . after seven years of this the Truman Fair Deal asks you to put your stamp of approval upon that appalling record of waste, inefficiency, dishonesty and failure, both at home and abroad."

The Republicans, he told his audience, propose to end waste, to overhaul and revise the existing machinery of government, to elect men who will regard office as a public trust, and not as a personal possession for private looting . . . and to establish a carefully thought-out foreign policy.

But perhaps the biggest departure from the Goldwater stereotype erected by today's critics was his discussion of what he termed "the social gains which have been made in the past 20 years." He praised the Securities Exchange Commission, saying it helps protect the individual investor. He praised the Reconstruction Finance Corporation. He applauded the establishment of the Social Security system, of unemployment insurance, old-age assistance, and aid to dependent children and to the blind. He spoke approvingly of the Federal Housing Administration. "These things have been of great benefit to the people," he said. "They were created by the Congress of the United States. And no responsible Republican has any intention or any desire to abolish any one of them."

Then Goldwater proceeded to ridicule McFarland's earlier claim that he was one of the four most powerful men in the U.S. One by one he enumerated individual cases in the Democratic mink coat and freezer scandals, and asked if the incumbent, as one of the four most powerful Americans, claimed 25 per cent of the corruption. He asked whether McFarland wished to take 25 per cent of the blame for the "inflation which has robbed your dollar of its purchasing power, forced prices up and up and up, eaten into your savings, and now forces you to pay $1.10 a pound for round steak, 92 cents a dozen for eggs, and 89 cents a pound for coffee."

He added:

"Will the junior Senator from Arizona take 25 per cent of the credit for increasing your taxes, for the fact that the federal government is now collecting 800 per cent more dollars in taxes than was collected in 1941?

"Will the junior Senator from Arizona, will this Fair Deal spokesman, who tells you he is one of the four most important men in the government of the United States, that he has power and influence—will he accept his share of the responsibility for the more than 117,000 American boys who have been killed, wounded, or captured in Korea?

"Now the junior Senator has kept silent on many things, but he has expressed himself positively and publicly on the Korean War. In Coolidge, Ariz., the junior Senator told a service club the Korean War is a cheap war because we are killing nine Chinese for every American boy. Then he added, it is the Korean War which makes us prosperous.

"I challenge the junior Senator from Arizona to find anywhere within the borders of Arizona or within the borders of these United States a single mother or father who counts our casualties as cheap . . . who would be willing to exchange the life of one American boy for nine Red Communists or 900 Red Communists, or nine million Red Communists."

McFarland realized that he had made a political error by adopting the Truman-like line of belittling the extent of the Korean War. The Senate Majority Leader was stung and no longer could afford to act as though his challenger didn't exist. So he hit back, ridiculing the businessman's inexperience and political ineptitude. Goldwater countered by charging, wrongly, that McFarland was a socialist. McFarland retaliated by having a Phoenix attorney, Frank Beer, read to a radio audience a letter Goldwater wrote to McFarland during the war requesting the Senator's aid in being transferred from the infantry to the air force. Goldwater exploded, charging that the implication of Beer's radio talk was that he had used influence to avoid combat duty.

"I have my combat wings," Goldwater replied. "I served overseas. I have more than two thousand hours of active military flying time. I volunteered for active service four months before Pearl Harbor, and I served continuously on active duty until after V-J Day, 1945. And when Truman started his war in Korea, I volunteered for active duty again, and was rejected for age and rank. This is the war McFarland, speaking in Coolidge in November of 1951, said was a 'cheap war.'

"My service is not unusual. Thousands of Arizona boys gave far more. At the specific request of Col. Ennis Whitehead, I asked for a transfer from the infantry reserve where I had held a commission since 1930, to the air corps and assignment to Luke Field Air Base on active duty. McFarland has published that letter requesting active service. Beer twists this request for active service into an evil, cowardly thing. Beer, speaking for McFarland, calls it 'influence seeking.'

"I confess I did everything I could to get assigned to active duty when my country was in danger. I went on active duty at Luke Field. I was transferred to Yuma to assist in the activation of the Yuma Gunnery School. And the first class of cadets to graduate from Yuma had a 20 point higher rating than those at my old station at Luke. From Yuma, I was transferred to the Ferry Command. I was one of ten men who volunteered to fly P-47's, single engine army pursuit aircraft, across the North Atlantic. For this assignment I was awarded the Air Medal.

"On my citation it says that I volunteered for an assignment which meant certain death in the event of engine failure.

"I served in the Mediterranean theater. I served in India and China. I came back to the United States assigned to the 4th Fighter Squadron as gunnery officer stationed at Van Nuys, Calif. My outfit was preparing to go back overseas when the war ended.

"I have no desire to capitalize on my war service and so far in this campaign I have minimized it. But I will not permit a cheap slur on my service to my country to go unchallenged, especially when it is motivated by political reasons, inspired by my opponent, and voiced by a man, Frank Beer, who was not in the service, who, in fact, was occupied during part of the war defending [a local man] against court-martial charges for allegedly stealing meat from the government."

As his campaign gathered momentum, at each whistlestop—or, in his case, at each country airport—Goldwater preached appeals for economy in government, for peace with honor in

Korea. At the insistence of campaign manager Stephen Shadegg, a knowledgeable politico who planned Democratic Sen. Carl Hayden's 1950 re-election campaign, Goldwater appeared often on radio and television (the latter a medium suited to his direct, personal approach). And he continued to challenge McFarland to debate, "soberly, seriously, and without name calling." McFarland, very much the front runner, refused. And Goldwater, in exasperation, accused his opponent of "ignoring every issue which concerns our future."

On a radio and TV broadcast, Goldwater contended that McFarland had said nothing about high prices, high taxes, and inflation, "or what should be done to restore the purchasing power of the dollar." Instead, the challenger said, McFarland's only issues were simply that "Goldwater is not a college graduate, owns a house in La Jolla, Calif. and was a society soldier." He then sketched briefly his military background, admitted to owning the house in La Jolla, and confessed that he was guilty as charged of not being a college graduate. He added, "As a matter of fact, my father died during my first year at college and I came home to go to work in the family business."

As the campaign was drawing to a close, McFarland was still the overwhelming choice to win the election, but his stock had been dropping steadily. Goldwater, on the other hand, was picking up support with each appearance. His partisans cheered lustily at every dusty watering stop along the way. And across the state, Goldwater workers installed 200 sets of Burma-Shave-like signs which taunted:

> "*Mac is for Harry*
> *Harry's all through*
> *You be for Barry*
> *'Cause Barry's for you."*
> —GOLDWATER FOR SENATOR.

When the tumult and the shouting ended, Goldwater defeated McFarland by 7,000 votes—36,000 fewer than Eisen-

hower's victory over Stevenson in Arizona. And although Goldwater often since has claimed that he was "the greatest coat-
tail rider in history," the fact remains that he ran an outstanding race against overwhelming odds.

Senator-elect Barry Goldwater arrived in Washington on his
44th birthday late New Year's night, for the opening of the
1953 congressional session. With him were his wife and
mother, both of whom wanted to witness the oath-taking ceremonies. Lame-duck Senator Ernest McFarland, whose term
didn't expire until noon on January 3, was still presiding over
the Democratic caucus which met to name minority Senate
officers. And Goldwater, the second Republican to be elected to
the U.S. Senate from Arizona since statehood, was more than
somewhat bewildered that soon he would be a member, if only
a very junior member, of the greatest deliberative body in the
world.

But Goldwater was not alone in his bewilderment. Ten other
Republican senators, including Thomas Kuchel (Calif.), John
Sherman Cooper (Ky.), and Prescott Bush (Conn.), were also
experiencing the agony of uncertainty and unfamiliarity. Goldwater's jitters were calmed when he was escorted, for the swearing-in rites, to Vice-President Alben Barkley's rostrum by
Arizona's senior Senator, Carl Hayden, who had been a legislator in the national capital longer than any other member of
the new Congress—ever since 1912.

It was inevitable that conservative Goldwater would almost
immediately become acquainted with "Mr. Republican"
Robert A. Taft, Ohio's tower of congressional integrity. And
they hit it off from the start. "I wanted a seat on the Interior
Committee," Goldwater said, "because of its importance to
the West. But, frankly, I didn't have any seniority, and besides
Taft wanted me on the Labor Committee. He said there should
be a businessman on it, so I took it." Goldwater's second committee choice had been Armed Services. But again he was out-

ranked. Thus on Jan. 13, 1953, nine days after the convening of Congress, he was assigned to the Labor and Public Welfare Committee and to the Banking and Currency Committee. Two weeks later he was named chairman of the Banking Committee's Subcommittee on Economic Stabilization, a post which handled price, wage, and rent control matters.

Goldwater's friendship for Taft was as genuine as his respect for the Ohioan was deep. Today he proudly points to the fact that his Senate desk formerly belonged to Taft. But he never blindly followed Taft. Just months before he became a U.S. Senator, Goldwater was one of 14 Arizona delegates to the national Republican Convention. And, although he personally favored Taft, he announced to the remaining delegates that he had decided to cast his vote for Eisenhower in protest over what he considered the high-handed tactics of the state pro-Taft faction. Three other delegates joined him.

Goldwater's first Senate speech, on Feb. 18, was a brief plea for freedom from government price supports in the cattle industry. His first major speech, delivered three months later, was a lengthy indictment of price controls. Armed with numerous statistical tables, charts, a consumer price index, wholesale price list, historical references, and personal observations, the Arizona businessman vigorously defended a free economy in a speech which proved a prelude to his incessant demand for freedom of consumer choice.

The first legislation sponsored by Goldwater was the so-called Bricker Amendment, a joint resolution proposing a Constitutional amendment designed to prevent abuses of Executive power in making treaties and other international agreements. The amendment was first introduced the previous year by Sen. John W. Bricker of Ohio, with the endorsement of 56 other senators. But, because of the impending national elections, the Senate did not find time to act on the amendment. Thus it lapsed with the adjournment of Congress in the summer of 1952. When Bricker again introduced his amendment the following year, Goldwater was one of 64 senators favoring the measure. After intensive hearings on the proposal, the Judiciary Committee, in June 1953, recommended adoption of the tripartite amendment.

Section 1 said that any part of a treaty which conflicted with the Constitution would be invalid. *Section 2* said that a treaty could become effective as internal law in the U.S. only through legislation which would be valid in the absence of treaty. And *Section 3* said Congress shall have power to regulate all Executive and other agreements with any foreign power or international organization, and that all such agreements shall be subject to the limitations imposed on treaties by that article.

The second section, because of its "which clause," was opposed by the new President, Dwight D. Eisenhower, and his Secretary of State, John Foster Dulles. The following year Bricker, realizing that his bill stood little chance of passage when it was opposed by the man who just months before received the largest popular vote in U.S. history, introduced a watered-down, substitute amendment. But it failed by nine votes to win majority approval. Then a substitute bill offered for the diluted amendment failed by one vote to obtain the two-thirds necessary for passage. Finally, after half-hearted attempts to revive the Bricker Amendment in 1955 and 1957, the issue was laid quietly to rest.

While it was being debated, few issues caused so great a national controversy as the Bricker Amendment. Its partisans claimed that it would protect the U.S. from hostile international organizations. Its enemies charged that it would alter our traditional treaty-making power and hamper the President in his constitutional authority to conduct foreign affairs. Dulles, in a speech to the American Bar Association (whose House of Delegates three times voted in favor of the amendment), warned that adoption would have "a calamitous effect" on the conduct of our foreign relations. Edward Corwin, historian and professor of Constitutional Law at Princeton, opposed the amendment. Noel T. Dowling, Harlan F. Stone Professor of Constitutional Law at Columbia, approved it.

The sudden interest in the treaty power was understandable, especially since America had emerged from her traditional isolationist shell only a decade or so earlier. Lend-lease, World War II, post and pre-war conferences, membership in the United Nations and other international bodies—all brought a new sense of international awareness to Americans. So, too, did America's participation in the Korean War, in which some 158,000 U.S. servicemen were killed or wounded. Supporters of the Bricker Amendment pointed out that Truman submitted the question of U.S. involvement in Korea to the U.N. Security Council, but not to Congress. Others noted that the government, in its belief in the steel seizure case of 1952, cited U.N. obligations in support of President Truman's action. And still others were bothered by a brief submitted to the Supreme Court in the Communist Party registration case, which cited the U.N. Declaration of Human Rights as part of its argument against the finding of the Subversive Activities Control Board and the constitutionality of the McCarran Act. Many Americans felt, as both Dulles and former Attorney General Mitchell pointed out, that the Convenant on Human Rights contained concepts alien to American law and American rights.

Goldwater felt that the Bricker Amendment would curb the potential of the President to commit America to possibly dangerous agreements. "I favored the Bricker Amendment from the start," he said, "and I was sorry to see it defeated. If I had it to do over again, I'd still vote for it."

Although new to Capitol Hill, Goldwater didn't hesitate to step on toes. The day Ike appointed California Governor Earl Warren as Chief Justice of the Supreme Court, Goldwater remarked, "I had hoped this position would go to somebody with high judicial experience, and while I have every respect for Governor Warren as a governor, I don't feel his experience qualifies him for this post. The Supreme Court of the United States should be composed of the outstanding judicial brains of the county, regardless of politics."

During his first trip back home since he left for Washington, Goldwater learned that the Arizona House of Representatives passed a resolution urging Congress to appropriate revenues from tideland oil properties for a fund to aid the nation's schools. Goldwater, who favored state ownership of the tidelands, said the resolution wouldn't influence his opposition. "I'm not going to retract my stand on the question, House resolution or no House resolution," he told newsmen. "The people of this state elected me knowing full well that was my position. If the government can take over the tidelands, it also has a right to come into any state and take over rivers, minerals, forests—anything we have of value, on the ground or under it."

In a statement a few months later, after a lengthy Senate filibuster over disposition of the tidelands, Goldwater amplified his stand on the tideland bill. "This matter transcends dollars and cents, or oil rights, or gas or mineral rights," he said. "It gets squarely down to the question of whether our states retain their Constitutional freedoms and sovereignties or whether the federal government shall seize them. If the federal government has paramount rights in these tidelands, then by the same arguments the federal government would have paramount rights in our Colorado River and other navigable streams and waters of Arizona. We would then have, in addition to California, the federal government to contend with in our search for justice in this matter.

"The acceptance of the federal doctrine would place the ultimate balance of power in the federal government and it is my belief that the less federal government we have molesting and interfering in our state government the closer we will approach the original intent of the Constitution. I call these things to the attention of Arizonans because it is my sincere belief that in this filibuster we saw developed the real plans of those who would make the federal government supreme over the states. It is a danger that is with us, and as long as men propose those dangerous actions we must remain alert.

"I feel that this filibuster has pointed up the real domestic issue of the present day. It has clearly placed on the one side the advocates of the teaching of the New and Fair Deals of the past 20 years, who say that only the federal government can give us what freedom has always provided, and, on the other side, where I stand, the advocates of states' rights with a minimum of federal interference. As I stated in my campaign, I was for the states having the title to these lands, titles that through years and years have been recognized as belonging to them. I am co-sponsor of the Holland Bill to recognize these titles.

"Nothing that has transpired, in the course of a month of filibuster and hundreds and thousands of words, has changed my mind on the matter. My vote was for this bill, just as it always will be for those measures intended to protect our freedoms as states and individuals and against those who would tamper with the freedoms that have made us the great nation we are."

Soon afterwards, on May 22, Ike signed a bill granting coastal states title to all submerged lands within their boundaries three miles out to sea, except in the Gulf of Mexico, where the claims of Florida and Texas would extend to a 10½-mile limit.

When Goldwater arrived in the Senate, a self-proclaimed conservative—the result of both his earlier reading and his having been strongly influenced towards the Jeffersonian democratic tradition by Uncle Morris—he found that by and large the liberals had won the field. Few of his colleagues were philosophical conservatives, although a handful of them had fought occasionally successful rear-guard battles against liberalism. Fewer still were, like Taft, prepared to label themselves conservatives. Goldwater was beginning to wonder whether John Stuart Mill had in fact been right when he described conservatives as "the stupid party." And he wondered whether Lionel

Trilling could have been correct when he wrote in 1950: "In the United States at this time liberalism is not only the dominant but even the sole intellectual tradition."

The absence of any determined conservative consensus, similar to the well-organized liberal consensus, troubled the Arizonan. For he felt that the perceptible drift to the left was endangering America, and that only a body of determined, dedicated conservatives—congressmen willing to eschew political expediency to defend the public weal—could both resist the liberal advance and begin to mount a successful counterattack.

A few years before, Goldwater had read Prof. F. A. Hayek's indictment of collectivism, *The Road to Serfdom*, and was deeply moved by the author's arguments in defense of the individual and the Rule of Law. Originally written in England before the war, the book warned that the prevailing shibboleths —"social planning," "general welfare," "freedom from want"— were even then nudging the Western democracies down a totalitarian road. Hayek claimed that the contempt for the 19th century liberalism which at that time was evident in England and the United States, was similar to the contempt displayed in Germany during and after World War I. The forces which destroyed freedom and unleashed totalitarianism in Germany were now at work in England, Hayek said. Yet few were ready to recognize that the rise of Fascism and Nazism was not a reaction against the socialist trends of the preceding period but an outcome of those tendencies. The democracies, Hayek argued, had progressively been moving away from the basic ideas on which Western civilization had been built; they had progressively abandoned that freedom in economic affairs, without which personal and political freedom has never existed in the past.

Hayek's book has since come to be regarded as a minor classic of anti-collectivist thought.* Goldwater had thoroughly famil-

---

* A former Communist leader, who is now an active anti-Communist and an intellectual spokesman for conservatism, credits the book as being

iarized himself with its arguments, but was aware that the most influential publications, professors, and politicians still inclined heavily toward collectivism of one kind or another. And, he reasoned, this trend could be reversed only if conservative spokesmen are willing to brave the slings and arrows of outrageous—and outraged—criticism in trying to sell an anti-socialist program. He knew that he alone could never hope to make conservatism the dominant political philosophy in America, but once in Congress he decided that he would do whatever he could to preach this creed in areas where it had been wholly drowned out by the left.

Understandably, some liberals pointed to their dominance in political and educational life, and in the communications media, as evidence of liberalism's intellectual superiority. But Goldwater was influenced by Hayek's argument, published in The University of Chicago Law Review in 1949, which explained why so many intellectuals embraced socialism—an argument which, by extension, can be applied to other more or less rigid versions of the collectivist ideology. Hayek noted that it is neither selfish interests nor evil intentions but mostly honest convictions and good intentions which determine the intellectual's point of view. In fact, he said, "on the whole, the typical intellectual is today more likely to be a socialist the more he is guided by good will and intelligence, and that on the plane of purely intellectual argument he will generally be able to make out a better case than the majority of his opponents within his class." Usually, Hayek admitted, it is the more active, intelligent, and original men among the intellectuals who now most frequently incline toward socialism, while its opponents are often of an inferior caliber. And the same

---

one of the most profound in crystallizing his intellectual break with Communism. Even before his apostasy, while reviewing the book in 1944 for the Communist publication New Masses, he pointed out that Hayek raised problems with which "progressives" (i.e., Communists) must come to grips.

is the case among successful teachers, by itself an important factor in bringing members of the younger generation into the socialist camp.

"The socialist will see in this merely a proof that the more intelligent person is today bound to become a socialist," Hayek noted. But, he adds, the main reason for this state of affairs is probably that, for the exceptionally able man who accepts the present order of society, a multitude of other avenues of influence and power are open. While to the disaffected and dissatisfied, an intellectual career is the most promising path to both influence and power. And even more than this: the more conservatively inclined man of first-class ability will in general choose intellectual work (and the sacrifice in material reward which this choice usually entails) only if he enjoys it for its own sake. He is, in consequence, more likely to become an expert scholar rather than an "intellectual" in the specific sense of the word; while to the more radically-minded, the life of an intellectual is more often than not a means rather than an end, a path to exactly that kind of wide influence which the "professional intellectual" enjoys exercising. It is therefore probably true, Hayek said, not that the more intelligent people are generally socialists, but that a much higher proportion of socialists among the better minds devote themselves to those intellectual pursuits which in modern society give them a decisive influence on public opinion.

Realizing this was no great comfort, however, when Goldwater saw his political position everywhere misunderstood or misinterpreted. And for a long while he could find no way to counter the argument that conservatives were blindly wedded to the past and fearful and distrustful of the future.

Then the intellectual tide in America began to turn, slowly at first but perceptibly. One of the earliest indications of this was the reception accorded Russell Kirk's *The Conservative Mind*. Published in 1953, to almost uniform high praise, Kirk's history of conservative thought in Britain and America stated a strong case against any connection—rather, he said, there was an incompatibility—between conservatism and the extreme doctrines with which critics had frequently associated it: red-neck segregation, anti-Semitism, and cultural, political or economic atavism.

In short, Kirk's fair-minded book, which criticized capitalists ("The American businessman is inordinately vain . . . he has reason to be ashamed of his record as a cultured man") as well as egalitarians, did much to destroy the stereotyped image of conservatism and to endow it with a degree of intellectual respectability. Kirk argued, in part, that for conservatives, the important concerns of man are religious consolation, family ties, private property and its fruits, and the assurance of a stable social order. Whereas the typical social planner of recent years, Kirk charged, is inclined to sweep away completely the whole idea of religion, with its concepts of mystery, sin, redemption, and hope, only to substitute for it a blueprint answer for human problems. This planning mentality disregards the important role of the family and community, would negate the right to personal disposal of one's own property and turn human society into a kind of ant society. Kirk concluded that the social planner goes against a deep-seated human wish for stability and permanence—the assurance that things will be with a man pretty much as they were with his father.

And Goldwater agreed with that aspect of conservatism presented by Russell Kirk. "I think Kirk has stated a case for conservatism better than any other contemporary scholar," Goldwater commented. "He has appealed to conservatives where no politician ever could hope to appeal to them."

Two years after publication of *The Conservative Mind*, William F. Buckley, Jr. launched his *National Review*, the witty, irreverent, and cogent magazine which is today the bible of many conservatives and the bane of most liberals. If the magazine is superfluous, in a country widely assumed to be a bastion of conservatism, publisher Buckley wrote in the initial issue, it is so because, "It stands athwart history yelling Stop, at a time when no one is inclined to do so, or to have much patience

with those who so urge it. . . . Radical conservatives in this country have an interesting time of it, for when they are not being
suppressed or mutilated by the liberals they are being
ignored or humiliated by a great many of those of the well-fed
Right. . . . We begin publishing . . . with a considerable stock of
experience with the irresponsible Right, and a despair of the
intransigence of the liberals, who run this country; and all this
in a world dominated by the jubilant single-mindedness of the
practicing Communist, with his inside track to History. All
this would not appear to augur well for *National Review*. Yet
we start with a considerable—and considered—optimism. . . .

"It is at this point that we steal the march. For we offer, besides ourselves, a position that has not grown old under the
weight of a gigantic, parasitic bureaucracy, a position untem-
pered by the doctoral dissertations of a generation of Ph.D's in
social architecture, unattenuated by a thousand vulgar promises
to a thousand different pressure groups, uncorroded by a cynical contempt for human freedom."

Gradually a conservative movement became discernible. One
curious phenomenon—which to this day confuses both critics
and friends of conservatism—was that no two conservatives arrived at their respective positions by the same route. Many were
attracted by Goldwater and his tireless espousal of conservatism.
Many enlisted under the banners of political theorist Hayek,
or economists Von Mises and Friedman, or social critic Kirk.
Others followed *National Review*, or were attracted by the
weekly newspaper *Human Events* or the monthly journal *The
Freeman*. Still others were converted by Ayn Rand, whose *The
Fountainhead* and *Atlas Shrugged* championed a spirited anti-
collectivist philosophy. Many students were brought to conservatism by the Intercollegiate Society of Individualists, an
organization conceived in 1950 as an antidote to the Intercollegiate Society of Socialists of 45 years earlier (which lists
among its alumni Max Lerner, Walter Lippmann, Ralph
Bunche, Walter and Victor Reuther, David Dubinsky, and
James Wechsler).

This move to conservatism by numbers of Americans sent established critics in search of explanations. Some of the reasons offered for Goldwater's conservatism—which became the focal point of conservatism—included the charge that he was a captive of amorphous and unnamed "vested interests," or the charge that he came from a state where many old people go to retire (and conservatism "ipso facto" appeals to this group)—a canard uttered by columnist Marquis Childs and, during election night 1960, by NBC's Sandor Vanocur.* Such glib attempts at explanation ignored the growing support for Goldwater and for conservatism among American students. In 1962, Goldwater was one of eight winners of the Robins Award for his inspiration to youth of America, especially for his "demonstrated interest in promoting political activity among young people" on nearly every college campus in the U.S. Columnist Morrie Ryskind observed, "This is no mere bobby-sox affair, replete with the shrill whistles given Frank Sinatra and Elvis Presley. If Barry has their hearts, it is because he has appealed to their minds, too. These are young people dedicated to a cause—the restoration of individual freedom from the shackles of the welfare state—and they see in Barry the Moses who will lead them out of slavery into the promised land."

Both Barry Goldwater and the conservative creed he preached so tirelessly have come a long way in the short decade when critics dismissed him as a temporary political aberration and assigned conservatism to the spot in American history reserved for the Equal Rights Party, Greenbackers, Free Soilers, Anti-Masons, Anti-Monopolyites, Antirenters, and the Loco-Focos.

* According to Valley National Bank figures of November 1961, "More than half of Arizona's present population is under 25 years of age. . . . It is not generally realized that the average age of Arizona residents is considerably below the national average and . . . that less than 100,000 of them are 65 years of age or over."

CHAPTER 7

Organized Labor

"Government, long hostile to other monopolies, suddenly sponsored and promoted widespread labor monopolies, which democracy cannot endure, cannot control without destroying, and perhaps cannot destroy without destroying itself." —HENRY C. SIMONS

"First we close down this guy's outfit where the trouble is. However, if he doesn't settle we close him down in the surrounding states. Then if he still won't settle, we close him down across the whole goddam country." —JAMES R. HOFFA

A FEW minutes before 11 a.m. on November 4, 1955, William Nelson left his $40,000 home in northeast Phoenix, walked to his pickup truck parked outside the garage, turned the key in the ignition, pressed the starter button, and was blown through the top of the truck.

Nelson's dead body, hurled 15 feet in the air, landed beneath an orange tree in his front yard. His right leg and right hand were torn off, his left leg was badly mangled. A 7-carat diamond ring, blown off his finger by the blast, was found 100 ft. from where the body landed. His watch, found near the scene, fixed the time of the explosion at 10:59 a.m.

Some of Nelson's neighbors thought the blast signaled the beginning of World War III. Others, whose windows were shattered, thought the explosion took place in their own yard.

And all were shocked when they learned of the dynamiting of Nelson, a retired cattle buyer who, they had been led to believe, dabbled in the stock market and lived a sequestered life. They were even more disturbed when they discovered the following day that "William Nelson" was really Willie Bioff, a convicted labor racketeer who had turned state's evidence some years before and was responsible for sending members of the Capone gang to prison.

During his early days in Chicago, Bioff had been a pimp. But he was a bright, ambitious racketeer and before long he wound up in Hollywood where he became a special representative of George Browne, president of the International Alliance of State Theatrical Employees and Motion Picture Operators. In this capacity Bioff forced union members to kick back 10 per cent of their salaries, and he was known to have charged up to $5,000 for the union initiation fee. He pressured motion picture studios into paying him off—about $200,000 a year for major studios, smaller amounts for smaller production companies—as a favor for keeping wages at a low level. Bioff admitted to a New York grand jury that he had extorted more than a million dollars from film producers and late in the 1930's he frequently boasted "I'm the boss now. Those producers do what I tell them to do, whenever I say."

About that time, columnist Westbrook Pegler began checking into the background of Bioff and discovered that he had been mysteriously released from a Chicago jail 18 years earlier after serving only eight days of a six months' sentence for pandering. Pegler repeatedly demanded that Bioff be extradited to Chicago to serve out his sentence, and his demands got results. Bioff was returned to Chicago, but in a style befitting the uncrowned boss of Hollywood: he was given a private office in the city workhouse and was accorded other special comforts—including a daily tub of iced beer.

Pegler kept hammering away at Bioff and soon the federal government stepped in. In 1941, he and union leader Browne were convicted of extortion. Bioff was fined $20,000 and sentenced to 10 years in prison; Browne received eight years. But both were released from prison three years later, after turning state's evidence against five Capone hoodlums (who received 10-year terms and were fined $10,000). Both were told to get out of town and a federal court—knowing that Bioff's life was in jeopardy—gave him permission to change his name. Soon afterwards Willie Bioff, alias William Nelson, arrived in Phoenix.

Not everyone in Phoenix was surprised to learn that the reclusive, law-abiding William Nelson was in fact ex-racketeer, ex-con Willie Bioff. Barry Goldwater had known Nelson—Bioff—for some time. "I met him through Peggy's uncle," he said. "He said he wanted to contribute to my campaign, and a few days later he gave me a check for $1,200. I even gave him an autographed picture, which a mutual friend requested. But three days afterwards, Nelson—or the person I thought was Nelson—walked in the office with the picture. 'Do you know who I am?' he asked. I said, 'Sure I know who you are, you're William Nelson.' And that's when he told me he was Willie Bioff. He said he didn't want to expose me to the risk of a scandal, so he tore up the picture right in front of me."

During the months after he made himself known to Goldwater, the two conversed extensively, holding approximately a half-dozen meetings over a three-year period. "He never revealed any names," Goldwater said, "but he told me how unions could and did abuse power, and he described for me how goons posing as labor leaders used illegal and coercive practices. He was a valuable source of information and I've never forgotten the lessons he taught me.

"In fact, Peg and I ran into him and his wife one night at the airport in Las Vegas. I went up to speak to the American Mining Congress when we ran into him. He asked if I'd fly him and his wife back and I said sure. By then I knew who he was, of course, and rather than run the risk of having someone recognize the two of us, and then have it all over the country that I was criticizing labor racketeers on the one hand and chauffeuring around an ex-labor racketeer on the other, I got smart for once in my life. When we landed I phoned Westbrook Pegler and told him about it. But nobody ever mentioned it. I was vacationing in Egypt when I heard that he'd been blown up."

No one mentioned it, until late last year when a book—charging that gambling in Las Vegas is controlled by organized crime syndicates—sought to link Goldwater with Bioff and another Las Vegas racketeer, Gus Greenbaum (who, with his wife, was stabbed to death in his Phoenix home on Dec. 3, 1958). The authors charged that Goldwater was a friend of both men and that he personally chauffeured Bioff in his private plane all over the southwest to attend various parties. Goldwater, promptly labeling the book's charges "trash," explained his association with Bioff. And he said that he knew Greenbaum as a grocery store operator in Phoenix long before he operated a Las Vegas casino.

When Goldwater arrived in Congress he had little knowledge of the problems or prerogatives of organized labor. His major involvement with the labor movement was his participation, almost seven years earlier, in Arizona's successful effort to pass a right-to-work law. But Goldwater's stores were not organized ("because the employees proved they didn't want to be organized," Goldwater said). And, although industry had been moving into the Grand Canyon state at an accelerated pace, particularly since the war, Arizona was—and is—a relatively non-unionized state. "I didn't know anything about labor matters," Goldwater admits. "Besides, I had my heart set on the Senate Armed Services Committee [an ambition that was to elude him until 1962, when he joined it after resigning his post with the Interior and Insular Affairs Committee] but Bob Taft said the Republicans wanted a businessman on the Labor Committee and that was that."

Goldwater's assignment to the Senate Labor and Public Wel-

fare Committee in 1953—together with another freshman
Senator, John F. Kennedy—was to prove to be an important
milestone in his career. Not only did it enable the Arizonan
to come under the influence of Taft, a man Goldwater long
had admired, but his work on the Labor Subcommittee, beginning in 1955, confronted him with what ultimately was
to become the issue that would first bring him to the public's
notice.*

For more than two years Goldwater listened to testimony
and talked with staff members whose opinions about labor
union affairs he respected—especially to Mike Bernstein, GOP
counsel for the Senate Labor and Public Welfare Committee
and, according to Goldwater, "the person who knows more
about labor law than any man I know." Then, during fall of
1955, in a speech to the Republican National Committee
School, he struck a theme he was to repeat often. He rapped
compulsory union political contributions for purposes of electing Democrats. He scored organized labor's direct influence in
Congress. And he enumerated—and graphically illustrated—
acts of violence perpetrated by unions during strikes. But, as
he was careful to do in every subsequent speech scoring labor
officials, he exonerated the rank-and-file worker and also made
clear that he was in favor of the trade union movement.

Not long afterwards, in his role as chairman of the Republican Senatorial Campaign Committee, Goldwater circulated a
report accusing labor leaders of preparing for "massive use of
political slush funds on a nationwide scale" to influence the
1956 elections. He charged that unions were forcing rank-and-
file members to support Democrats through compulsory union
dues and assessments.

Labor fired back, accusing Goldwater of being anti-labor, of

* Goldwater had been in office only three months when he walked
out of a Phoenix meeting with representatives of the Communist-domi-
nated International Union of Mine, Mill, and Smelter Workers, after
an out-of-state union representative tried to take control of the conference.

trying to harass the labor union movement in the United States, and of "neo-fascism." The AFL-CIO gave him a "zero" rating for some 20 important issues on which it claimed he voted "wrong" from the union point of view in 1956. (Goldwater retaliated by claiming that the AFL-CIO's Committee On Political Education—COPE—was issuing biased and slanted voting records of congressmen in an attempt to influence voting.) The *Washington Post* in 1957 quoted a COPE official as saying that "a large share of the money, men, and pamphlet resources will be devoted to attempts at unseating Goldwater...." And in February, 1958, organized labor named Goldwater as the Senator it most desired to beat in the coming elections.

As early as 1955, a Senate committee had uncovered examples of kickbacks and other abuses of union welfare funds by union officers. But it wasn't until after the 85th Congress convened in 1957 that Congress, on January 30, established an eight-member Select Committee on Improper Activities in the Labor or Management Field. The purpose of the "McClellan Rackets Committee," as it came to be known, was to inquire into union and management racketeering in order to determine whether changes were needed in federal laws. Barry Goldwater was one of the eight members, joining Republican Senators Joseph McCarthy (Wis.), Irving M. Ives (N.Y.), Karl E. Mundt (S. Dak.), and Democratic Senators Sam J. Ervin, Jr. (N.C.), John F. Kennedy (Mass.), Pat McNamara (Mich.), and John L. McClellan (Ark.). Robert F. Kennedy was named Chief Counsel.*

Throughout the 1957 hearings, the committee principally looked into the illegal dealings of Dave Beck, West Coast boss

---

* Senator McCarthy, who died in office, was replaced by Sen. Carl T. Curtis (Neb.). Senator McNamara resigned from the committee and was replaced by Sen. Frank Church (Idaho). Senator Ives left the Senate in January, 1959 and was replaced by Sen. Homer E. Capehart (Ind.).

of the International Brotherhood of Teamsters—and into the involved financial dealings of Teamster President James R. Hoffa and his lesser Teamster officials. While network television covered the hearings, investigators revealed how Beck stole hundreds of thousands of dollars from the union treasury, how he controlled gambling, pinball, and tavern operations in some northwest cities, and how he exacted kickbacks from large corporations. And they worked feverishly to pin down the elusive Hoffa, who somehow always managed to keep one jump ahead of the investigators. Reports of corruption within the hierarchy of powerful unions, stories of intimidation . . . of beatings . . . even of murder, began capturing headlines. Often in the limelight was a very vocal Barry Goldwater.

Because of the Rackets Committee revelations, and because some Teamster officials took the Fifth Amendment during the hearings, the AFL-CIO convention expelled Hoffa's powerful union in 1957. While there was general agreement that the Committee had done a good job, the Republican members of the Committee now began demanding an equally vigorous look into the dealings of the United Auto Workers, a union presided over by Walter Reuther, longtime political backer of liberal Democrats.

Republicans were irked for these reasons: First, that Robert Kennedy seldom consulted with them about witnesses he planned to call. ("If we sent someone around to ask Bobby," Goldwater said, "he would give us the information. But he never volunteered anything and it became darned annoying.") And, second, they were aware that Robert Kennedy, who had resigned from the Permanent Investigations Subcommittee in 1956 in order to campaign for Adlai Stevenson, waited until after Beck and Maurice Hutcheson (leader of the Carpenters Union) declared that they would support Eisenhower before announcing preliminary plans to investigate the Teamsters and the Carpenters. Finally, Republican members were quoted as saying that the Democrats were afraid to investigate Reuther because he was a power in Democratic circles. "This idea," wrote Robert Kennedy in his book, *The Enemy Within,* "was fertilized by publicity initiated by the Teamsters and Jimmy Hoffa, who were anxious to draw the Committee's fire from the Teamsters and direct it at the UAW; away from Hoffa and at Reuther."

If the idea was in fact fertilized by the Teamsters and Hoffa, it fell upon receptive Republican ears. For GOP members were disturbed that the Committee had no plans to look into the lengthy UAW strike against the Kohler Company of Wisconsin, in which strikers imported from Michigan by the UAW beat and kidnapped non-strikers, dynamited autos and buildings, fired shotgun blasts through windows and doors, hurled acid and paint bombs into workers' homes, threatened wives and children of non-strikers, and generally caused widescale rioting during the picketing. One 230-lb. UAW member beat and trampled a 125-lb. worker so badly that he crushed his chest and pierced a lung. (While the union member served 13 months in prison, the UAW, which had paid his legal expense dutifully paid half of his normal $100-a-week salary to his wife.)

Another striker beat a 65-year-old man so badly that he not only was hospitalized for 18 days, but he had to return to the hospital seven times after that. The man never recovered his health, and died two years later. When the assailant fled to Michigan, Democrat Gov. G. Mennen Williams refused to extradite him to Washington to stand trial. And when priests spoke out against the reign of terror, Emil Mazey, Secretary-Treasurer of the UAW, accused the Catholic clergy of being "not men of integrity."

In his book, Robert Kennedy took a detached attitude toward the violence. He wrote: ". . . mistakes had indeed been made. For instance, in the early days of the strike, the union had formed mass pickets at the plant and with a human blockade had kept workers out. And it had erred in other ways: the

record showed some 800 instances of violence, threats, telephone calls, 75 per cent of which had been directed against the
non-strikers."

But, contrasted with his style when writing about Beck and
Teamster racketeers, Kennedy appeared especially eager to
avoid offending the UAW terrorists. He acknowledged the
guilt of UAW officials by saying "there is no great evidence that
they took major steps to try to stop the violence." His use of
litotes caused raised eyebrows, however, when he said of the
roving goon squads, the union "did permit some 10 or 12
organizers to come in and lend a hand. Of itself, there was
nothing wrong with this. However, two or three of these were
big hulking men, and the testimony revealed they were under
no direct instructions and were permitted by the UAW to do
exactly what they wished. The result was that two of them
caused considerable trouble and got into serious trouble."

Republican attempts to nail Reuther aside, the Committee
revelations, including testimony from 1,526 witnesses whose 14
million words filled 40 volumes, outraged the conscience of the
nation. (It was true that these examples of brutality and il-
legality were confined to a relatively small part of the labor
union membership. But it was also the case that examples of
violence could be found in many sections of organized labor.)

In his book, *Crime Without Punishment*, Senator McClellan noted that never before in the history of Congress had an
investigation drawn so much mail. "Estimates made by veteran
members of the Committee staff," he said, "placed the total
number of communications received by the Senate Select Committee somewhere in the neighborhood of two hundred
thousand. The figure . . . does not include the routine incoming
mail connected with the administration of the Committee's
offices, nor does it cover the many thousands of messages and
telephone calls received by investigators in the field, nor their
interviews with informants and possible witnesses all over the
United States."

The overwhelming percentage of mail was sent by rank-and-file union members. Letters and telegrams often bore multiple signatures—as many as 10 to 15 pages of names. And almost all of them were favorable to the work of the Committee.

"They called for help against racketeering and against totalitarianism," McClellan wrote. "They spoke of brutality and coercion, of kickbacks and shakedowns, of rigged elections and fraudulent vote counts. They asked the Committee to put an end forever to bestial tactics of goon squads. They were philosophical and patient; they were outraged and frantic; they were strident and they were quietly courteous; they were remarkably erudite and they were naively simple; they were belligerent and they were timorous. Yet in their multitudes, they cried out the same plea: 'Help us'. . . .

"These were the subjects that cropped up day after day in thousands upon thousands of letters: fear, threats, undemocratic procedures, rigged elections, disappearances of union funds, assessments for political purposes without consultation of the rank and file, discrimination by reason of race, creed, or color, 'sweetheart' contracts that callously sold the membership down the river, kickbacks, Communism, domination by known racketeers, locals placed in trusteeship (often unjustly and for the sole purpose of protecting the national leaders' positions of power) for periods of one to twenty years . . .

"The letters cried out about violence and intimidation, bombings, graft paid to public officials, withholding of union books and membership cards, featherbedding, coercion upon small businessmen to join unions under threat of violence, failure to audit union books for periods ranging from one year to a quarter-century, no meeting notices, no meetings, boycotts, goon tactics, self-perpetuating dictatorships, shakedowns, paper locals, vandalism."

McClellan made two other relevant points: That receipt of more than 200,000 communications indicates that the Committee received one letter, one phone call, or one telegram for every 100 union members in the nation. And that it was a saddening reflection upon the integrity of too many union leaders that approximately one-half of the men and women who wrote to the Committee, and whose livelihoods and welfare are in trust to unions, were afraid to sign a letter addressed to the Senate of the United States.

Like all of the other Rackets Committee members, Goldwater received many such letters, and was disturbed by the power of organized labor to commit these offenses in the name of the working man, with apparent impunity. "I believe the laboring man has contributed an enormous amount to America," he said. "I want him to enjoy his fair share of this nation's prosperity, I want him to have a house, a car, and money in the bank. My objection is not to the worker, but to the boss—the powerful union official who takes advantage of him and, under the guise of fighting 'for the little man,' takes advantage of every other American."

Robert Kennedy saw in the revelations an indictment of American society. "The revelations of the McClellan Committee, were, in my estimation, merely a symptom of a more serious moral illness," he said. "For our nation to survive in the period of heightened international competition, we must reaffirm some of the basic values of our forebears, values that are deeply rooted in the history of our country and in its rise to a position of strength and respect in the community of nations. . . . Dangerous changes are taking place in the moral fiber of American society."

Goldwater agreed that the examples of graft and corruption were an indictment of society. But *he* reviewed them as syndromes of the enormous economic and political power concentrated in the hands of union leaders—power he believed the majority-party Democrats, for political reasons, were unwilling to challenge. He was disturbed that, as Prof. F. A. Hayek put it, "the public has certainly not yet become aware that the existing legal position is fundamentally wrong and that the whole basis of our free society is gravely threatened by the powers arrogated by the unions." Specifically, Goldwater believed the privileged position of organized labor was epitomized by UAW President Walter Reuther.

Early in 1958, Goldwater journeyed to the Masonic Temple in Detroit to speak before a United Republican Dinner. In a particularly heated address he accused Reuther of using his union and the union movement in general, merely as a convenient stepping-stone to further a political creed. He quoted from a research project of The Industrial Relations Center of the University of Chicago which in turn quoted Michigan newspapers to the effect that organized labor took over the Democratic Party there with the aid of armed squads and baseball bats. And he generally laid the financial and economic ills of Michigan at the doorstep of Reuther.

When Governor Williams criticized Goldwater for coming into Michigan and making "unfound charges against Walter Reuther and the labor movement," the Arizonan replied, "Reuther's not the property of Michigan, he's a national labor leader and a national menace. I don't want to wish him on Michigan, but I would be happy if Michigan could contain him and keep his menacing tactics from overflowing into the other 47 states."

A year earlier, at a Salute-to-Eisenhower dinner in Detroit, Goldwater charged that Reuther "is more dangerous to America than the Sputniks, or anything Russia might do." Reuther quickly fired back that Goldwater was "this country's number one political fanatic, its number one anti-labor baiter, its number one peddler of class hatred."

"I worked very carefully on that speech," Goldwater remembers, "because it was going to be on radio. But it turned out to be thirty seconds short and during my impromptu remarks I made that statement. It was one of those spur-of-the-minute things and if I had it to do over I never would say it."

Reuther, Goldwater said, "has a very strong influence on the

Democrats, through the left-wing Americans for Democratic
Action. But his influence in the labor movement isn't as strong
as he thought it would be. The more conservative labor leaders,
like George Meany, have stayed in charge and kept him in line.

"I don't know Reuther personally. I can't doubt his honesty
and sincerity. He's said to be a fine family man, he has a good
mind. I just disagree with his economic theories."

The Reuther-Goldwater controversy continued throughout
the early months of 1958. At one point, during a press conference in the Senate caucus room, Reuther accused Goldwater
of being a "political hypocrite and a moral coward." Goldwater,
stung by the remark, replied that same afternoon, "Reuther
accused me today of being a moral coward. In my section of
the country when one calls a man a coward he smiles. I could
not tell whether Mr. Reuther was smiling or not, because he is
such a coward he locked the door and would not let anyone in
except members of the press."

The feud continued cross-country from Detroit to Washington, and across the desks of congressional investigating committees. A standing-room-only crowd squeezed its way into hearings to hear Goldwater say to Reuther, "Some day you and I
are going to get together and lock horns." Reuther evenly reminded Goldwater that, "We're together right now, Senator."
Goldwater countered that they were in a place where "I'm asking the questions." But he suggested that they debate sometime in the future. Shortly afterwards, on a network television
show, Goldwater challenged Reuther to a public debate in
Phoenix—"where the warmth and sunshine can get into his
soul"—on the subject of the right-to-work law or unions in
politics, proceeds of the debate to go to the Samuel Gompers
Clinic in Phoenix. Soon afterwards he challenged Reuther to a
debate in Detroit. And a few months later the labor leader
agreed to a radio debate, for which Goldwater insisted on paying half the cost. Then, according to Goldwater, the UAW
changed it to a half-hour show, then to a television show; finally,

two days before the debate, Goldwater was told that Reuther couldn't make it and that he would have to settle for a UAW vice-president. Goldwater accepted, but only after publicly criticizing Reuther—"the man who called me a moral coward" —as having run out on him.

At the conclusion of the Rackets Committee hearings, Reuther claimed that the United Auto Workers had been exonerated. The Republican minority claimed otherwise. In a separate report, the four Republicans said that the Committee's investigation of the Teamsters Union "was vigorous and productive. . . . It was a job well done. Legislation was enacted incorporating recommendations of the committee."

But, it added, in investigations into UAW activities, it was a different story. There, the four said, "The Committee failed properly to investigate pertinent allegations, failed to examine key witnesses, failed to affix responsibility, and failed to submit constructive corrective recommendations." The report accused Robert Kennedy of divorcing himself from probes into the UAW, and with providing an inadequate investigative staff. And it charged the committee with refusing "to probe into areas which would have fixed the responsibility for the clear pattern of crime and violence which has characterized and has generally been associated with UAW strikes."

Whenever an investigation touched upon the domain of Walter Reuther, the report said, "a double standard of committee morality prevailed: one procedure was employed for the unions not connected with Walter Reuther and a different procedure was employed for the investigation of activities of the UAW." Furthermore, the Republican members said they were convinced, on the basis of testimony, "that corruption, misappropriation of funds, bribery, extortion, and collusion with the underworld has occurred within the UAW."

The main thrust of the Republican argument was contained in the following statement:

"The authors of the report from which we dissent create the

impression that this committee investigated the UAW for corruption with the same staff and zeal it has shown for other unions and employers in previous and later hearings (actually only a mere handful of our large investigative staff were ever permitted to work on any investigation of UAW improprieties), instead of acknowledging the fact that the committee limited its investigations here into the UAW's participation in the labor disputes; and on the sole basis of a cursory invited examination of a small part of the UAW's financial records by one member of the staff, the authors proceed from this fragmentary and entirely inadequate and incomplete investigation to issue a clean bill of health to Reuther, the UAW International, all of its officers, and to its more than 1,200 locals and many joint councils.

"We resent this obvious attempt to place the power and prestige of a committee of Congress at the disposal of Reuther so that he, having resisted all attempts to inquire into the books, records, and spending of enormous sums of dues by his union, can, as he has already, cite this committee report as evidence of his self-serving and oft-repeated hyperbole that the UAW is the model of what a 'clean and democratic' union ought to be.

"We must say that if Walter Reuther desires a 'clean bill of health,' he must first submit the body of the UAW to the X-ray machine of public scrutiny. Such scrutiny in order to be adequate and penetrating would also have to investigate the so-called flower fund of the UAW and its use of dues moneys on a wide variety of political activities."

Robert Kennedy has denied the Republican charges. "Why didn't you do to Reuther what you did to Beck and Hoffa, I have been asked," he wrote. "The reason is very simple. . . . Reuther and the UAW have made mistakes, as I have pointed out, but as a general proposition the UAW is an honest union and Walter Reuther is an honest union official who attempts to run an honest union. For some people that is unfortunate but nevertheless it is true. . . . The sooner this fact of life is

accepted in the country, the better off we shall all be." Goldwater disputes this explanation and still maintains, "Bobby
Kennedy whitewashed Walter Reuther."

The Rackets Committee hearings, especially those concerning the activities of the Teamsters, had so outraged public
opinion that Congress decided that new legislation was needed.
When the mild Kennedy-Ives bill failed to pass in 1958, John
Kennedy and Sam Ervin the following year introduced a bill
ostensibly aimed at remedying the cause of this corruption.
Goldwater, whose own reform bill had been rejected, denounced it as "a sweetheart bill which does nothing to curb the
abuses uncovered by the McClellan Committee. It is a hoax
on the public." Nevertheless, the bill passed the Senate on
April 25, 1959 by a vote of 95-1. Only Goldwater voted against
it. "If I had to select the vote I regarded as the most important
of my Senate career, it would be the one I cast on the Kennedy-
Ervin 'Labor Reform' Bill . . ." Goldwater wrote the following
year. "The measure had been advertised as a cure-all for the
evils uncovered by the McClellan Committee investigation. I
opposed it because I felt certain that legislation which pretended to respond to the popular demand for safeguards against
union power, but actually did not do so, would preclude the possibility of meaningful legislation for some time to come."

A few months later, after the House rejected the Kennedy-
Ervin measure, and after President Eisenhower appealed to the
nation on August 6, 1959 to ask Congress to pass a truly effective
measure, saying that the bill passed by the Senate failed to come
to grips with "blackmail picketing" and other abuses, Senate
and House conferees worked for almost three weeks before
adopting what is now the Landrum-Griffin Bill—a bill that
passed the Senate 95-2, this time with the support of a mildly
disappointed Goldwater. Even at the time he voted for the
measure, Goldwater contended (as Senator McClellan and
others today agree) that it was inadequate to deal with the
many abuses uncovered by the Rackets Committee. The bill
did not go to the heart of the labor union monopoly problem,

Goldwater said, although he voted for it because he realized there was no hope of getting a strong bill out of Congress and because with all its faults "it was far better than the weak, toothless Kennedy-Ervin bill."

Goldwater's stand against several of the leaders of labor brought him a great deal of favorable publicity. It had been a long time since anyone had publicly criticized the power of organized labor and before long the Goldwater name came to be widely known. A *Saturday Evening Post* article described the Arizonan as the freshman with "more leadership potential than any other Republican in the Senate during the past 10 years." His lone vote against the Kennedy-Ervin bill did not go unnoticed.

Goldwater continued traveling from state to state to make speeches about the problems of monopoly unionism. Only now he could point to support for his position from what seemed an unlikely source: the nation's colleges and universities. It was no secret that much—perhaps the most important part—of organized labor's moral support came from the intellectuals. For years the prevailing attitude was such that anyone who criticized the monopoly powers or coercive methods of unions found himself unpopular with influential academicians. The nation's professors seemed to believe what Harvard Prof. Edward Chamberlin termed "the prevailing public attitude of the post-depression years, that labor had been held back for so long that it was sure to be 'right,' and therefore must always have enough power to win." This point of view is still common among scholars, but in recent years opinion has started to shift.*

* In October, 1963, The Chase Manhattan Economic Research Department mailed a questionnaire to 460 academic economists. Replies were received from 321, representing more than 140 schools in 44 states and the District of Columbia. Of these, 54% felt anti-trust laws should apply to labor unions. And 44% felt that labor union monopoly now constitutes a major problem in the U.S.—almost twice the number who find business monopoly a major problem.

Roscoe Pound, former Dean and Professor Emeritus of the Harvard Law School, spoke critically of the immunities of labor unions and their members and officials "to commit wrongs to person and property, to interfere with the use of highways, to break contracts, to deprive individuals of the means of earning a livelihood, to control the activities of the individual workers and their local organizations by national organizations centrally and arbitrarily administered beyond the reach of state laws, and to misuse trust funds—things which no one else can do with impunity." The University of Chicago's Prof. Milton Friedman noted that the important difference between labor and enterprise monopoly was that, "While there seems not to have been any upward trend in the importance of enterprise monopoly over the past half-century, there certainly has been in the importance of labor monopoly."

When labor unions used their power to shut down newspapers in New York City and Cleveland, to tie up public transportation in Philadelphia, and to interrupt service of airlines and railroads across entire sections of the country, even the opinion of those whose friendship toward labor was unquestioned seemed to reflect upon the idea contained in a statement attributed to Jackson: "Equal rights for all—special privileges for none."*

In 1958, after extensive speech-making, Goldwater introduced a bill making national right-to-work legislation mandatory. But, in 1963, he reversed himself on grounds that section 14(b) of the Taft-Hartley Act gives the states the right to pass

* During the recent New York newspaper strike, James Reston, Washington Bureau chief of the *New York Times*, wrote: "The President of the U.S. cannot censor the New York papers. The Congress is specifically forbidden to abridge their freedom. But Bert Powers, the boss of the New York printers, cannot only censor them but shut them down. What is 'free' about a press that can be muzzled on the whim of a single citizen?" The *Times*, not wishing to provoke the unions in the midst of touchy labor negotiations, killed the column and requested syndicate subscribers to do likewise.

such laws, and therefore he felt it would be a violation of states rights for the federal government to usurp that prerogative. He remains in favor of state right-to-work laws ("No law in the U.S. should compel a man to join any organization or group," he said. "Neither should a man be denied the right to join any group whose purposes are lawful. Some men want to belong to unions. Some do not.") And he favors outlawing union shops in states which do not have laws specifically providing for such an arrangement.

Goldwater has also changed his mind on the question of applying anti-trust laws to unions. In *The Conscience of a Conservative* he said that he was at a loss to understand why anti-trust legislation had never been applied to labor unions. "If it is wrong for a single corporation to dictate prices throughout an entire industry," he wrote, "it is also wrong for a single union—or, as is the actual case, a small number of union leaders—to dictate wages and terms of employment throughout an entire industry."

But during an interview conducted by *Congressional Quarterly* in August 1963, Goldwater said he no longer felt it was a workable proposal because the laws are far too cumbersome. If you have to apply the anti-trust monopoly laws and procedures to determine whether or not the union is acting in restraint of trade or in a monopolistic manner during a strike, it might take years, he said. He suggested that the way to curb union power would be to amend the Labor-Management Act to remove the sources of power—powers which were needed by labor in the early 1930's but which now enable unions to abuse both management and the public. Goldwater's eagerness to curb the power of organized labor is tempered by an understanding of labor's historical role and present importance. Last summer, during a threatened nationwide railroad strike, he opposed the frequent talk of compulsory bargaining, arguing that it would deprive labor of its principal legitimate weapon, the right to strike.

Goldwater's principal bête noire has remained Walter Reuther's COPE, which he terms "the best political organization I have seen." Although both corporations and organized labor are prohibited from engaging in federal elections, Goldwater charges that the courts have permitted COPE to circumvent these proscriptions by ruling that they are "educational efforts," whereby unions divert members' dues to finance partisan political efforts.

"It is impossible to say just how much unions spend on political campaigns," Goldwater said. "Certainly one can't tell from the amounts officially reported, which invariably present a grossly distorted picture. In 1956, for example, labor officially acknowledged expenditures of $941,271. According to that official report, $79,939 of the total was spent in the state of Michigan. However, a Senate investigating committee obtained evidence that in that year each of Michigan's 700,000 union members had been assessed $1.20 as a contribution to a 'citizenship fund,' and that this money was made available for political activities. This suggests that labor spent, from that one source alone, almost a million dollars in Michigan instead of $79,000. By projecting the difference on a nationwide scale we get a more realistic idea of the size of labor's political contributions."

Goldwater charges that direct financial contributions are one of organized labor's smallest political endeavors. The bulk of their money and energy is spent in performing the functions of a regular party organization: making phone calls, driving cars, manning the polls—chores for which members are more often than not reimbursed from union funds. Furthermore, he says, unions sponsor radio and television programs and distribute reams of printed material designed to support the candidate of the union's choice. All of these activities are illegal when directed in behalf of a particular candidate or party.

Goldwater's main contention is that individual union members are denied the fundamental right to decide for themselves how to spend their own money. "Is it morally permissible to take the money of a Republican union member," he asks, "and spend it on behalf of a Democrat?"

In order to obviate criticism that compulsory union dues were being spent for political purposes, the United Auto Workers established a procedure whereby a member could write a registered letter once a year to union headquarters asking that no part of his dues be used for "educational" purposes. After he notified his local, the national headquarters would earmark his money for a cause it considered nonpartisan. "A union worker would almost have to be a fool to stick his neck out like that," Goldwater said. "Anybody in his right mind knows that not more than a handful of Reuther's members have ever made, or would dare make, that kind of request."

"In order to achieve the widest possible distribution of political power," Goldwater has suggested, "financial contributions to political campaigns should be made by individuals and individuals alone. I see no reason for labor unions—or corporations—to participate in politics. Both were created for economic purposes and their activites should be restricted accordingly."

There probably is no way of knowing exactly how much of that "large share of . . . money, men, and pamphlet resources" COPE promised to spend to unseat Goldwater in 1958 ever was actually spent. A *Chicago Tribune* reporter, after spending several weeks in Arizona during the campaign, estimated the figure to be $500,000 in cash, time, and services. Whatever the precise figure, it wasn't enough. For Goldwater, although considered the underdog by most analysts and publications despite his being the incumbent, overwhelmingly defeated Ernest McFarland (who won the governorship in 1954 and was re-elected in 1956), winning 56.1 per cent of the vote (164,593 to 129,030) and carrying 11 of the state's 14 counties.

But it took considerable campaigning on Goldwater's part. Even today knowledgeable political observers in Arizona insist that McFarland had the edge until just a few days before election when Goldwater made an unorthodox television appearance. He came on camera by crashing through a curtain of union newspapers. Then, with dramatic embellishment, he asked the viewers to "take a good look—see if I have horns and tail." With that he turned slowly around. From there he proceeded to blister "the union bosses" who say "let's you, the working man, and Goldwater fight."

He alternated his pejorative remarks toward labor officials with praise for the working man; he struck out at COPE, which he called "the mastermind of hate," but spoke warmly about boyhood friends whose parents were laboring men; he scored James Hoffa as "one of the most powerful and dangerous men in the United States," then described rank-and-file union member as "the forgotten man." And he stated. "The issue in this campaign is not whether Barry Goldwater is a Republican or a Democrat. It is whether a United States Senator must be completely subservient to labor bosses and, because of political fear, accede to their every demand."

The appeal was effective. And the campaign saw more unorthodox activity. A COPE organizer from California, a man with a police record for criminal violence, was discovered in Arizona trying to marshal opposition to Goldwater. Another man, an admitted ex-Communist, a 20-year veteran of the labor wars who had then been last employed by the UAW, spent two months in Arizona during the election campaign and—according to a signed affidavit—was seen in the Phoenix COPE offices. (The ex-Communist, John T. Watkins, whose contempt of Congress conviction had been reversed by the U.S. Supreme Court the summer before, said he had been in Arizona hunting a job, not on union political business.) And Goldwater claimed that, "We'll probably never know whether outside union money is pouring into the state to help Governor McFarland because we know that he once forgot to report a previous $4,000 contribution from the Teamsters Union."

This was a reference to Dave Beck's admission to the McClellan Committee in 1957 that his union contributed $4,000 to McFarland's 1954 gubernatorial campaign. At the time, McFarland said he could not recall having received the money but investigators produced a canceled check disclosing the contribution. Goldwater expressed skepticism over McFarland's forgetfulness, saying, "In Arizona politics a check for even a thousand dollars is one remembered forever and a day, believe me."

During the 1958 campaign Goldwater's major entanglement with organized labor came as the result of what Arizonans and newspapers dubbed the "Joe Stalin cartoon case." On a weekend soon before election day an anonymous leaflet had been deposited in and on autos throughout Phoenix. On it was a caricature of a grinning Joe Stalin, pipe in mouth, outlined with a hammer and sickle, knowingly asking, "Why not vote for Goldwater?" And it explained that Goldwater was lauded by the Mine-Mill-Smelter Union, which had been expelled from the AFL-CIO in 1950 because of its Red-tinged leadership. In their zeal to link Goldwater with Communism, the authors of the leaflet had violated a federal law—punishable by a year in jail, a $1,000 fine, or both—requiring persons publishing and distributing campaign statements to print their names on the literature.

Before long, hundreds of the leaflets found their way to Goldwater's campaign headquarters, brought there by indignant Goldwater partisans demanding to know who was responsible for the smear. Soon the press, radio and television reported the leaflet's appearance, and an inevitable rash of accusations began. Republicans said the Democrats were to blame, the Democrats claimed the leaflets came from Goldwater backers who were bidding for sympathy, the Arizona COPE disavowed knowledge, and Governor McFarland requested an investiga-

tion by the Senate Privileges and Elections Subcommittee.
James H. Duffy, the Chief Counsel of that subcommittee—on
order from Chairman Theodore Green (D.-R.I.)—was sent
to Phoenix to investigate.

What followed was a performance Ringling—or, more likely,
Barnum—would have envied. Arriving in Phoenix the Friday
before the election, Duffy—after telling reporters the leaflets
were "the worst of this sort I have ever seen"—began an investigation, a two-day affair, after which he concluded that neither
Goldwater nor McFarland was to blame. He said that the only
evidence he had uncovered of large scale distribution of the
leaflets was an admission by Goldwater's campaign manager,
Stephen Shadegg, that he had mailed copies to everyone on
the Senator's mailing list. Shadegg had mailed a number of
the leaflets to the state's news media when they were first
brought to Goldwater headquarters, in order to publicize the
attempted smear. But he claimed this was far less than the four
or five hundred attributed to him by Duffy.

Goldwater backers questioned Duffy's impartiality. Not only
did he tell a newspaper reporter, "Of course I'm a Democrat,
and I hope McFarland is elected," but his last words to Shadegg, after he issued his report and presented McFarland with a
statement absolving the Governor of responsibility, were, "I
hope Governor McFarland wins by a substantial majority!"

Duffy's investigation—in which he didn't bother to interview anyone who had found a leaflet in his car, didn't ask the
assistance of the FBI, and didn't even contact Senator Goldwater—might have gone unnoticed outside Arizona if it hadn't
been for the efforts of Sen. Carl Curtis, minority member of
the Privileges and Elections Subcommittee. Branding Duffy's
action "A violation of all political principles" and "a cheap
political trick," the Nebraskan commented that the improprieties committed by Duffy were as bad as those he was sent to
Arizona to investigate. Duffy had no authority to make a statement on the eve of an election in an attempt to influence vot-

ing, Curtis charged; furthermore, Curtis said that Duffy not only failed to advise the minority counsel as to the results of his inquiries, as provided by the written rules of the Committee, but denied to the minority counsel and to Curtis' administrative assistant that he was going to Arizona.

Incensed by both the leaflets and Duffy's mission, Goldwater charged in his election eve telecast that the smear and the "investigation" were pre-arranged, saying "this operation has been planned for a long time, deliberately planned, diabolically planned, by those outside forces who have been here since long before the beginning of this election." As soon as the election was over, however, the "Joe Stalin cartoon case" lapsed into obscurity, and remained dormant for some three months.

Then on Feb. 10, 1959, Frank Goldberg, a former official of the International Association of Machinists and a county Democratic committeeman, and Earl N. Anderson, Grand Lodge Representative of the Machinists Union (with headquarters in Los Angeles) and former Arizona state chairman of the Machinists Nonpartisan Political League, both called a press conference and publicly admitted responsibility for the leaflets. As they had told the FBI almost a month earlier, they alone claimed responsibility for the violation—neither Goldwater's opponent, nor COPE, nor the IAM had anything to do with the Stalin cartoon. (A subsequent federal grand jury investigation in Los Angeles, to determine whether the IAM actually was behind the leaflets, was shortly abandoned.)

When news about their testimony to the FBI leaked out, said Goldberg, he and Anderson were approached by one Leland Glazer (assistant county Democratic Chairman who had voluntarily undertaken chairmanship of the state Democratic committee investigating the leaflet case) and were asked to put the blame for the leaflets on Shadegg. This charge implicating Glazer was wired to Senator Green and to FBI Director J. Edgar Hoover. And Goldberg—noting earlier Democratic claims that Glazer had broken the case—wired Goldwater:

"Such statements are untrue. In fact, Democratic officials have contributed nothing to the case except confusion."

After a two-day silence, Glazer issued a statement which made much of the fact that McFarland was hurt by the leaflets, that COPE was absolved (IAM is not affiliated with COPE, but has, instead, its own political league), and that Shadegg had mailed out some of the leaflets—in short, Glazer spoke of everything except his alleged attempt to have the defendants blame the Goldwater organization.

If the investigation surrounding Goldberg's and Anderson's apprehension was confusing, their reason for preparing the leaflets was even more so. After witnessing what he called the "political smears and character assassination" of the local newspapers (presumably their coverage of organized labor's dubious activities in the election), Goldberg said they decided to "call public attention to the strange bedfellows politics has made." The leaflets, he said, were not directed at Senator Goldwater, but were "an individual's idea designed to needle" the newspapers for their unwanted influence in the political future of Arizona.

According to their story, later sworn to at the trial, Goldberg contacted Anderson in California and asked him to arrange for printing the cartoon in that state. (The caricature of Stalin was originally used, with a different text, by a California aircraft union to fight a right-to-work measure.) Fifty thousand cartoons were subsequently printed in a union shop in Santa Monica, Calif. But the union label was not used—because, said Goldberg, it would have carried the name of the state where they were printed and he did not want to bring California into an Arizona election. After arranging for a retired IAM representative to deliver the leaflets to him in a Yuma hotel, Goldberg—unaware, he said, that his act was illegal—distributed some in Yuma the Thursday before the election and others in Phoenix on Friday. While driving to Tucson on Saturday, to distribute more leaflets, Goldberg claimed he heard a radio newscast say that the leaflets were illegal; whereupon he telephoned Anderson, and, together they decided to dump the remaining bundles in a field outside Phoenix.

Both Goldberg and Anderson readily accepted responsibility for their actions and in June of 1960, both were found guilty and fined $1,000.

Goldwater supporters concluded that it was totally unrealistic to think that someone who wanted only to "needle" the local papers would wield such a sharp knife, and would exercise such extreme precautions to remain anonymous. They also pointed out that it was naïve to believe that these two men, both of whom were former union officials, both of whom had been actively engaged in politics, both of whom knew enough to keep the California union label out of Arizona politics—were unaware their actions were illegal.

Goldwater realizes that the leaders of organized labor will be solidly aligned against him during any future elections. Last summer, COPE said in its weekly newsletter that if Goldwater became President it would be "goodby to social security, jobless pay, minimum wage and progress." A UPI survey of AFL-CIO leaders last October found them "solidly lined up in opposition to Senator Goldwater." California Gov. Edmund (Pat) Brown told 1,000 union leaders at a Los Angeles banquet given by COPE that the two greatest problems facing American labor "are automation and Arizona Sen. Barry Goldwater." And the fifth biennial convention of the AFL-CIO last November warned against the "growing threat of the right wing," and left no doubt in anyone's mind that it meant Goldwater and his followers. "By branding Mr. Goldwater as the tool of the 'radical right' bent on union destruction," observed a *Wall Street Journal* reporter, "labor politicos figure they can stir an 'anti-' fervor among union members. . . ."

Goldwater's relationship with Arizona union members is somewhat similar to Robert Taft's relationship with organized labor in Ohio. A majority of union men will vote against him, but he will be supported by a sizeable number—35 per cent was the estimate given by Al Kane of Phoenix, a member of the Painters Union for 28 years. However, those union workers who do support Goldwater are unlikely to do so outside the privacy of the polling booth. For they fear, rightly or wrongly, that union pressure will be brought to bear on them.

An example of how pervasive this fear actually is can be seen from the following incident: For many years the Goldwater stores awarded the outstanding graduate of each Phoenix high school an engraved watch. Carver High School, an all-Negro school until the Phoenix board of education voted in 1953 to end racial segregation, was included in this award.

Last summer *The Arizona Republic* received from a young woman a copy of a letter she had written to Goldwater, thanking him for a favor he had done. She had received the Goldwater Award from the Senator himself during graduation ceremonies at segregated Carver High School early in 1950 (before Goldwater ran for the Senate). Early last year she accidentally broke the watch. When her boss suggested that she write and tell Goldwater about it, she did.

"I wish it could be repaired or replaced because it was a high school gift of achievement from you that I wanted to treasure forever," she wrote to Goldwater. Not long afterward she received a letter from a Goldwater aide telling her to take the watch to Rosenzweig's Jewelers where it would be repaired free, compliments of the Senator.

The watch was repaired and the woman was very grateful —so grateful that she wrote to Goldwater saying, "I consider this a very high class favor that you certainly did not have to do and I want you to know I'm grateful, Senator. I am heartily reinforced and proud to know you are a man who is aware of the ordinary citizen. I shall always be delighted to tell others about what you did. Thanks again."

Three days after receiving the original letter, *The Republic* received another letter from the girl. She admitted that she had wanted her original letter to Senator Goldwater publicized. However, she wrote, "since that time I have changed my mind and *do not* want you to publish this letter or any information relative to it in any form." Her reason? "My husband," she explained to an inquiring columnist, "is afraid he might lose his job. His union is opposed to the man who presented the watch."

Goldwater feels that this attitude on the part of organized labor will be difficult to surmount, but he maintains that he will continue to hammer away at what he believes to be an inordinate concentration of power in the hands of a few men. "The time has come, not to abolish unions or deprive them of deserved gains," he wrote, "but to redress the balance—to restore unions to their proper role in a free society. . . . The enemy of freedom is unrestrained power, and the champions of freedom will fight against the concentration of power wherever they find it."

CHAPTER 8

Domestic Views

"If you permit appeals to unity to bring an end to criticism, we endanger not only the constitutional liberties of our country, but even its future existence."
—ROBERT A. TAFT

W HEN freshman Sen. Barry Goldwater rose on the Senate floor on April 8, 1957, he did so with mixed emotions. He was about to criticize publicly the spending policies of the Eisenhower administration, especially its proposed $71.8 billion budget, at that time the largest peacetime budget in history. Yet, as he had openly admitted, he owed his seat in the U.S. Senate to the political appeal of Dwight D. Eisenhower.

What made his decision doubly painful was the fact that that very morning, shortly before he left for Capitol Hill, an Eisenhower aide had telephoned and invited Goldwater to cocktails at the White House that evening. "I felt badly about it," Goldwater remembered, "but it was something I felt I had to do. After all, we Republicans had promised a change from the big-spending policies of the Democrats, and we were simply promising more of the same."

Nevertheless, Goldwater's decision was fraught with political risk. For Ike, who less than six months previously had been overwhelmingly re-elected, was an undeniably popular President. A war hero to many, a smiling, kindly paternal figure to others, a symbol of the end to 20 years of Republican frustration to still others—Dwight Eisenhower was all these, and in April of 1957 he was enormously popular.

Until the GOP convention in 1952, Ike's political views were virtually unknown, but after wresting the nomination from Taft after a bruising primary campaign, Ike sounded every bit like a fiscal conservative. On Oct. 1, 1952, the Republican presidential hopeful told a Lansing, Mich. crowd, "We believe . . . that the deficits must be eliminated from our national budget." Three days later, at Fargo, N.D., he said, "If you have the kind of government that this crusade is determined to offer you, you will have a government that will examine, with a critical eye, all of these crazy spending programs of the national government. It will eliminate deficit, as its first step toward bringing down taxes and making the dollar sound."

This was what Taft, and all conservatives, wanted to hear; and for a while it held conservative criticism in check. But before long the gap between Ike's promises and performance disenchanted many of his most ardent conservative admirers. *National Review*, which for the first 11 months of its existence was generally content to treat Ike with a resigned tolerance,* raised the question, in pro and con articles by editors just before the 1956 elections, of whether conservatives should vote for Eisenhower. And William F. Buckley later summed up the extent of conservative disenchantment when, in 1959, he wrote:

"Under the Eisenhower Program one can, simultaneously, declare for a free market economy and veto the gas bill which aims at a free market on gas; stand by a policy of liberation and go to Geneva; lucubrate over constitutional rights and freedoms

---

* Of the sort epitomized by William Buckley's barbed quip (during a review last year of Ike's book): "My guess is the Communists moved with whatever caution it can be said they did between 1953 and 1960 because they hadn't the least idea what Eisenhower was talking about, and thought a little prudence might be in order."

and forever abandon captured American soldiers; and over the whole package—and this is Mr. Eisenhower's historical skill—there is suffused a general benignity of a kind that, at least until very recent days, bewitched the multitude of the voters."

Thus, Barry Goldwater was taking a political risk by making himself one of the leaders of the anti-administration forces. With what he describes as "the greatest personal reluctance," he dissected the proposed 1957-58 budget:

"Let there be no misunderstanding . . . as to the political implications of my remarks. Just as I campaigned against waste, extravagance, high taxes, unbalanced budgets and deficit spending in the recent Democratic administrations, so shall I also, if necessary, wage a battle against the same elements of fiscal irresponsibility in this Republican administration.

"It is, of course, with the deepest sorrow that I must pass this judgment upon my own party. . . . Until quite recently, I was personally satisfied that this administration was providing the reliable and realistic leadership so vital to the maintenance of a strong domestic economy which, in turn, is a vital factor in maintaining world peace.

"Now, however, I am not so sure. A $71.8 billion budget not only shocks me, but it weakens my faith in the constant assurances we have received from this administration that its goal is to cut spending, balance the budget, reduce the national debt, cut taxes—in short, to live within our means and give our citizens the maximum personal benefits from their own endeavors.

"Mr. President, the Republican Party is pledged by principle to strengthen the basic economy of this nation by the achievement of these aims. To do otherwise constitutes a betrayal of the people's trust. Yet, here we have this abominably high budget request which is the epitome of inconsistency, when compared with statements made by me, by many of my colleagues, and by the President in 1952."

There was no mistaking Goldwater's words, even enveloped as they were by references to harmony and Republican principles. Goldwater took a stand, not against Ike personally, but against those policies adopted by the Eisenhower Administration which Goldwater felt were inconsistent with traditional GOP promises. And he told his colleagues that if he did not survive the 1958 elections, "it will not be because [I have] broken faith with either the American people or the principles of the Republican Party in this almost frenzied rush to give away the resources and freedoms of America, whether in federal spending programs at home or economic aid efforts abroad."

Throughout this speech devoted to domestic economic policy, Goldwater contended that the Republicans, more particularly the "Modern Republicans," were becoming obsessed with the view that the government had a right—a duty, in fact —to interfere increasingly in the lives of citizens. "I have heard discussed on the floor something about the rights of American citizens," he said. "The question is asked, 'What rights have we lost?' Let me name one right we have lost. We have lost the right to decide for ourselves how to spend about 30 per cent of our income, because that is about what is going into taxes today. Thirty per cent of the income of the people is regulated by the federal government. We have lost the right to decide for ourselves where we are going to spend it."

And he concluded by saying that every item in the proposed federal budget could and should be reduced; then "we can begin the long march to the restoration of that right and every other privilege of American citizenship which has been submerged beneath these outrageous federal spending programs. It is my earnest hope that the President and my colleagues in the Congress will give serious and penetrating thought to this question. We may not, any of us, be here to witness the ultimate consequences of a continuation of this trend, but history would not forget that ours was the challenge forfeited."

For all his smiling countenance and his assertion that Goldwater was entitled to speak his mind, Ike was piqued by the criticism.* And he was reported doubly annoyed when, a few days afterward, newspapers quoted his brother Edgar, a Tacoma, Wash. lawyer, as also being unhappy at the size of the budget. "Edgar has been criticizing me since I was five year old," a visibly embarrassed Ike rejoined at a subsequent news conference.

Goldwater's attack on the Eisenhower budget may have been unorthodox politics, and at that time was doomed to certain defeat, but it was derived from his strongly held conviction that the government does not have an unlimited claim on the wealth of the people. "One of the foremost precepts of the natural law," he noted, "is man's right to the possession and the use of his property. And a man's earnings are his property as much as his land and the house in which he lives. Indeed, in the industrial age, earnings are probably the most prevalent form of property."

In *The Conscience of a Conservative*, Goldwater noted that Ike had agreed with Taft that the federal budget should be reduced from the $81 billion proposed by Truman to approximately $70 billion in fiscal 1954 and $60 billion the following year. And he observed that, "The only way to curtail spending substantially, is to eliminate the programs on which excess spending is consumed." Invoking the principle of subsidiarity

* A minor contretemps developed during the fall of 1963 over Goldwater's remark that "one Eisenhower [for President] in a decade is enough." Ike, in turn, told the *New York Herald Tribune*, that: "I am unclear on precisely what Senator Goldwater's present views are." The following day Goldwater replied: "It is difficult to understand how President Eisenhower can be unclear about my position in view of the wide publication my views have received." (And *Newsweek* quipped: "To some, it seemed that Eisenhower could hardly be as unclear about Goldwater's views as the nation at large was about the general's views in 1952— right up until the Presidential campaign began.") The following week, however, after Goldwater and Ike had a talk at Ike's Gettysburg farm, and after the Arizonan explained that he intended nothing personal by the remark, Eisenhower said that he probably misunderstood Goldwater's views.

formulated by Pope Leo XIII, Goldwater contended that the federal government must begin withdrawing from activities that could be better performed by lower levels of government or by private institutions or by individuals—whichever could best perform them.

The economy-mindedness Goldwater displayed, even as a member of the Phoenix City Council, toward spending public funds has punctuated his political career. Deprived of the availability of unlimited tax funds, Goldwater believes politicians would necessarily exercise greater frugality with public money. But when there is nothing to restrain them from voting still another spending program, except perhaps an easily subdued conscience, the temptation is usually irresistible. "It takes someone with greater will power than most politicians have to refrain from taxing and taxing, spending and spending, in the hope of electing and electing," he said, paraphrasing Harry Hopkins.

To clarify the basis of Goldwater's 1957 break with the Eisenhower spending policies, and the sources of his unending call for consumer choice and other manifestations of individual liberty, we must again return to the ideological battle waged during the past decade and a half. "Throughout history," Goldwater noted several years ago, in striking a persistent theme of the conservative counterattack, "government has proved to be the chief instrument for thwarting man's liberty. Government represents power in the hands of some men to control and regulate the lives of other men. And power, as Lord Acton said, tends to corrupt men."

It is this single belief, that government has in the past invariably proved to be the chief instrument for thwarting man's liberty, which primarily motivates Goldwater's votes on domestic issues. And it is this belief which prompted Goldwater to say that, "Liberalism today is a walking contradiction . . . which believes in irreconcilables—freedom and collectivization.

Having to choose between them liberals usually embrace collectivization first, hoping somehow that freedom will win out also. The trouble with the typical liberal is that he views freedom not as independence of the arbitrary will of another, but as independence of the wiles and snares of chrome-covered cars with tail fins, sold to him against his will by high pressure Madison Avenue hucksters who will go to any lengths to keep the world safe for Wall Street brokers."

Goldwater's conservatism usually focuses on economic freedom, which he maintains is the freedom most often exercised in today's industrial society. To be controlled in our economic pursuits means to be always controlled, says Prof. F. A. Hayek. "Whoever controls economic activity controls the means for all our ends and must therefore decide which are to be satisfied and which not. Economic control is not merely control of a sector of human life which can be separated from the rest; it is the control of the means for all our ends. And whoever has sole control of the means must also determine which ends are to be served, which values are to be rated higher and which lower—in short, what men should believe and strive for." "One of our principal tasks," says Goldwater, "is to reverse the thinking responsible for the notion that commercial enterprise is disreputable, the making of a profit immoral—the idea that the employment of a hundred or a thousand people is exploitation, but to politically command the same number is considered honorable."

Goldwater concurs with Hayek's statement that, "Once you admit that the individual is merely a means to serve the ends of the higher entity called society or the nation, most of those features of totalitarian regimes which horrify us follow of necessity. From the collectivist standpoint, intolerance and brutal suppression of dissent, the complete disregard of the life and happiness of the individual, are essential and unavoidable consequences of this basic premise. . . ."

The alternative position has been eloquently stated by

Prof. Sidney Hook, Chairman of the Graduate Department of Philosophy at New York University. "Socialism as we understood it when the word was young was not only a program for the economic reorganization of society, but faith in a moral ideal," he says. "We became socialists in a time of relative prosperity, not depression. The economic program—socialization—was conceived of as the instrument of achieving the moral ideal of social equality in the most comprehensive sense of that phrase. We were socialists, not because we wanted wealth, but because we hated proverty; and we hated poverty because it degraded human beings, and because we took it, in an oversimplified way, as a symbol of the arbitrary power of man over man, of the irrationality of social existence in an age of science and potential plenty."

But Hook, whose intellectual integrity is unquestioned among conservatives, and who reflects the beliefs held by today's liberals, is not a devotee of the Total State. "The question *how far* planning must go is yet to be decided," he says. "Even if *total* economic planning were socially more efficient than any other form, it would not necessarily follow that it would be acceptable if it seriously interfered with those rights and freedoms of the person which we wish to see preserved."

This contention brought from Max Eastman, formerly a pure socialist, the observation that under a free economy political freedom is possible, while under a state-controlled economy it is impossible. "Hook's notion that society might stop halfway in adopting this mode of life, or that anyone would be the gainer if it did, seems especially impractical," he said. "It seems a little like hoping a boa-constrictor will eat only half of your cow." Nevertheless, Hook contends that freedom under a planned society, even a totally planned society, is not impossible, although difficult. "Its potential dangers to democracy are so great, however, that it is the better part of wisdom to discard total planning as an ideal of social reform,"

Hook believes. "The best alternative available to us, he maintains, is a "partially planned economy, in which certain areas are planfully left to free enterprise, and in which every further step in socialization is tested by its probable consequences on the democratic life of the community."

Those who disagree with Sidney Hook's contentions do not doubt his pledge to oppose any restriction of political democracy. Goldwater maintains, however, that the economic policy championed by liberals—even those many liberals who reject pure socialism—places too much power in the hands of government. For while a particular government might at any given time be wise, judicious, and circumspect, the powers transferred to government are seldom if ever surrendered, regardless of the wisdom of giving them up.

One of the most scathing jeremiads directed toward Goldwater and his domestic program came last summer from the pen of Walter Lippmann, who had earlier acted as though neither Goldwater nor the views he represented existed. When Lippmann finally did "discover" Goldwater, however, he abandoned the thoughtful and irenic approach for which he has become noted. Goldwater's candidacy, he wrote in his *Newsweek* column, "strikes at the heart of the American party system."

And a few weeks later, in his syndicated newspaper column, Lippmann labeled the Arizonan an "extremist," saying the "Goldwater philosophy is radically opposed to the central tradition of the Republican party, and is wholly alien to the moderate and conservative character of the American party system." Then he levelled his severest indictment, charging, *inter alia*, that Goldwater, if elected, would repeal the progressive income tax ("a measure so extreme that it would dismantle the national defense and destroy the credit of the United States") and would repeal welfare measures ("as fast as he could, thus opening the country to vast misery and vast disorder"). "Senator Goldwater," Lippmann noted, "is a more serious threat to the Republican Party than he is to the Democratic."*

Three weeks later, after the Gallup Poll had noted Goldwater's growing popularity with even Independent voters (those "whose political views generally fall somewhere in between those of Democrats and Republicans"), Lippmann used a different approach. Goldwater, he said, "is now engaged in remodeling his ideas, in moving away from the far right and toward the more moderate center." This time he added, "Senator Goldwater, who is not a fanatic of the extreme but an ambitious politician, is now in the process of reshaping himself for the political realities of this country. It is interesting to watch him and comforting to think that the system is working so well."

This *volte-face* on the part of a decidedly anti-Goldwater columnist prompted *Time* to suggest that it was Lippmann who was making a "sedate sort of turnabout," and to note that whereas the columnist had practically excommunicated Goldwater from the GOP, he now "seemed to be un-excommunicating Barry."

Goldwater enjoyed the controversy—not because his views had been misrepresented (Lippmann said that Goldwater had changed his mind about asking the repeal of Social Security—a position he never held) but because, "For years the press buried my statements back by the want ads; now people are beginning to pay attention to what I've been saying. And even those who don't agree with me are beginning to understand what I've said, and why they don't agree."

The Arizonan's views on both the income tax and on welfare measures were set forth in considerable detail long before Mr.

---

* Goldwater, amused by Lippmann's putative solicitude, said: "I didn't know he was so concerned with the fortunes of the Republican Party. Could it be that finally even Lippmann has seen the light?"

Lippmann unleashed his blast; as early, in fact, as 12 years ago in the speech kicking-off Goldwater's Senate campaign. Government, he said in *The Conscience of a Conservative*, has *some* claim on our wealth—"the problem is to define that claim in a way that gives due consideration to the property rights of the individual." But its rightful claim was an equal percentage of each man's wealth, the principle behind property, excise, and sales taxes. "The idea that a man who makes $100,000 a year should be forced to contribute 90 per cent of his income to the cost of government, while the man who makes $10,000 is made to pay 20 per cent, is repugnant to my notions of justice," he said.

Goldwater maintains that the graduated tax is confiscatory, and that its effect, and to a large extent its aim, is to force men to stay at a common level. "Many of the leading proponents of the graduated tax frankly admit that their purpose is to redistribute the nation's wealth," he said. "Their aim is an egalitarian society—an objective that does violence both to the charter of the Republic and the laws of Nature. We are all equal in the eyes of God but we are equal *in no other respect*. Artificial devices for enforcing total equality among unequal men must be rejected if we would restore that charter and honor those laws." In addition, Goldwater noted that the revenue collected because of the graduated features of the tax amounts to less than the federal government spends on agricultural subsidies.

During a Chicago speech to the National Federation of Republican Women late last year, Goldwater related his philosophy toward taxation—namely, that it would be unwise and impractical to repeal the income tax, but that it would be desirable to eliminate the progressive features. Where progressive rates under the present income law became punitive in nature, he noted, they destroy initiative and incentive and have "a speakeasy effect on the morals of the American people." He suggested an overhaul of the complex federal tax laws which blur the line "between what a taxpayer legally owes his government and what he morally owes his government."

It is unlikely that Goldwater was prepared for the liberal criticism of his proposal to repeal the progressive features of the tax law. For it seems accurate to say that, as two University of Chicago Law School professors (Walter J. Blum and Harry Kalven, Jr.) phrased it, "Progressive taxation is now regarded as one of the central ideas of modern democratic capitalism and is widely accepted as a secure policy commitment which does not require serious examination." Even so, as the title of their probing study—*The Uneasy Case for Progressive Taxation*— indicates, a clear case for such taxation has not yet been made.

In fact, both the case *for* and the case *against* the progressive income tax seem to be relatively uneasy. Harvard's Dean Erwin Griswold wrote that "ability to pay" is the principal justification for progressive taxation, and a majority of people whose attitudes toward progressive taxation were analyzed by a University of Chicago Law School project agreed. Yet despite a general popular feeling that "ability to pay" is sufficient justification for imposing a progressive income tax, Goldwater believes an ethical standard is primarily what is at stake. English economist J. R. McCulloch expressed this idea more than a century ago: "The moment you abandon the cardinal principle of exacting from all individuals the same proportion of their income or of their property, you are at sea without rudder or compass, and there is no amount of injustice and folly you may not commit."

There are other arguments surrounding progression. Goldwater's assertion that its aim is egalitarian was contradicted by a University of Chicago Law School study, which found that virtually no respondents associated taxes with envy or hostility to the rich or with concern over economic equality. Bertrand de Jouvenel, whose *The Ethics of Redistribution* is a counterpoise to *The Uneasy Case* . . . , wrote that "redistributionism is not descended from socialism; nor can any but a purely verbal link be discovered between it and agrarian egalitarianism."

The complexity of the issue can further be indicated by the fact that even the conservative Hayek concedes that there can be a valid argument in favor of progression to compensate for the tendency of many *indirect* taxes to place a proportionally heavier burden on smaller incomes. He believes a reasonable solution would be to fix the maximum admissible rate of direct taxation at that percentage of the total national income which the government takes in taxation. (Thus if the government took 25 per cent of the national income, 25 per cent would also be the maximum rate of direct taxation of any part of individual incomes.)

Professor Milton Friedman contends that it is not clearly inappropriate for persons with higher incomes to pay higher absolute payments for government services, on ground of benefits conferred. Yet, his suggestion for obviating a situation where a majority could vote to impose on others taxes that did not also affect their own tax burden, would be a flat-rate tax on income above an exemption, with income defined very broadly and deductions allowed only for strictly defined expenses of earning income.

Goldwater recognized the overall complexity of the income tax laws, and of the pro and con arguments which prevail, when he told an interviewer last summer, "I am against the progressive feature of the income tax, but I wouldn't reduce the progressive feature and nothing else, because this wouldn't work. What I would propose is a complete study of the whole tax problem by a compact group of academic counselors, businessmen, labor people and legislators who could devote all the time needed to it. When the package is ready, then sell it to Congress. When Congress is sold, introduce it, pass it, and throw the old one out." Included in that new package, he said, would either be "an elimination or a drastic cutting of the progressive features, where they become punitive."

During the summer of 1962, Goldwater's long held position, that progression helps curb incentive, hinders investment, and brings in little revenue (Friedman avers that a flat tax of 23.5 per cent on taxable income, as presently defined, would yield as much revenue as the present tax rate)—was tacitly admitted by President Kennedy not long before Lippmann accused Goldwater of being unrealistic. When he announced plans to seek a tax cut, the President said: "Our present tax system is a drag on economic recovery and economic growth, biting heavily into the purchasing power of every taxpayer and every consumer. . . . Our tax rates, in short, are so high as to weaken the very essence of the progress of a free society—the incentive for additional effort."

Lippmann's other two major criticisms of Goldwater—that he would "repeal welfare measures as fast as he could" and that he changed his mind about repealing Social Security—were of a quite different nature. Goldwater has never advocated repeal of Social Security. He has, however, suggested that participation be made voluntary. "I realize that most Americans favor Social Security," he said, "and no President is going to take it away from them. But there should be some provision made to put it on a voluntary basis—to let those who have provided for their old age withdraw from what is now a compulsory program." Aside from the fact that *compulsory* participation in the Social Security program is antithetical to his view of the role of government, Goldwater is especially mindful of the fact that, by 1970, ten per cent of the worker's basic wage will be diverted into Social Security. "I suspect that about 1969 or 1970 we're going to see a revolt start among the working people, the salaried people, against the Social Security concept," he said. "And I think we're going to have to do some revising." Milton Friedman put it another way when he said, "the number of citizens who regard compulsory old age insurance as a deprivation of freedom may be few, but the believer

in freedom has never counted noses." Those who believe in freedom, he wrote, must believe also in the freedom of individuals
to make their own mistakes. "If a man knowingly prefers to live
for today, to use his resources for current enjoyment, deliberately choosing a penurious old age, by what right do we prevent
him from doing so? We may argue with him, seek to persuade
him that he is wrong, but are we entitled to use coercion to
prevent him from doing what he chooses to do?"

The Lippman-Goldwater argument over welfare measures
is to some degree an extension of the larger, liberal-conservative
controversy. But Goldwater has never indicated that he would
repeal all welfare measures "as fast as he could." Nor would
he permit the infirm, the poor, or the unfortunate to go un-
aided. He would, however, seek to impress upon people the
need to make welfare a private concern—of individuals, families, churches, private hospitals, religious service organizations,
community charities, and similar organizations. "If the objection is raised that private institutions lack sufficent funds," he
said, "let us remember that every penny the federal govern-
men does *not* appropriate for welfare is potentially available
for private use—and without the overhead charge for process-
ing the money through the federal bureaucracy. Indeed, high
taxes, for which government welfarism is so largely responsible,
is the biggest obstacle to fund raising by private charities."

If none of this is sufficient to meliorate the problem, then, he
says, the job should be done "by local and state authorities that
are incapable of accumulating the vast political power that is
so inimical to our liberties."

For these reasons, Goldwater has opposed medicare programs
to provide medical care for the aged financed through Social
Security. Initially he was one of two senators to vote against
Kerr-Mills, a limited medical aid program providing for match-
ing federal-state grants to cover medical expences of the in-
digent aged. Since that time, however, he finds that "The
Kerr-Mills seems to be working—at least it would be far better

than the omnibus medicare plan." In a minority report made to the Senate Special Aging Committee last fall, Goldwater, together with Senators Dirksen and Frank Carlson, questioned the contention of Committee Democrats that Kerr-Mills did not and could not effectively solve the problem of medical aid to the aged. The minority report cited the widespread availability and use of voluntary health insurance, existence of state and local programs, and contended that "the program will work if given full support." A month earlier, during debate on the Senate floor, Goldwater charged: "It is common knowledge that the present administration, in its attempts to couple a medical assistance program for the aged to the Social Security system, has thrown up every roadblock at its command to hobble and shackle the Kerr-Mills Act."

Early in the summer of 1961, a national debate was provoked over public welfare programs, not with respect to the problem of slum sections in a major industrial city, but concerning the New York community of Newburgh. This Hudson River town of 31,000 people found itself faced with a mounting city budget. City officials estimated that unless they could find a way to trim costs, real estate taxes would have to be boosted a whopping 30 per cent. One way to cut back, suggested City Manager Joseph Mitchell, would be to tighten up on welfare programs, which were costing almost $1 million—more than the combined cost of police and fire protection—out of every single annual budget. One reason for Newburgh's heavy welfare load was the number of migrant workers who followed the summer harvest north to Newburgh's fruit farms and then settled down for the winter. Because most of them were uneducated, and because Newburgh lacked jobs to absorb them into the labor market, most of them were idle during at least half the year.

On July 15, 1961, Newburgh put into effect a 13-point plan adopted by the City Council. It provided, among other things, that:

—Welfare payments would, where possible, be converted to food and rent vouchers (in an effort to prevent relief funds from being spent in saloons).

—All male reliefers who were able to work would be employed by the city on a 40-hour basis, and anyone who refused would be striken from the relief rolls.

—No one who quit his job would be entitled to welfare.

—The relief income of any one family would not be allowed to exceed the income of the lowest-paid city employee with a family of comparable size. (Seventeen Newburgh families had received more than $200, tax-free, per month. Others received allotments ranging up to $365 per month, and one family received $1,000 in one month.)

—Mothers of illegitimate children who had additional offspring out of wedlock would be deprived of public charity (the children, it is presumed, becoming wards of the community should the mother be unable to provide for their well-being).

—Aid to dependent children cases would be reviewed monthly by the city attorney.

—New applicants for relief payments must prove they didn't come to Newburgh just to get on the welfare rolls.

—And a three-month limit was to be placed on welfare aid, except in cases involving the aged, blind, and disabled.

Even before July 15, the battle lines had been drawn. Thousands of letters poured into Newburgh, both praising and damning the city's program. Most Newburgh voters were aligned solidly behind the new measures. The Gallup Poll found that 85 per cent of Americans interviewed backed such key aspects of the Newburgh plan as city work projects for relief recipients and denial of relief for those who refuse jobs. And Barry Goldwater, describing the Newburgh plan "as refreshing as the clear air of Arizona," said he would like to see every city adopt a similar plan. In a letter to City Manager Mitchell he said: "The abuses in the welfare field are mounting and the only way to curtail them are the steps which you have already taken . . . more power to you."

On the other hand, welfare departments of most states opposed the Newburgh plan. New York State officials feared that it would jeopardize the state's $150 million federal welfare reimbursement, inasmuch as federal law requires states to administer welfare aid in a uniform manner. Abraham Ribicoff, at that time Secretary of the Department of Health, Education, and Welfare, described the plan as "demagogic," saying it was a "destructive approach that will solve nothing." The National Urban League denounced it as a "false idea, ignorantly or maliciously contrived." Various NAACP chapters objected to the plan because they considered it a not-so-subtle slap at Negroes (who comprised two thirds of Newburgh's migrant population).

And the *New York Times* editorialized: "Newburgh is flagrantly, willfully in the wrong . . . it is pursuing an inhumane policy and it is following an outlaw course. It is punishing innocent children in the name of 'morality' and driving . . . the unfortunate off the relief rolls because the taxpayers are weary. . . . The voice of man's inhumanity to man is loud in the land. . . . Who will take a stand also for the cause of decency, of mercy, of food and shelter for the poor—even the imperfect poor . . . ?"

Not long afterwards the State Supreme Court, in litigation instituted by state officials, invalidated 12 of the 13 points; the Newburgh controversy ended with a barely audible whimper. Yet critics and supporters alike claimed victory—critics, because the court ruling prevented Newburgh city officials from implementing what were believed to be excessive, even inhumane rules; and supporters, because the controversy effected a saving of $126,000 in 1961 and permitted a city tax cut the following year. Furthermore, on December 11, 1961, Secretary Ribicoff ordered revision of the federal public welfare program to eradicate abuses. (Among his proposals to Congress: That able-bodied men be required to work for their relief payments, and that vouchers be used instead of cash payments for some relief families.) Ribicoff said the proposed revision had nothing to do with the Newburgh imbroglio. Nevertheless, supporters of the Newburgh plan said the action proved the existence of systemic welfare abuses which were badly in need of reform.

That there was a victory in the Newburgh controversy was dubious. For still unresolved are the important questions of whether cutting off aid to a mother who has more than one illegitimate child will help curb promiscuity (or at least a major consequence of promiscuity) or whether it will merely serve to harm the child, and whether there should be an arbitrary time limit for welfare aid, regardless of the availability of jobs. Regardless of "who won" however, a national debate was joined which served both to inform the public about the nature of public welfare in this country and to highlight aspects of the conservative response to the problem.

In 1961, when there was considerable congressional agitation to raise and extend the federal minimum wage, Goldwater set forth his case against such a law in an article in the *Reader's Digest*. He pointed out that he was not against good pay, and that in his own family mercantile business the lowest-paid part-time worker received a higher wage than the then-proposed federal minimum. But, he contended, the minimum wage was complete economic nonsense. "More money going into circulation without a corresponding increase in production simply bids up the price of goods and services. Result: higher prices, belt-tightening, unemployment." Furthermore, he said, once again striking a familiar note, "it permits the hand of federal bureaucracy to reach down into the states and fumble with the economic structure. Result: violation of the 10th Amendment in the Constitution's Bill of Rights—which guarantees preservation of states' rights, the keystone of our republic."

Goldwater explained how a minimum wage law primarily harms the low wage earners, those it is supposed to help, by citing two examples. In the first, he recalled that the owner of a chain of small department stores in the South testified before the Senate Labor Committee that if the wage-and-hour law were extended to cover his business he would be compelled to fire about 100 of his 1,000 employees, including all 50 high school students employed part-time. Their services, the entrepreneur said, were simply not worth the proposed minimum—not worth even $1 an hour—in terms of their productivity. Therefore, instead of providing additional income for fringe employees, the law would deprive them of whatever income they then had. In the second case, the owner of variety shops in Mississippi and Louisiana implied that he would have to lay off some of his 150 full-time workers and 125 part-time workers if the minimum wage were applied to his business.

"And there are many other similar examples," Goldwater said. "All of them prove that passing minimum wage laws hurts exactly those people it is supposed to help. The only reason these laws don't do more damage is because they usually lag behind the supply-and-demand minimum wage, the true minimum wage established by the market place. But that's no justification for imposing minimums by federal government fiat. They are still wrong in principle." If people still want such laws, Goldwater says, "The responsibility for this legislation rests with each state, not with the federal government. No federal bureau is wise enough to decree a law that judiciously can take into consideration the problems and conditions in every hamlet or even in every state in the U.S."

Goldwater's opposition to federal aid to education arises from reasons somewhat similar to those supporting his opposition to federal minimum wages: his belief that both are unconstitutional and that both constitute heavy-handed, and potentially disadvantageous, federal interference in local or state matters. But he also opposes federal aid to education because he believes it fosters the illusion that federal money is free, because he claims that figures released by the Department of Health, Education and Welfare and by the Office of Education are too often examples of unsupportable statistical magic, and because he believes that federal participation is unnecessary—except to such areas as aid to Indians (where the U.S. is committed by virtue of treaty), aid to impacted areas ("where the federal government itself has created the problem and thus has the responsibility of solving it," he said), and support of education for children of servicemen.

In 1963 Goldwater had his staff look into the disposition of funds available in the form of fellowships under the 1958 National Defense Education Act. "This act was passed and these funds were made available," Goldwater said, "in a desire on the part of Congress to aid the Cold War effort. And what do we find? We find that of the first 3,840 fellowships given under the act, less than 20 per cent are for students pursuing fellowships in science and engineering. Thirteen fellowships were for purposes of studying folklore, 39 were in theology, including four in Buddhist studies, and 108 were in sociological studies. The *Wall Street Journal* even had an article about graduate students using NDEA fellowships to learn the finer points of glass blowing.

"Now these all may be very fine pursuits. But can anybody tell me in all honesty what they have to do with the defense effort. How are a bunch of beatnik-type folk singers going to help us in the Cold War, unless we expect to win it by charming the Russians with our singing?"

But his principal objection is his belief that federal aid inevitably will lead to federal controls—and, he says, it could and *should* not be otherwise: "Congress cannot be expected to appropriate the people's money and make no provision for how it will be spent. Congress would be shirking its responsibilities to the taxpayer if it distributed his money willy-nilly, without regard to its use."

Goldwater believes the federal government has a part to play in education, "but a reduced role—not the one being mapped for it by the U.S. Office of Education." Federal research funds for colleges are both wise and necessary, he admits, as are some college fellowships. "It's at the local level that I don't like to see the federal government extending its control," he commented. "It just isn't necessary. If there is a financial squeeze on local taxpayers or local school districts, it's because the federal government is taking the money to Washington. If Washington would permit some of that money to remain with the taxpayers, there would be no financial problems."

Goldwater's position on education is not unlike his approach to agriculture—that the federal government should not interfere except in case of inordinate conditions (or to get the farmers painlessly out of a situation created by the federal government). The federal government's unconstitutional intrusion into agriculture has not brought us any closer to a solution of the farm problem, Goldwater maintains. Farm incomes were declining when federal intervention was undertaken, but today, many farm incomes (excepting those of gigantic corporate nature) are still low. And there are now the additional problems of restrictive production controls, high consumer prices, large crop surpluses, and a gigantic tax bill.

The solution, Goldwater said, is a prompt but painless termination of the farm subsidy program over a period of several years. Since the government got the farmers into their present state, he says, it has the responsibility to make the transition back to competitive farming an easy one.

Goldwater did find some humor even in the now tangled farm subsidy program, however, and in 1959 he introduced into the *Congressional Record* the following spurious letter:

"Dear Mr. Senator:

"My friend Bordeaux over in Pima County received a $1,000 check from the government this year for not raising hogs. So I am going into the not-raising-hog business next year. What I want to know is, in your opinion, what is the best kind of hogs not to raise? I would prefer not to raise razorbacks, but, if that is not a good breed not to raise, I will just as gladly not raise any Berkshires or Durocs.

"The hardest work in this business is going to be in keeping an inventory of how many hogs I haven't raised. My friend Bordeaux is very joyful about the future of this business. He has been raising hogs for more than 20 years and the best he ever made was $400 until this year, when he got $1,000 for not raising hogs. If I can get $1,000 for not raising 50 hogs then I will get $2,000 for not raising 100 hogs.

"I plan to operate on a small scale at first, holding myself down to about 4,000 hogs, which means I will have $80,000. Now, another thing: These hogs I will not raise will not eat 100,000 bushels of corn. I understand that you also pay farmers for not raising corn. So will you pay me anything for not raising 100,000 bushels of corn not to feed the hogs I am not raising? I want to get started as soon as possible as this seems to be a good time of the year for not raising hogs.

Octave Broussard

"P.S. Can I raise 10 or 12 hogs on the side while I am in the not-raising-hog-business—just enough to get a few sides of bacon to eat?"

Each of the foregoing Goldwater positions—on education, welfare, taxes, and agriculture—tends to be counter to prevailing liberal thought. (The *New Republic*'s strongly anti-Goldwater "T.R.B."—in reality, Richard L. Strout, staff reporter for the *Christian Science Monitor*—recently termed the Arizonan an "economic illiterate.") Goldwater, of course, did not originate the battle over the many economic issues which divide Americans; he merely joined it at a time when it appeared that the battlefield had been left solely to those who called for a permanent policy of government control or direction of investment, creating employment by deficit spending, cheap money policies, large public works programs, and rejection of fiscal thrift—in short, to those who adopted what today are called "Keynesian" economic views. It was true, examined either by the direction of governmental economic policies since the advent of the New Deal, or by the beliefs of most academicians, that "Keynesianism" had won the day. But if the anti-Keynesians had been routed, they had not been extirpated.

In 1948 a handful of economists, historians, journalists and political scientists journeyed to Switzerland to establish the Mont Pelerin Society. Their reason, according to a charter member, was that believers in a free market society were few and far between. Each felt intellectually isolated in his own country and thought it would be desirable to provide some form of professional association which would provide the intellectual stimulus through interchange of ideas that was lacking in their own country's professional associations and journals.

Milton Friedman, a charter member of the society, remembered that, "In the late 1930's, the University of Chicago was about the only institution in the U.S. at which there was a substantial group of believers in a free enterprise system. There were isolated individuals elsewhere, most of them survivors of an earlier day. Most of the members of the faculty who were below the ages of 40 or 50 had been converted to New Dealism or socialism or to planning in one form or another."

Today, however, this situation has been changed. The original function of the Mont Pelerin Society has largely disappeared, Friedman says, because the "radical" doctrines which were espoused at that time by so few people, are now espoused by many, in every nation in the world. And because "vigorous teachers of a free market persuasion are much more widely spread over the country. There is hardly an institution where there is not one or two, and there are several places other than Chicago where there is quite a collection." He points to the failure of Socialist economic organization in the Soviet Union, as well as to the impact of Hayek's *The Road to Serfdom*, as the principal reasons for the beginning of the trend away from collectivism.

Critics of Keynes have blamed the English lord for nearly every economic malady of the past century—even though Keynes's epochal *The General Theory of Employment, Interest and Money* wasn't published until 1936. And pro-Keynesians countered with the charge that theories of the nature of those proposed by Keynes single-handedly preserved the capitalistic system by helping America and Europe finally surmount the Depression. The argument, inevitably, was soon joined by those people who denounced Keynes as a Communist and Socialist, and by those who—while worshiping the general theory as hagiology—thought that catallatic principles could be discarded like last year's fashions in the search for the economic Grail. (One is reminded of New Jersey Sen. Clifford Case's non sequitor to the effect that nobody reads Ludwig von Mises anymore, therefore his economic theories are passé.)

While the whole debate can be said to remain still unsettled, it seems accurate to state that the overall controversy has been turned toward the question, Should the constant application of Keynesian economic theory remain a permanent policy of the federal government, or, Is Keynes's contribution merely that of a collection of specific policies applicable to unusual economic situations (and then only on a temporary basis, to avert a snowballing disaster such as was the 1930's depression). In this connection, in a review of a specifically anti-Keynesian book last summer, *New York Times'* economics specialist Edwin Dale noted that "it is entirely possible to quarrel fundamentally with the Keynesian revolution in economics. In brief, from John Maynard Keynes to Kennedy, the moderns could still be dead wrong, and the evidence is not yet decisive either way. The civil war in the profession still rages." Not being an economist, Goldwater is unqualified to argue the technical aspects of economics—as are all his senatorial colleagues with the possible exception of Paul Douglas, former University of Chicago economist.*

Yet it is not merely statistical data which are involved in public discussions of economics. At issue also are those things of life which Prof. Wilhelm Roepke, architect of West Germany's economic miracle, described as being "beyond supply and demand and the world of property," which "give meaning, dignity, and inner richness to life, those purposes and values which belong to the realm of ethics in the widest sense."

To Roepke, Keynes—for all his numerous talents, his personal appeal, and his many substantial contributions to economic theory—was a "representative of the geometric spirit" which looked upon men as little more than statistics to be manipulated by government planners. Adam Smith, on the other hand, viewed economics as "an organic part of the larger whole of the intellectual, moral, and historical life of society." He was, Roepke says, "a representative of the humanist spirit of the 18th century." On the lesser level of economics, Roepke maintains, "the road from Adam Smith to Keynes has doubtless been one of progress in many respects; on the higher level of total intellectual and spiritual development, it is equally certain that the road has been one of reaction and regression."

Social envy, the desire to take from some and give to others,

* A reporter's unfamiliarity with Keynesian economics accounted for what Goldwater described as the worst experience he ever had with the press. "During a press conference before a speech to the National Interfraternity Council in California two years ago," he explained, "I said that Harvard was the seat of Keynesianism. During the question and answer period after my talk I said that many of our leaders came from fraternities. The next day one of the wire services carried a story saying that I said Communism flourishes where fraternities are prohibited. I contacted the bureau chief right away and he obtained a radio transcript and replayed that part, and sure enough it said Keynesianism. Then the reporter admitted he didn't know what Keynesianism was; he thought I said Communism. I got two fraternity paddles in the mail from Harvard, and I'm still being asked by students what I meant by that equation."

has always been active, Roepke said. But all these and similar tendencies had, since time immemorial, been kept in check by their generally bad intellectual and moral reputation. People were always too prone to sin in those respects, but they did so with bad conscience and with the knowledge that respectable economics was against them. But Keynes, Roepke says, became one of the first minds of our time to relieve people—all those eager to spend, to soak the rich, or to despise financial and monetary discipline—of their bad conscience.

In other words, these "economics" questions had as much to do with prudence, sagacity, and integrity as with the statistical norms of production, saving, and investment. Goldwater was not alone in realizing that if politics is far too important to be left solely to politicians, economics is far too important to be left solely to economic planners.

A few weeks before the November 1963 off-year elections, Rep. Richard Fulton (D-Tenn.) wrote Goldwater a letter asking whether the Arizonan was serious about his earlier proposals that the Tennessee Valley Authority (TVA) be sold to private interests. Goldwater, knowing why the legislator hoped to put him on record, nevertheless replied: "I am quite serious in my opinion that TVA should be sold, for, among other benefits of such a transaction, I believe it would be a great boon to the State of Tennessee to have this enterprise placed on the tax rolls."

Goldwater's candor was received with less than uniform pleasure. "Why don't you go all out, Barry, and advocate the selling of the U.S. postal system?" asked an irate Tennessee Republican, in a letter which reflected the tone of much of the mail that descended on Goldwater's Washington office. After the subsequent election, the defeated Republican candidate in the Mississippi gubernatorial race said Goldwater's statement cost him about 25,000 of the 380,000 votes cast (although he hastened to add that without Goldwater's general political appeal he never would have come close to winning the 38 per cent of the vote he did, thereby establishing a modern record for a Mississippi Republican). Among other newspapers, the *Washington Post* and the *Philadelphia Inquirer* accused Goldwater of inconsistency in urging the sale of TVA while concomitantly co-sponsoring the $1 billion Central Arizona Project bill. Dwight Eisenhower said that he opposed selling the project, although he declared himself opposed to additional TVA's.

This flood of criticism confirmed that TVA is still a touchy, emotional political issue—as it has been ever since its inception in 1933 as a flood control project (dealing also with reforestation and navigation). Since that modest beginning, TVA has been progressively enlarged into a major power producer (fourth, on the basis of total investment, only to Consolidated Edison Co. of New York; Pacific Gas & Electric Co.; and Commonwealth Edison) serving customers in seven states: Tennessee, Alabama, Georgia, Kentucky, Mississippi, North Carolina and Virginia. And it has endeared itself to its customers by providing them with electricity subsidized by the remainder of the nation's taxpayers (.94 cents per kilowatt-hour for TVA customers, compared with a national average of about 2.5 cents).

Despite the storm of controversy he provoked, Goldwater refused to back down. When he was asked why he didn't wait until after the election to reply to the Democrat's letter, or why as a potential GOP presidential candidate he didn't sidestep the issue entirely, the Arizonan replied: "It's better for a candidate to be honest rather than dishonest. I wouldn't want to offer myself as a candidate anywhere with a lie under my hat. This TVA is a socialistic venture which has been perpetrated on the American public without their knowing what they're getting into. I'm not going to keep my mouth shut about it."

In the heat of the discussion it was generally lost sight of that

Goldwater had not suggested that TVA be turned over in its entirety to private business. He proposed that only the specifically nongovernmental operations of TVA—the fertilizer plant and the steam-generated power plants—be restored to private ownership. The hydroelectric operations, flood control, and navigation projects should, he said, remain in federal hands but be returned to government agencies already established to handle such functions.

In disposing of the steam-operated power plants, Goldwater suggested that the states in the Tennessee Valley be given first call upon them. If, within five years, they failed to exercise their option, then the plants would be offered for private sale to bidders. "I don't know whether any group in the country can manage a financial transaction this big," he said, "but I'd like to find out." If none can, he suggested the creation of a quasi-governmental corporation, similar to the Telstar Communication Satellite Corp., in which the federal government and private investors would share ownership.

Goldwater pointed to suggestions by the late Secretary of the Interior, Harold L. Ickes. "Ickes proposed ending duplication of existing services by TVA," Goldwater noted. "He said the Agriculture Department should run the soil conservation operations and forestry aspect of TVA; the hydroelectric power should be sold through the Interior Department. He said this would save money and make for better administration of the national programs for the benefit of *all* citizens of the U.S." (Goldwater might have reminded Ike that he once described TVA as "creeping socialism," or that another revered Republican, Herbert Hoover, noted in his 1952 memoirs that TVA had become "a radiating headquarters for socialism.")

Goldwater also had his defenders: Raymond Moley, one-time Cabinet member in the New Deal, characterized the proposal as "wholly reasonable," and the *Wall Street Journal* commented: "True, we don't expect Senator Goldwater to get very far with his suggestions; by now there are probably too many vested interests wedded to what is. Nonetheless, we find it refreshing to see some fresh thought brought to bear on a stale controversy."

The charge that Goldwater was inconsistent—in opposing TVA while simultaneously favoring congressional passage of the Central Arizona Project bill—was valid only if it could be demonstrated that Goldwater ever opposed federal reclamation projects, which he has not. Perhaps because he was raised in the sere Southwest, he long has been aware of the importance of reclamation. Even while serving on the City Council, he and two other Phoenicans, in a brief history of Phoenix written as a preface to the city code, hailed President Theodore Roosevelt's reclamation acts as invaluable steps in the march of progress.

In a letter rebutting the *Washington Post*'s editorial, Goldwater pointed out that TVA and the Central Arizona Project are wholly unrelated, both in conception and in practice. TVA, he said, produces and merchandises power and fertilizer which are heavily subsidized by federal investment and exempted from federal taxes, whereas CAP is truly a reclamation development. "Under a recent Supreme Court decision, Arizona is entitled to additional water from the Colorado River," he wrote. "The purpose of the CAP is to conduct this additional water into central Arizona, not for the purpose of expanding agricultural production in the state, but for the purpose of preserving an existing economy. Testimony clearly shows that not one additional acre of land will be brought into production through the use of this water."

Goldwater further called attention to statements by the Bureau of Reclamation which in June of 1963 said: "Without additional water, a substantial part of the presently irrigated lands will be forced out of production, and growth and development of the area will be retarded." In addition, the report stated that the water is estimated to be within the payment ability of water users, and the rate for commercial power would be competitive with alternate sources. The payout schedule, the report noted, indicates that reimbursable federal costs could be paid out in 50 years from water sales and power revenues. "I think that any responsible analysis of the Central Arizona Project," Goldwater wrote, "would clearly show it to be a life saving project to deliver water to Arizona with virtually all the project costs returned to the federal government in 50 years."

Where Goldwater appears to have made what Arizonans—including pro-Goldwater Arizonans—consider a tactical error was in telling Representative Fulton that Arizona was "ready, willing, and able," to tax itself to pay for the water project. In the face of mild criticism from some state leaders, Goldwater correctly pointed out that the suggestion was not original with him—that when current Secretary of the Interior Stewart Udall was a member of the House of Representatives from Arizona, he made a similar suggestion. And it was conceivable that Arizona would, in the event Congress refused to appropriate funds, have to tax itself the $1 billion necessary to protect its economy. But at the moment Goldwater made his apparent *gaffe*, Arizona's senior Senator, Carl Hayden, chairman of the powerful Senate Appropriations Committee, was flexing his political muscle—a combination of cajolery, pressure, and salesmanship—to steer the CAP bill past the shoals of the Senate.

The chairman of the Arizona Power Authority agreed with Goldwater that the state could finance the project. And Goldwater had in his possession a study from a New York firm which he said showed the "complete feasibility for financing on the state level." Nevertheless, Arizonans were apprehensive. For they knew there would be trouble enough getting the bill through Congress in view of the opposition of the 40-man California congressional delegation, which was miffed when the U. S. Supreme Court in June of 1962 settled a 12-year-old law suit between the two states by awarding Arizona twice as much Colorado River water as it now uses. But were Congress to conclude that Arizona really could go it alone, even congressmen who had no feelings about the bill one way or the other might well decide to allow her. And most Arizonans realized that $1 billion would be a staggering cost to be faced with, especially for a project most considered a traditional federal undertaking.

Tactical mistake or no, Goldwater came through the affair unscathed. And if in future Arizona elections he could not be assured of an "almost unanimous" victory (the phrase New Jersey political boss Frank Hague once used to describe his crushing 110,743 to 6,798 re-election victory as mayor of Jersey City), it was evident that the conservative spokesman was nowhere more popular with voters than in his home state.

CHAPTER 9

The Negro Revolution

"My mother bore me in the southern wild,
And I am black, but O! my soul is white."
—WILLIAM BLAKE

STARING out over blinding footlights at a predominantly white audience, a young Negro drags nervously at his cigarette. He pauses, squints, then remarks, "Look at the size of this crowd! To hell with the show, let's march on Georgia."

The young man is Dick Gregory, a social satirist who in little more than a year climbed from the status of a $10-a-day car washer to that of a $5,000-a-week commentator on the foibles and follies of *boobus Americanus*—and all because he now says to audiences from coast to coast the same things he used to say under his breath.

Perhaps no comedian of recent times has so pricked the conscience of a nation while simultaneously tickling its funnybone. For whereas the meteoric rise of Gregory is a modern phenomenon—who could have guessed that the former mail clerk who used to drop in the "foreign" slot letters addressed to Mississippi, would today be a national celebrity?—the conditions which made possible his success are age-old. For it is the controversial area of race relations to which Gregory addresses himself. Yet when he speaks of Freedom Rider Roulette ("You pick from six bus tickets—five to go to Chicago and one to Birmingham") or a Freedom Rider Martini ("Three and you get stoned"), the gleam in his eyes takes the edge off a topic both Negroes and whites usually dislike being reminded of in public.

Gregory manages to evoke a smile instead of bitterness when discussing the Ku Klux Klan ("the Mafia with a drawl"), his daughter's skepticism of Santa Claus ("even at 2 years old, she knows damn well ain't no white man coming into our neighborhood at midnight"), or the recondite benefits of lynch mobs ("I've got a brother who can run a half-mile faster than any white boy in the world"). In mock seriousness he talks about those old Civil War movies on TV ("The ones where, at the end, all the slaves are weeping and wailing, 'cause the South lost. Now ain't that somethin'? That's like Jimmy Hoffa pulling for Bobby Kennedy"). And in the next breath he solemnly assures his audience that the NAACP has had the atom bomb for three or four years (and when the South *does* rise again, he says, is it gonna have a surprise).

But beneath the veneer of humor, satirist Gregory's thrusts have a biting edge. "I went to one of those separate but equal schools down South," he says. "I don't know how old the textbooks were, but they sure kept me out of the Navy. If people wanted to sail off the edge of the earth, I sure wasn't gonna be one of them." At another point, he notes, "Down South they don't care how close I get as long as I don't get too big; and up North they don't care how big I get, as long as I don't get too close." When Negroes congregate in large areas in the North, he states, and it looks as though they might control the votes, "Northerners don't say anything to us—they have a slum clearance." And on the subject of housing, Gregory can be heard to remark, "Now that we've come into a little loot, my wife wants to move to the country. I think she's out of her mind. We could have the only decorator-designed slum in Chicago."

And so it goes. Whether acceptance of Gregory's barbs can be attributed to an ingrained guilt or whether it mirrors a masochistic tendency on the part of his audience, is a question best left for those who probe the human psyche. But, in addition to proving that there exists an effective middle ground for social protest Gregory's success is indicative of something else: America, in the decade of the 1960's, is thinking about what is now referred to as "the Negro revolution."

The revolution began modestly in Montgomery, Ala. in 1955 when the Rev. Martin Luther King, applying the Gandhian concept of non-violence to a mass movement, led the Negro community in a boycott protesting a city bus system which relegated Negroes to the rear. That successful act of defiance kindled Negro hopes throughout the nation, and was followed in short order by sit-ins, lie-ins, wade-ins, pray-ins, swim-ins, stand-ins, Freedom Rides, civic rallies, racial picket lines, and countless other means devised to call attention to Negro grievances. By the summer of 1963 the disparate demonstrations became less sporadic and uncoordinated; they were brought together under the disciplined well-organized leadership of heretofore relatively unheard of Negro organizations bearing the names of CORE, SNCC and others.

The summer protest culminated in a freedom march on Washington in late summer, during which an estimated 200,000 marchers, carrying placards and signs demanding equality, made their way in orderly fashion down Constitution and Independence Avenues from the Washington Monument to the Lincoln Memorial. There, together with actors and folk singers, clergymen and politicians, Negro spokesmen demanded passage of the administration's proposed civil rights bill, a Fair Employment Practices Act outlawing job discrimination, integration of all public schools, and a federal job retraining program.

With the close of the march and the summer of demonstrations came a national accounting: included in the ledger book, in addition to the enormously successful marshaling of the nation's moral resolve to act on basic Negro grievances, were the killing of NAACP leader Medgar Evers and the bombing of Negro children in Birmingham; growing Negro resentment in northern cities which provoked often violent white retaliation. Capping the summer's activity, both for good and ill, however, was the ever-persistent question: Where do we, as a nation, go from here?

Barry Goldwater reflected his understanding of the deep Negro exasperation when, three months before the Washington Freedom March, he told students at Phillips Academy, "If I were a Negro, I don't think I would be very patient." And from its inception he had endorsed the Washington march as a wise move in keeping with the right of petition. "Anybody has the right to come to Washington and visit his congressman," he stated. "I'll be in my office to receive people from my state."

But, despite his pronouncements and his record in favor of Negro claims for equality, Goldwater became a prime target of civil rights leaders (and those out to make political hay at his expense). At the 55th annual Governors' Conference in Miami Beach last July, California's Edmund G. (Pat) Brown labeled Goldwater a segregationist (and when he returned to Sacramento the following week, was picketed outside his Governor's mansion by Young Republicans). Nelson Rockefeller, at that time Goldwater's most persistent GOP critic, engaged in rank political opportunism by saying he "didn't really know whether Goldwater was or was not a segregationist."

Jackie Robinson, who first broke the color barrier in major league baseball, expressed alarm that the GOP under Goldwater would become a "white man's party" and promised to campaign tirelessly against Goldwater should he be nominated. Walter Lippmann did not promise to go out on the stump in an effort to defeat Goldwater, but he made a Stakhanovite effort to alert his readers that in the event of the Arizonan's nomination, "The party of Lincoln would have become the rallying point of the racists." And Gallup and similar pollsters disclosed that Goldwater, as well as other Republican candidates for President, would receive negligible Negro support.

If the reasons for all of this were understandable, they were nonetheless ironic. Few men not deliberately courting minority bloc votes have expressed their sympathy for Negroes—verbally and through action—more often than Goldwater. As a member of the Phoenix City Council, politician Goldwater voted to desegregate the restaurant at Sky Harbor Airport. As chief of staff of the Arizona Air National Guard, Colonel Goldwater in the spring of 1952 handed down an order that segregation was henceforth to be banned in the air guard. On Oct. 21, 1951, at a mass NAACP rally in Phoenix's Eastlake Park, businessman Goldwater donated $200 cash; on Feb. 7, 1952, he donated a $200 check, both donations to be used for the legal defense fund of the Maricopa County (Phoenix) NAACP in an effort to speed integration of public schools. He was a member of both the Phoenix and Tucson NAACP, but, he explains, "I got out when they started attacking me politically." He is today a member of the Urban League, a national organization of Negro and white employers and professional men whose main activity is overcoming job discrimination against Negroes.

When a Southern editor questioned him about his donations to the NAACP, Goldwater wrote: "My firm conviction in this matter is that desegregation should be conducted at the state level without federal intervention. Therefore I felt that by contributing to the local group [NAACP] as a private citizen, I was helping its chances of resolving the problem."

During debate over the proposed civil rights bill last summer, Goldwater was quoted in a front page *New York Times* story as saying it was unquestionably "morally wrong" to deny Negroes equal access to public accommodations. Nevertheless, he said, an attempt to correct this moral evil by law "will not solve anything"; such a law would only "upset individual rights and states' rights."

Almost two years ago Joseph Alsop wrote that Goldwater, under the guise of "states' rights," has "always taken the kind of stand on racial desegregation that pleases Southern Democratic voters"—meaning, segregationists. Yet if segregationists and racists were pleased by Goldwater's opposition to the Supreme Court's 1954 desegregation decision (*Brown v. Board of Education*), or by his opposition to public accommodations laws, they could take scant comfort in his reasons for adopting his position. For Goldwater has always unequivocally declared his opposition to segregation. In *The Conscience of a Conservative* he wrote: "It so happens that I am in agreement with the objectives of the Supreme Court as stated in the Brown decision. I believe that it is both wise and just for Negro children to attend the same schools as whites, and that to deny them this opportunity carries with it strong implications of inferiority." But, he maintains, the actual matter of school integration must be left to the states if the 10th Amendment to the Constitution is not to be subverted.

In a *Harper's* column on Goldwater, William S. White quoted the Arizonan as saying, "It is morally and ethically wrong to segregate white and Negro children in schools or elsewhere; segregation does result in inferior opportunity for Negroes." In articles on Goldwater in both *Fortune* and *True*, Goldwater's opposition to segregation was set forth clearly. Even liberal playwright Gore Vidal, in a demeaning article in *Life* in June of 1961, admitted, "Personally [Goldwater] sees nothing wrong with Negro and white children together in the same schools." And in the *Yale Political* for the summer of 1962, Goldwater once again is quoted as saying, "Morally, I don't think that segregation is right. I think that it is wrong. I don't care where it is practiced or how it is practiced or between whom it is practiced. . . . I don't like the fact that many places in the South still practice segregation. I don't like the segregation that's being practiced in New York City."

Confusion reigns, however, with respect to the ultimate

meaning of Goldwater's approach to the Negro problem. One attempt to clear the polemical air was made by the conservative *National Review*: "If it is true that Goldwater, because he believes in private property and states' rights, can therefore be called a segregationist in effect, then by the same token it is true that . . . Herbert Hoover, because he was opposed to intervention during the late '30s, was a Nazi in effect; that the American Civil Liberties Union, because it opposes ex parte legislation in Georgia, is in favor of the Ku Klux Klan, in effect." The magazine noted that Republicans can come nearer to the truth by charging that Democrats who approve the civil rights bill with its anti-discrimination in commercial facilities clause, are in effect opposed to personal control over one's private property, inasmuch as the bill was, in this single aspect, a direct assault on private property. If the Democrats, in their anxiety to discredit Goldwater and the conservative wing of the Republican Party, hammer away at the theme that such sentiments as Goldwater's add up to an anti-Negro policy, the magazine noted, then the disastrous (for the Negro) may result: those who side with Goldwater may begin reconstructing their habits of thought, and arguments, and eventually their policies. "Thereafter, they might proceed, resignedly, on the assumption that what is anti-Negro and what is traditionally American are apparently one and the same thing. And that therefore one must now choose between staying free, and truckling to the Negro vote."

Furthermore, *National Review* made the observation that some of the bill's provisions were not so much as mentioned by the President or by any other Democratic Party officials—let alone put forward as legislative proposals—three months before the actual agitation for the bill. It added, "It is undiscriminating to insist that the question of constitutionality has not been raised and to dismiss constitutionally-based arguments against the bill as presumptive anti-Negroism."

After Roy Wilkins, executive secretary of the NAACP,

scored Goldwater for his stand on the civil rights issue, Edward
Banks, Negro publisher of the *Arizona Tribune*, wrote that it
was unfair to liken Goldwater to Governors Barnett and Wallace. Wilkins, said Banks, "overlooks the progress made in the
Senator's home state in the field of human relations." In a letter sent to (but not published by) the *Saturday Evening Post*,
as a rebuttal to the Jackie Robinson article, Banks said that
Robinson's comments were "grossly unfair." Goldwater may
not go as far and as fast as some of us might wish, Banks said,
"but he has a strong, true history here in Arizona on problems related to the Negro and I believe in him as one who
knows him well. I am sorry that Mr. Robinson, whom all of us
regard highly, has allowed himself to become the instrument of
a political faction which is intent on smearing an honest and
upright man who knows and understands the Negro problems
and whose achievements here in Arizona are solid."

In a subsequent conversation, Banks expressed the view that
Goldwater "is basically a liberal when it comes to civil and human rights. He has done a great deal for Negro integration in
Arizona and he should be judged on that record. Arizona is
one of the most liberal states in these United States when it
comes to race relations, and Goldwater's influence has been a
major factor. He has done more for Arizona Negroes than any
other Arizona politician." After an interview with Goldwater,
Chuck Stone, editor of the national Negro weekly *Afro-Ameri-
can*, said about the Arizonan that "in the area of civil rights,
the lines become blurred and his deep feeling about racial
equality again and again rises to the surface whenever he
touches upon this critical subject." In the event Goldwater
became President, Stone wrote, "one thing is certain: Colored
people will have a sympathetic ear to their demands."

Goldwater's brother Bob said, "Barry has always been very
much for the Negro. He and I grew up here in Phoenix, played
football and baseball with them. We had a lot of Negro
friends, and hope we still do." When a picket in a Phoenix

march, sponsored last summer by the NAACP, carried a sign saying, "Goldwater's hires no Negro sales personnel," Bob Goldwater pointed out that the Goldwater stores (which had by then been sold to a New York firm) employ 17 Negroes, several in jobs of supervisory nature, out of a total of some 400 employees. This amounted to slightly better than four per cent in an area where Negroes comprise less than a half of one per cent of the population—a percentage far more liberal than quotas demanded by the NAACP during last summer's nation-wide protest marches and demonstrations.

Goldwater's boyhood friend and finance chairman, Harry Rosenzweig, said, "When citizens in our town felt it was time to end segregation in the schools, the Catholic leader of that effort—a man far from Barry in political matters—received a generous check from Goldwater to help that effort."

When the late President Kennedy requested discretionary authority to withhold federal funds from programs in which discrimination is practiced, a position advocated in the interim report of the Commission on Civil Rights, Goldwater advocated making such a denial of funds mandatory. He felt that a merely discretionary cut-off would give the President too much personal political leverage. As he put it, discussing the result of such a definite policy, it would be interesting to see "how long a state would push for segregation if federal funds for roads 'got lost.'" And such a position would be in keeeping with the due process clause of the Constitution as it is now interpreted.

Goldwater's position on the disposition of federal funds was warmly supported by Frederick D. Patterson, president emeritus of Tuskegee Institute, who wrote in a letter to the *New York Times*: "Whereas the President's message to Congress requested discretion in denying federal funds, Senator Goldwater would make this a mandatory requirement and has supported his position by saying that he doubted if many states would refuse the millions of dollars which come to them from the federal government for road-building programs, if the elimination of discrimination was the small price they would have to pay to secure this largesse.

"I think Senator Goldwater's position is absolutely sound and emphasizes the fact that no state is going to be willing to do without federal monies in order to preserve segregation and discrimination, when it comes down to the hard reality of eliminating these proscriptions or doing without the money....

"The purpose of the legislation is not to deny states money but to see to it they disburse it equitably. And this is exactly what will happen if such action is taken. In my opinion Senator Goldwater, who is reputed to be careful not to offend the South, was willing to take a forthright position on this issue—not because he anticipated the withholding of funds but because he realized that despite the furor that such reaction would create, it would in the end result in compliance. And once compliance is established, the animus associated with the change would soon be forgotten. This has been the history of civil rights changes in the South."

But for every one defense of Goldwater's position in the press, there were countless brickbats. Walter Lippmann, carrying on his incessant (and somewhat inexplicable) attack, criticized the Arizonan's unwillingness to give the federal government power to prevent discrimination in public accommodations. This, Lippmann said, was a conception of private property which Blackstone described as the "sole and despotic dominion . . . over the external things of the world, in total exclusion of the right of any other individual in the land." Furthermore, Lippmann said, no civilized society has long tolerated the despotic theory of private property, which is "alien to the central truths of Christendom."

It is doubtful that Lippmann and those who pursued similar arguments were really arguing for some sort of dissolution of private property. Nevertheless, Goldwater felt that any arbitrary attempt to regulate private businesses in the fashion prescribed by the proposed civil rights bill, was at least a major step in the direction of the abolition of private property. (Max Eastman once confessed, "It seems obvious to me now—though I have been slow, I must say, in coming to the conclusion—that the institution of private property is one of the main things that have given man that limited amount of free and equalness that Marx hoped to render infinite by abolishing this institution.")

The argument over a public accommodations law was not confined solely to academic argument over private property, however. An important further aspect was noted by Cornell University's Andrew Hacker, who wrote in the December 8, 1963 *New York Times Magazine*: "Legislation, if and when passed, may create as many problems as it solves. Backed by the authority of government, Negroes will have access to places formerly closed to them—access, indeed, to the facilities and opportunities of white America. But white Americans will grow increasingly resentful at such intrusions, and tensions will continue to mount. The problem will have to resolve itself, and the changes that take place will be largely outside the realms of law and politics." This, in brief, is in large measure Goldwater's attitude, and the reason for his opposition to the proposed rights law and the claims advanced regarding its pressing importance.

As the result of rethinking the constitutional problems involved in the question of the federal government's right to force school integration, Goldwater has modified one of his original positions. In *The Conscience of a Conservative*, he argued that whereas he believed it both wise and just for Negro children to attend the same schools as whites, he was not prepared to impose his judgment on the people of Mississippi or South Carolina. Furthermore, he said at that time that he was not impressed by the claim that the Supreme Court's decision on school integration is the law of the land. The Constitution is what its authors intended it to be, the Arizonan argued, not what the Supreme Court says it is. "I therefore support all efforts by the States, excluding violence of course, to preserve their rightful powers over education."

Since then, however, Goldwater, when asked how a state might resist Supreme Court school segregation decisions, replied: "The idea is not to resist it. There is nothing in our Constitution that says a person can violate the law. Neither is there anything that says a state can violate the law. If the states feel that states' rights have been tampered with, you have the amendment process or the elective process. Either one is open." Furthermore, while declaring that he would first try moral persuasion to obtain compliance with federal court decisions directing schools to integrate, Goldwater conceded that he felt a law should be passed giving the Attorney General the power "to use a very tightly drawn law aimed like a rifle at this precise problem in a school district." He would, he said, use whatever federal authority was legal, including federal troops or marshals to carry out the courts' decisions, only as an extreme resort rather than as a matter of policy.

This, admittedly, represented a change in Goldwater's position. His revised thinking would appear to be in line with that of Milton Friedman, his economic advisor, that if forced to choose between the evils of enforced segregation or enforced integration in education, he would find it impossible not to choose integration. Goldwater points out, however, that—contrary to claims of critics—he has consistently opposed state or local segregation in bus, airline, or railroad terminals engaged in interstate commerce. And also contrary to critics' claims, he has often denied that Republican strategy aimed at capturing Southern states in 1964 is designed toward writing off the Negro vote. "We want Negro votes," he explained. "Sure we want all the votes we can get. But we don't intend to make wild promises like the Democrats. And another thing—I just can't see this idea that the liberals are peddling that if the Republicans carry Southern states it's an example of racism, but it's just plain good politics if the Democrats carry them."

Goldwater also looks with disapproval on proposals for a Fair Employment Practices Commission. "I agree that it is wrong, morally wrong, for people to discriminate in employment because of color or race or religion or any other reason," he explained. "But if the govenment can forbid such discrimination, it is a real possibility that sometime in the future the same government can *require* people to discriminate in hiring on the basis of color, or race or religion." He believes, with Milton Friedman, that it is no more desirable that momentary majorities decide what characteristics are relevant to employment than what speech is appropriate. Indeed, Friedman asks whether a free market in ideas can long be maintained if a free market in goods and services is destroyed. "The ACLU," Friedman noted, pointing out the absurdity of the government's trying to decree employment practices, "will fight to the death to protect the right of a racist to preach on a street corner the doctrine of racial segregation. But it will favor putting him in jail if he acts on his principles by refusing to hire a Negro for a particular job."

State sovereignty, remarked Justice Salmon P. Chase, died at Appomattox; and millions of Americans, either out of conviction or by rote, today echo his sentiments. Others, undeniably in the minority, deny Chase's contention. And, nearly a hundred years after the stillness at Appomattox, the debate over states' rights continues to elicit heated response.

Barry Goldwater is, as he has been during his entire congressional career, on the side of states' rights—and because of this stand he has been branded a segregationist. He remains insistent, however, that the 50 states are, in effect, 50 laboratories in which men independently test and probe the ways of civil government, developing new tools and techniques and developing their own skills. There are those who say that the cost of 50 governments is too great to bear in this complex age, he says. And yet, he asks, how better to meet complexity than with a diversity of resource? How can we measure the cost of what we gain from our states against any scale of dollars that might be re-channeled and centralized as a result of weakening state responsibilities? The ledger sheet that the structure of state power must satisfy, he says, is the well-being and the freedom of the people who live in those states. Regard for the federal system, and the 50 states that make it a system, is in his view first of all a regard for the due process of law. It is a regard for the wisdom of the people themselves. It is confidence in their ability to use that wisdom to solve their problems, in their own best ways. "The federal system, with its base in the states," he says, "tolerates many differences without, of course, tolerating impairment of nationally agreed upon freedoms. It does not demand, in other words, that all citizens adopt a single best answer to any problem—but it does tend to prevent them from adopting any single worst answer."

Passions surrounding the race issue have become dangerously incendiary on the question of the Supreme Court's school de-segregation decision. What disturbs Goldwater is that Chief Justice Warren admitted in his ruling in the Brown case that the court was legislating. "In approaching this problem," Warren said, "we cannot turn the clock back to 1868 when the amendment was adopted. . . . We must consider public education in the light of its full development and in its present place in American life throughout the nation." This admission, the Arizonan believes, could accurately be described as judicial irresponsibility. If we condone the practice of substituting our own intentions for those of the Constitution's framers, he maintains, we in effect reject the principle of constitutional government and endorse—whatever the immediate issue at hand— a rule of men rather than laws.

Many non-conservatives, Sidney Hook among them, concede that the Supreme Court legislated in the Brown decision, saying that the Court always has legislated. "The ultimate question," Hook said, "is the character, grounds, and wisdom of its legislation. . . . That the Supreme Court decision overturns earlier precedents is true. This is not unusual. The real question is: Should the precedents be retained or overturned?" This view holds that not merely slavery but all the institutional restraints and indignities which constituted servitude must be abolished. Segregated education, these spokesmen say, is inherently cruel, unjust, and degrading to the group discriminated against, in the same way that the yellow patch or badge of inferiority, the mark of the pariah, the stigma of the outcast, are degrading. This school of thought believes that even if the physical facilities of Negro education were actually better than those set aside for the whites, segregation would still be degrading for the same reason, as Hook put it, "that we regard a well-fed slave as still a slave."

While agreeing with this, Goldwater contends that the ultimate question is *not* whether Supreme Court legislation is wise or just, as Hook maintains. The question is whether the Constitution is, as Charles Evans Hughes said in 1926, "What the Supreme Court says it is." Goldwater says no, that Article I, Section II of the Constitution vests all legislative powers in Congress, and that Article V explicitly describes the manner in which the States have the power to amend the Constitution.

The purpose of the 10th Amendment, Goldwater says, was and is to restrict the federal government, to hold it within the circumscribed boundaries of delegated powers. The constitutional system, he says, does not mean that the will of the people will be thwarted, only that *immediate* objectives will be subordinated to *long-range* objectives. He notes approvingly that the Senate Judiciary Committee, commenting on the 1937 attempted court-packing plan, said that inconvenience and even delay in the enactment of legislation is not a heavy price to pay for our system. Preservation of the American constitutional system, the Committee said, is "immeasurably more important . . . than the immediate adoption of any legislation however beneficial."

"The reason the word 'no' is used as a direct restraint on government 26 times in the original 7 Articles of the Constitution, and five times more in the Bill of Rights," Goldwater says, "is to limit the scope and size of federal government, so it can't become tyrannical. If we expect to remain a free people, we have to see to it that states' rights are not permitted to disappear, even if sometimes we are perplexed at the actions of certain states."

Attempts to depict Goldwater as a racist, segregationist, or a bigot—all three charges have been lodged against him, directly and by implication—have not deterred some of the nation's more militant bigots, racists, and segregationists from attacking Goldwater. The May 1963 publication of the National States Rights Party labeled Goldwater a "kosher conservative," and, not far from its advertisement of the spurious Protocols of Zion, linked him with "Jewish espionage artists." During the National Draft Goldwater Rally in Washington on Independence Day, leaflets were passed out describing Goldwater as "the Arizona Israelite," proclaiming, "Hear Goldwater tell lie after lie to get your vote." And last August, two California members of the American Nazi Party picketed Goldwater for President headquarters in Phoenix. They carried signs, lettered on both sides, reading: "Lincoln Rockwell for Presindent" (sic), "Goldwater is a Race Mixer," "Goldwater Supported the Red NAACP," and "Communism Is Jewish." The Nazis, wearing swastika armbands and one wearing cap, boots, and the traditional Nazi storm trooper khaki uniform, continued picketing until a group of irate teen-agers forcibly closed their sidewalk marching route by forming a human chain, and finally forced them to their car amid threats and shaking fists.

"I'm used to kooks like that picketing me," Goldwater said amusedly. "If they ever stop, I'll wonder what I've done wrong."

CHAPTER 10

The Left and the Right

---

*"Revolutionary movements attract both
the best and worst elements of society."*
—GEORGE BERNARD SHAW

W HEN self-proclaimed Marxist Lee Harvey Oswald assassinated President John F. Kennedy on Nov. 22, 1963, he plunged the United States into a period of mourning and confusion from which it has not yet fully recovered. And the nation will be a long time forgetting the pictures of the young Chief Executive—one minute smiling and waving to a warm, enthusiastic Dallas crowd which lined the streets to cheer him along the path of the motorcade, and the next minute slumped in his wife's lap in the back seat of a convertible speeding him on a hopeless mission to Parkland Hospital.

The initial reaction of most Americans, after they realized the enormity of the crime, was to ask who could have done such a terrible deed. And why? Until the capture of Lee Harvey Oswald, who was himself murdered two days later, and posthumously adjudged guilty by reason of overwhelming circumstantial evidence, the motives and identity of the assassin could only be guessed. But within minutes after the shooting most radio and television newscasters knowingly laid the blame at the doorstep of "right wing extremists." The Soviet Union blamed it on "a well-planned action of Fascist forces of the ultra-right-wing." The Communist governments of East Germany, Poland, and Cuba also blamed the American right wing. And the U.S. Information Agency, in its broadcasts to Russia, said that the assassination had taken place in Dallas, which it described as a center of right wing extremism.

Even when it was learned that Oswald—who had spent some time working in a factory in Russia, who had applied for Russian citizenship and who married a Russian—had no connection with the right wing, but instead belonged to the outer fringes of the far left, the charges against the right did not diminish appreciably. Bishop James A. Pike said that in fixing the blame for the assassination "we must include all those who, by their race hate and extreme radical right propaganda, have consistently supplied the fuel which would fire up such an assassin." Columnist Max Lerner said: "When right wing racist fanatics are told over and over again that the President is a traitor, a Red, a 'nigger-lover,' that he has traduced the Constitution and is handing America over to a mongrelized world-state, there are bound to be some fanatics dull-witted enough to follow the logic of the indictment all the way and rid America of the man who is betraying it."

As a result of this sophistical and inflamatory reasoning, much of the grief and emotion Americans felt was directed against anyone—politicians, newsmen, private citizens—who had opposed the policies of the slain President. Sen. John Tower received so many threatening letters and telephone calls that he temporarily moved his family out of his home. An anonymous caller threatened to kill Sen. Tom Dodd, a domestic liberal who had helped expose the pro-Communist background of the Fair Play for Cuba Committee to which Oswald claimed allegiance. And abusive letters and threatening phone calls were received by Barry Goldwater, blaming him for the assassination.

It seemed not to matter that just the month before Goldwater asked his personal friend John F. Kennedy if he had any political advice to give, and the President responded, "Don't announce your candidacy too soon. And don't get mixed up in those damn primaries." Nor did it seem to matter to those struggling to pin the blame for the assassination on Goldwater that just two months before the assassination, during ceremonies in the Rose Garden of the White House before a gathering of congressional and military leaders, the President called, "Barry!" when he spotted the Arizonan, beckoned Goldwater to join him, and said to everyone within hearing distance, "We are all friends."*

"The abuse heaped on me and other conservatives resulted from inaccurate comments by some radio and television announcers, immediately after the assassination, that right wing elements may have been responsible," Goldwater said. "I was surprised that some persons would make charges like that which were so quickly disproved by the facts." One newscaster who made inaccurate comments, but proved big enough to apologize, was CBS newsman Walter Cronkite. On the day of the assassination he told his nationwide audience that Goldwater, enroute to a political meeting, had brushed off the assassination with a "no comment." When Cronkite learned that Goldwater was in fact enroute to his mother-in-law's funeral in Muncie, Ind., and could not be reached for comment, he immediately sent a letter acknowledging his "gross error," adding: "You had indeed had a most heart-touching comment, and of course we know you were enroute to a moment of grief of your own. . . . I cannot tell you how deeply I regret this episode in a day of such sorrow, and I can rest easy only with the knowledge that you are a forebearing and forgiving man."

What bothered most conservatives was not that these very

*The *New York Times* reported that after the ceremony the two "shook hands and Mr. Goldwater clasped the President's shoulder as photographers' shutters clicked madly. They laughed together but their exchange could not be overheard."

persons, who would have fastened on any right wing associations of Oswald to extirpate the entire conservative movement, discerned no connection between the assassin's pro-
Communism and his political proclivites. ("In his alienation,
Lee Oswald turned to the left," said Walter Lippmann. "But
that was incidental.") For as near as can be determined, the
assassination *was* the independent handiwork of a fanatic
whose sympathies just happened to lie left—far left—of center.
The conservative objection was primarily that many of the
same people who had rabidly opposed Goldwater even before
the assassination were, under the guise of objective analysis
and doing scant justice to a political moratorium established
out of respect for the dead President, trying to destroy the
Arizonan by repeating that his political popularity would suffer because of "his connections with the far right," or because
there would be "an inevitable move away from extremism."

This ploy did not pass unnoticed. Goldwater said, "It was
just more than the political left wing could bear to discover
that Oswald, the accused assassin, actually was a professed Communist." Other conservatives pointed out that in allegedly
counseling against "hate," these commentators were attempt-
ing to whip up hatred against those who disagreed with their
prevailing view. The *Wall Street Journal* commented, "To
make the assassination of a President an occasion for character
assassination does worse than confuse issues." And Senator
Tower reminded the public that Oswald's mind was not shaped
by our society, but by Communist propaganda. "Let us remember," he said, "that in talking about extremists, in talking about
the purveyors of hate, the real purveyors of hate in this world,
the real fomenters of class war and bigotry among people are
the Communists, and the real disease of this world is Communist imperialism." (When "TRB," who regularly fulmi-
nates about the thunder on the right, attempted the standard
anti-conservative agglutination in the *New Republic*, Dwight
Macdonald was moved to reply: ". . . the awkward thing for

liberals about Oswald was that he was a crackpot leftist. . . .
There may be 'brooding Oswalds' of the right but so far they
have not taken action, which, as an old-fashioned believer in
the Bill of Rights, I think is the important thing. The only
Oswald we have had was of the left. . . . I agree it was a great
pity that the assassin turned out to be not a lunatic Birchite, as
we all assumed in that first hour of shock, but a lunatic
'Marxist.' But such was the fact. Oswald is our baby, not
theirs.")

That there were and are fanatics and moral bankrupts on the
far right is something few conservatives would deny. The political right, like the political left, has attracted as many odd-
ball exhibits and freaks as can be found along the midway of a
circus: The anti-Semites, the anti-Negroes, those who see a
Red hand directing every move made in Washington, those
who—in Democratic Congressman Morris Udall's memorable
phrase—foolishly warned that "the U.S. Army is training can-
nibals in Georgia to invade our country and enforce integration
and intermarriage." And then there are those who, for whatever reason, have clambered aboard the right wing bandwagon
to conduct their personal vendetta against fluoridation ("If the
doctors say it's all right," Goldwater said, "I have to take their
word for it"), against the "pro-Communist" National Municipal League ("total nonsense," commented NML Vice-President Goldwater), and dozens of similar bogeymen.

The absurdity of these right wing fringe groups has been well
covered by at least a half dozen books, every major publication, and all three major television networks. Almost without
exception, these "exposés" indiscriminately lumped respectable
conservatives with the Ku Klux Klan and the American Nazi
Party, leaving the unwary with the impression that the "radical
right" was on the verge of toppling the U.S. government (a
popular theme among novelists and moviemakers) just as soon
as the Imperial Wizard and George Lincoln Rockwell could
decide on a *modus operandi* acceptable to Goldwater and his

followers.* One CBS documentary on the far right so angered Goldwater, because it linked him by implication with every known or reputed right extremist, that he flatly informed officials of the network he would have nothing more to do with them.

Strangely, for a media which seemed almost anthropophagous when it came to ferreting out pockets of right wing resistance, not once in the past half-dozen years has a major publication conducted a similar exposé of the political left. In fact, until the assassination it was generally agreed by the important communications media that extremism existed only on the right. When a reader asked an official of Cowles magazines whether *Look* would run a piece on the far left similar to its article on the far right, the official responded with what seemed to be the general feeling: "We discussed doing a similar piece on the far left. Our researches led us to the conclusion that there really is no Far Left in the United States except for the Communists."

The argument about extremists can be said to have begun in earnest on February 9, 1950, when the junior Senator from Wisconsin, Joseph R. McCarthy, told a county women's Republican club at Wheeling, W. Va. that he had in his hand the names of a number of Communists working in the State Department. To this day the argument rages whether the number of supposed Communists was 57 or 205. But this and subsequent allegations that Communists, agents of a foreign power, had wormed their way into positions of power and influence in the U.S. State Department and Army, ignited a controversy which was to leave deep lesions and painful scars on the American body politic.

* Those who preached this line only have to look as far as Texas, supposedly a hot-bed of right wing reaction, where far right Gen. Edwin Walker finished a pitiful last in a 6-man race for Governor in 1962, to see the foolishness of this fear.

The bitter debate over what came to be known as "Mc-Carthyism" was not without its comic aspects. England's Bertrand Russell charged that McCarthy had made it unsafe for Americans to read Thomas Jefferson. When Robert Hutchins, as late as 1954, insisted that "professors everywhere will hesitate before they express opinions contrary to those of Senator McCarthy," liberal Prof. Sidney Hook, who not only read Jefferson but in 1961 delivered the Jefferson Memorial Lectures at the University of California, observed: "When other individuals, right-wing extremists, have charged, on the basis of the fact that some professors have been members of the Communist party, that our universities are hotbeds of communism, they have been regarded as creatures of the intellectual underworld. Even a few hundred teachers . . . is a very small percentage of the total. But what shall we say of the statement that *all* professors have been intimidated by McCarthy into silence at a time when any honest observer on the campuses of America could testify to the loud, continuous and unrestrained criticism of McCarthy voiced by students and teachers alike? Actually, it is the lone and rare supporter of McCarthy who has been the genuine non-conformist in academia."

The excesses on the pro-McCarthy side were equally exaggerated—and, from the viewpoint of almost a decade, equally laughable. For too many, McCarthy became *the* symbol of anti-Communism, while other equally tough anti-Communists of the liberal left—Hook, Sen. Paul Douglas, Bertrand Wolfe—were often ignored or deprecated by the Wisconsin Senator's followers. And too many were too prone to accept even McCarthy's more blatant misstatements and exaggerations as Gospel, according to St. Joseph.

Columnist William S. White felt that McCarthyism involved "a profound and memorable test of true liberalism and true conservatism alike," and on that issue he was aligned with liberalism. But there was simply no such convenient line separating Caliban from Prospero. (For McCarthy, who at one time was supported by more than half those who responded to a Gallup Poll, obviously had the backing of many nonconservatives.) And not all conservatives were pro-McCarthy. Ralph de Toledano, whose book (with Victor Lasky) on the Hiss trial stamped him as a "McCarthyite" in the minds of many who refused to turn their backs on Alger Hiss, said of the Wisconsin Senator, "I realized after my first talk with him that I had forgotten more about Communism and the minutiae of subversion than he would ever know."

And in a letter to this writer in 1959, the late Whittaker Chambers wrote:

"I have never published any comment about the late Senator McCarthy, or ever, voluntarily, mentioned his name in public. The reason for my silence is simple. I am not one of his admirers. But neither am I one of his vilifiers. My conclusions about Senator McCarthy are the result of close personal observation and direct personal experience. Any sense-making presentiment of them must take the form of a review of the intimate record. Perhaps the time will come when such a review will serve a purpose. I do not believe that the time has come yet.

"So, while my complete rejection of Senator McCarthy as a suitable symbol of the right is not a secret, I have preferred to keep it as private as possible. But I feel free to add here my belief that if a section of the right persists in finding in the Senator the true symbol of its cause and hopes, that section of the right will increasingly risk foreclosing its claim to be taken seriously. My hope has been that, with the Senator's death, and the press of new, tremendous issues, the symbol would fade in the natural course of things, and those who rallied to it would find a more effective symbol. . . .

"A faith in individual men, or factions, does not seem to me of decisive importance. Our need seems to me to be, not a faith in men, or even parties or causes, but a rigorous effort of the mind to grasp the nature of the forces shaping our reality, and their inter-relationships, in order to try to generalize from that reality a little helpful truth. Goethe's dying words never rang to me more meaningfully than now: 'Light! Light! More light!' "

As Chairman of the Senate Permanent Investigations Subcommittee, McCarthy subsequently headed an investigation of the Army loyalty program in what soon became known as the Army-McCarthy hearings. During the course of the televised proceedings, McCarthy charged that the Army loyalty program was lax. The Army, which had employed Boston attorney Joseph N. Welch, accused McCarthy of trying to destroy the reputation of a young assistant attorney to Welch by accusing him of being a Communist sympathizer.

As a result of the hearings, a motion was introduced into the Senate by McCarthyphobes to censure the Wisconsin Senator for contempt of the Senate or its committees, abuse of fellow senators, and abuse of Army Brig. Gen. Ralph W. Zwicker. An original 46 charges of misconduct were discarded in favor of the charges that, because of McCarthy's failure to appear before the Gillette subcommittee in 1952, he was in contempt of that committee (which, as a result of a resolution introduced by Sen. William Benton that McCarthy be expelled from the Senate, undertook to investigate his conduct), he abused congressional colleagues (McCarthy had characterized New Jersey Republican Sen. Robert Hendrickson as "a living miracle without brains or guts"), and that he abused General Zwicker while a witness before the McCarthy investigating committee.

Before long the charges against McCarthy were reduced to the case that he was contemptuous of the Gillette subcommittee. (McCarthy's attorney, Edward Bennett Williams, pointed out in his book, *One Man's Fight for Freedom*, that a witness is cited for contempt if he is subpoenaed to testify and declines to appear, or if he refuses to answer proper questions. Yet the Watkins committee's report charged that McCarthy declined

the "invitation" of the Gillette subcommittee to appear before
it in 1952. And never in Senate history had anyone been pun-
ished for declining an "invitation" to appear.)

But by then it was too late. Passions were too highly in-
flamed to get either of the Senate factions to consider the fine
points of law. On December 2, 1954, the Senate voted 67-22 to
censure Joseph McCarthy. Commented lawyer Williams, "History must show in one of its more ironical paragraphs that Sen.
Joseph McCarthy, whose name became an international by-
word for ruthless inquiries, was himself the casualty of a Congressional investigation that flouted the rules of fair play."

Freshman Sen. Barry Goldwater was one of the twenty-two
senators—all Republicans, incidentally—who voted against
censure. During debate on the movement Goldwater defended
McCarthy as having "the strongest voice now speaking in
America against Communism." To remove such a man from
honor and influence in America at this juncture, Goldwater
said, would be a strong victory for Moscow in the field of
American public opinion and a propaganda triumph for the
double-talking, co-existence-with-Russia crowd.

"All the discredited and embittered figures of the Hiss-Yalta
period of American dishonor have crawled out from under their
logs to join the effort to get even," Goldwater claimed. "The
news columns and the airways have been filled with their pious
talk about 'civil liberties,' 'ethical codes,' and 'protection of the
innocent,' while at the same time these people have dipped
into the smut pot to discredit Senator McCarthy and his work
against Communism."

Goldwater further claimed that if the Senate "still sees fit
to approve the censure resolution, then I suggest that there are
many here who will say to themselves in the undeceiving soli-
tude of their private thoughts, 'This has been the dirtiest day's
work of my life.' "

While Goldwater had never been an uncritical supporter of
McCarthy, he believed, as he told a Wisconsin Republican
State Convention in 1957, that "Because Joe McCarthy lived,

we are a safer, freer, more vigilant nation today." But he told his Senate colleagues, at the height of the McCarthy controversy, that, "If I were Joe, I would walk over to [Sen. Robert Hendrickson] and I would say, 'I'm awfully sorry about what happened.'" When Sen. Everett Dirksen worked out a compromise arrangement whereby the Senate would say only that it did not condone what McCarthy had done (although there had been no rules forbidding what he had done, and that such rules should be drafted making it mandatory to censure anyone violating these rules in the future) in return for McCarthy's apology to Hendrickson and Sen. Arthur Watkins, it was Goldwater who—together with lawyer Williams—spent several hours at McCarthy's bedside in Bethesda Naval Hospital (where he had undergone treatment for a severely infected elbow) in vain begging the controversial Senator to accept the proposed compromise resolution.

When, after the censure, McCarthy accused Dwight Eisenhower of congratulating senators who hamper "the exposure of Communism" and of putting up a "shrinking show of weakness" toward Red Chinese who "are torturing and brainwashing American uniformed men," Goldwater quickly criticized McCarthy and came to the defense of Eisenhower. When, nine months later, McCarthy accused Eisenhower of appeasing the Reds at Geneva and of offering "friendship to tyrants and murderers," Goldwater labeled McCarthy's remarks "unwise and untimely."

One reason Goldwater voted against censure of McCarthy was because he felt it would establish a bad precedent. He pointed out that through the years other senators were equally guilty of using intemperate, inflamatory language toward their colleagues and others. For example, Goldwater said, several years ago Oregon's maverick Sen. Wayne Morse "referred to Senators Lehman, Mansfield and Humphrey as 'gutless wondres.'" He labeled Ike "a demagogue, who was obviously willing to commit any expedient act for support," "the most dangerous man who has been in the White House," and a man "completely lacking in political morality." And, Goldwater said, Morse had labeled Secretary of State John Foster Dulles an "evil man, bent on war," termed Lewis Strauss "an enemy of the people . . . an enemy of democratic government," and cruelly browbeat Clare Boothe Luce at the time she was being considered as American Ambassador to Brazil.

Morse also wrote a letter to his late Oregon colleague, Democratic Sen. Richard L. Neuberger, blasting his "complete untrustworthiness" and his "amoral conduct." In a subsequent letter, Morse told Neuberger, ". . . I have had my fill of your deceit, trickery, and completely untrustworthy tactics. . . . My disrespect for you has become so complete that there is no basis on which you and I can work together."

Yet despite this intemperate language, every bit as vitriolic as that employed by Senator McCarthy, Goldwater felt—and still feels—that it would be wrong to censure the Senator from Oregon—"just as it was wrong to censure Joe McCarthy."

In an article in *Harper's*, William S. White paid a backhanded tribute to Goldwater for his defense of McCarthy, even while making clear his own abhorrence of the Wisconsin Senator. "I disagree with Barry Goldwater on many fundamental things," wrote White, "not the least that in his time he gave support to Joseph R. McCarthy. But it is necessary to say this, too: Goldwater was by no means alone in this; indeed, on the Republican side he was in a vast majority.

". . . if we are going to pursue people at this date for not having pursued McCarthy until it became safe to do so we shall have to chase a vast lot of them—including some famous Democratic 'liberals'. . . . Having gone along with McCarthy when McCarthy was riding high, Goldwater was at least one who stood there to the end, even after McCarthyism had been overwhelmingly rejected. He sought no storm cellar when the hurricane broke at last; he stood his ground."

By the time of the death of McCarthy in 1957, most Americans, tired of four years of bitter internecine warfare, were content to let the "McCarthy era" pass into history, where, as Whittaker Chambers phrased it, a "sense-making present-ment" might someday be possible. And for the most part vio-lent ideological hostility subsided—until one day early in 1961 when the American public discovered the existence of the John Birch Society. More precisely, it discovered that the leader of the John Birch Society (which by then was more than two years old) believed that Dwight Eisenhower was "a dedicated, conscious agent of the Communist conspiracy," and that Milton Eisenhower and the late John Foster Dulles were also Communists.

From that day on—on the Senate floor, in church pulpits, in newspaper editorials, magazine articles, books, and campaign speeches—the right-left issue was joined once again. And not only the head of the Birch Society, but the society's members (most of whom were unfamiliar with their leader's faulty assessment of Eisenhower *et al.*) and anyone holding views similar to those of the society were denounced as "right wing extremists." When it was learned that Birch leader Robert Welch favored Barry Goldwater above all leading presidential candidates, the anti-Goldwater forces went out of their way to tie Goldwater to the Birch Society apron strings.

From the very beginning of the controversy, Goldwater ex-pressed open disagreement with the idea that either of the Eisenhowers or Dulles was anything but a patriotic American. And he criticized Welch for what he called his "intemperate and unwise" views. But he refused to deprecate society mem-bers, saying that the ones he knew in his home town were responsible, interested citizens, and that so long as the group operated within the framework of the Constitution, it was perfectly legal. In a letter to T. M. Storke, editor and publisher of the Santa Barbara (Calif.) News-Press, Goldwater further explained: "The argument, in my opinion, against the Birch Society centers on Mr. Welch and for this reason I have no intention of denouncing members of the society, so long as their remarks are temperate and in keeping with the decency called for in American politics. Let's not berate the constitutional rights of Americans to say anything, as long as it doesn't lead to the overthrow of our government."

Early in 1962, an editorial in *National Review*—highly praised by the *New York Times'* James Reston, among others —said that "Mr. Welch, for all his good intentions, threatens to divert militant conservative action to irrelevance and ineffectuality." And it called upon conservatives everywhere to reject, "out of a love of truth and country, his false counsels."

The subsequent issue of *National Review*, on Feb. 27, carried the following letter from Goldwater:

"Let me congratulate you on *National Review's* article entitled 'The Question of Robert Welch.' I think you have clearly stated the problem which Mr. Welch's continued leadership of the John Birch Society poses for sincere conservatives. It is a problem which requires all of us who believe in the concepts of constitutional government and individual liberty to make it plain that we do not intend to depart from the truth in the pursuit of aims we believe are in the best interests of the American people.

"Mr. Welch is only one man and I do not believe his views, far removed from reality and common sense as they are, represent the feelings of most members of the John Birch Society. At least they do not represent the convictions of John Birch members with whom I am acquainted in my home state of Arizona. Because of this, I believe the best thing Mr. Welch could do to serve the cause of anti-Communism in the United States would be to resign.

"I am sure you realize this is a difficult suggestion for me to make, for I am well acquainted with Mr. Welch's dedication. However, we cannot allow the emblem of irresponsibility to be attached to the conservative banner."

This didn't satisfy the political and ideological wolves nipping at Goldwater's heels. When, during a speech in Los Angeles, the Arizonan quoted from poet Edwin Markham, *News-*

week gravely noted that these were the lines "used by Robert Welch, boss of the John Birch Society, to lead off the Society's bulletin for March 1962." (But a few weeks later when President Kennedy, in reply to a news conference question on the prospects of his priority items in Congress, quoted from Arthur Hugh Clough's "Say Not the Struggle Nought Availeth," *Newsweek* failed to remind its readers that lines from that very poem were used to lead off the Birch Society's bulletin for June of 1960.)

The Birch controversy, Goldwater contended, was meant to obscure the issues. "I don't know a member of the Birch Society working in a responsible position in the Republican party above the precinct level," he said. And he made it clear that he considered liberal "fear" of the right wing to be liberal fear that conservatism was becoming a potent political force. On the basis of dues received by the John Birch Society, *Newsweek* reported that "insiders now estimate the nationwide membership at 16,500." And it noted also that the only two congressmen who belonged to the Birch Society—California Republicans, Rep. John Rousselot and Rep. Edgar Hiestand— had been defeated for re-election.

Nevertheless, despite the limited nature of the Birch Society, the tide of criticism implicating Goldwater as a pawn of fanatic groups continued to swell. Ohio's volatile Sen. Stephen M. Young contended that "the radical right is an even deadlier threat to our democratic traditions and institutions than are the American adherents to communism." And during a 1961 exposé of far right groups—which turned out to be a variety of anti-Semitic, Fascistic, and segregationist groups—the *New York Times* commented, "The right-wing organizations have their own magazines—most notably, the biweekly *National Review*, edited by William Frank Buckley." The *Times* later apologized for its blatant below-the-belt swipe at *National Review*—but not before editor Buckley wrote: "Ours is a right-wing magazine, perhaps even a notable magazine, as would be, in my judgment, any magazine whose contributors include such writers as John Chamberlain, James Burnham, John Dos Passos, Max Eastman, Evelyn Waugh and Whittaker Chambers. To suggest that we have anything to say interesting to the membership of any organization whose heroes are three men [Castro, Hitler, and Nasser] who rate high among those most despised by the editors of National Review is, well, news unfit to print. No doubt you understand that our reaction to this incredible amalgam is as acute as yours would be if someone were to write that the New York Times is the most notable daily of liberals and Communists."

A few months later, in a dispute over the right of National Review to lease the facilities of Hunter College for its Forum, the Times and Mr. Buckley had a similar go-round. This time Buckley wrote:

"You begin [your editorial] by saying that National Review is a publication 'far off to the right.' It is your privilege, of course, to use your own political yardstick on these matters, but surely you are being arbitrary. One of National Review's regular contributors was an editorial writer for the Times (1934-36), and during that period often served, in fact, as acting editor. Another of our editors was, roughly over the same period, your daily book reviewer. Their views are the same today as when they were writing for the Times, indeed expressing the Times' policy—was the Times a dozen or so years ago far off to the right?

"We are far off to the right in the same sense that a couple of dozen Senators of the United States are far off to the right, and a quarter of the members of the House. Indeed, if one or two national commentators are correct in projecting Sen. John Tower's victory in Texas (he ran, so to speak, on a straight National Review ticket), we are far off to the right in the sense that the majority of the nation may be far off to the right. And the identification of National Review's position on world affairs becomes more difficult for your readers when you suggest that we and the Communist Party are complementaries. . . .

"The normal reader would surely [feel] that what is distinctive, and extreme, about the Communist party is that its members are agents of a foreign power; totalitarians; trained agents of deceit, treachery and subversion; and men who seek to ruin the processes of intellectual intercourse by consciously undermining the meaning of words and concepts and ideals.

"The coupling of the Communists with *National Review* suggests that these characteristics are also true of the writers for *National Review*. The writers of *National Review* are a troublesome lot. But I have no reason to suspect Russell Kirk is a right wing foreign agent, James Burnham a liar, John Chamberlain a totalitarian, Will Herberg a subversive, Henry Hazlitt a traitor."

Buckley's points were well taken. And they were echoed, to a degree, by William S. White who wrote in *Harper's*: "I have long uncomfortably suspected that conservatism—with or without the prefix 'ultra'—doesn't get too fair a hearing among many of us."

"Let the critics of the radical right point out what the rightists are doing that's dangerous. Let them name names and places that they hold in the Republican Party," Goldwater said. "The real radicals are those high in our government who want to collectivize our nation."

Goldwater has continuously repeated that the real danger to our country comes not from the extremists on the right, but from those on the left—and he contended as much long before the assassination of the President. The danger, he said in a lengthy article in the *Saturday Evening Post*, comes from "the leftists in our midst who even today counsel a 'soft' attitude toward Communism, both at home and abroad. I believe it comes from the muddle-headed 'do-gooders,' from the intellectual theorists, from the appeasers and the 'accommodators,' from the professional collaborationists and pacifists. It comes from organizations like the Americans for Democratic Action, whose 1961 policy statement reads like a brief for Red China and Castro's Cuba, and the American Civil Liberties Union, which would like Americans to think that the Senate Internal Security Committee and the House Un-American Activities Committee are more dangerous than Soviet espionage agents."

The leftists in our midst, Goldwater said, rigorously oppose any use of force, or any show of strength in a conflict where our antagonists understand only the element of power. These leftists support an intense internationalist propaganda line which downgrades American patriotism as something smacking of 'isolationism' or international adolescence.

The leftists, Goldwater noted, suggest—in the interest of "accommodation"—that we junk our opposition to the admission of Red China to the U.N., that we forswear our policy of "massive retaliation" (which he describes as "the only shield we have in practical terms against annihilation by the forces of international Communism"). The winds of appeasement blow from the left, Goldwater said. On that side of the political spectrum reside the voices which interminably counsel negotiation in non-negotiable situations where discussion would only lead to the sacrifice of our own or our allies' strategic interests. It was the leftists, he notes, who "hailed the rise of Castro in Cuba and obscured his early Communist dedication." It is they who say that any direct action to rid the Hemisphere of Castro would offend opinion in other Latin American countries. "And," he added, "the left wing in American politics certainly sparked the ridiculous and ill-fated effort to submit to Castro's prisoner-tractor deal."

At home, Goldwater said, the leftists are driving "for more and more central government control over the lives, affairs, and liberty of the American people." They are out to replace the judgment of the individual with the judgment of the state. And they are advocating programs of fiscal irresponsibility.

"Thus," he concludes, "through advocating a soft policy on the international front, American leftists comprise the genuine danger to our country at this critical period in history. They have sown the seeds of appeasement abroad and fundamental weakness at home. They have shown themselves to be incapable, philosophically and practically, of coming to grips with militant, ruthlessly aggressive Communism. They prefer to bury their heads in the sand or, like Don Quixote, spend their time jousting with windmills they call 'the radical right' rather than come face-to-face with the issues which will determine the destiny of America and the future of the world."

During the past few years Goldwater has pointed to other examples of what he considers the liberal double standard toward conservatism. Goldwater agreed with liberal Senator Dodd, who in praising the American press for bringing the Birch Society to light, said: "But for some reason which I cannot understand it has not used this weapon anywhere near as effectively against the Fair Play for Cuba Committee, the various offshoots of the Communist peace offensive, and the other Communist-front operations in this country. . . . There is a job of political balancing to be done. For my own part, I would be more than satisfied if our press devoted as much column space in coming months to exposing the subterranean operations of the Communist Party in this country as they have in recent weeks to exposing the excesses of the John Birch Society."

What seems to bear out Dodd's claim of a need for political balancing is the fact that when the Associated Press reported Dodd's anti-Birch remarks, his reference to the Fair Play for Cuba Committee was excluded. As Vice-Chairman of the Senate Internal Security Subcommittee, Dodd was in a unique position to study the operations of the Fair Play for Cuba Committee, and he called attention to its pro-Communist orientation long before it was revealed that Lee Harvey Oswald, acting on instructions written on stationery of the Communist Party of America, was in the process of establishing a local chapter of this committee in Dallas.

The Subcommittee revealed that most of the cost of a FPFC ad which appeared in the *New York Times* on April 6, 1960— seeking to convince Americans that Castro's Cuban regime was not Communist—had been paid for largely by the Cuban government. (Harry Gideonse, President of Brooklyn College, promptly and correctly labeled the ad "an affront to the American people." And he branded the committee's concept of fair play as benevolence toward a regime "which suppresses basic human rights and sanctions terror and official murder as an instrument of government.") It further revealed that the first director of FPFC—a former CBS newsman and a former convict—subsequently fled to Cuba to make propaganda broadcasts for Radio Havana; and his successor, who refused to answer Subcommittee questions about FPFC, fled to Algeria where he now serves the left-leaning government of Ahmed Ben Bella.

Dodd also had called attention to a Madison Square Garden rally, sponsored in May of 1960 by the New York Committee for a Sane Nuclear Policy, which was found to have been organized and promoted by a veteran member of the Communist Party. The SANE national committee directed its New York chapter to surrender its charter when the fact was called to its attention. But the press was also silent about the Communist infiltration.

Conservatives were further exercised when it became evident that the news media were not at all concerned with the implications of the publication of *The Liberal Papers*—a collection of essays, which claimed to express the liberal viewpoint on important political problems, prepared at the request of 12 congressional liberals. Among other things the essays declared that, "As the cold war continues, it becomes increasingly difficult for decent Americans . . . to be outspokenly and genuinely anti-Communist." Other essays demanded that the U.S. invite Russia to plug in on our early warning attack system, abandon further nuclear testing, press for Red China's admission to the U.N. (followed by economic aid), surrender our Japanese bases, disarm Quemoy and Matsu, expel Nationalist China from its U.N. Security Council seat, and demilitarize central Europe.

"Reasonable men can disagree about cold war strategy," Goldwater said. "But this kind of recklessness—where most recommendations echo Communist demands, and where the theme of the essays is that the West is equally to blame with Russia for the Cold War—rightly deserves to be classified as extremist. And the press pretends not even to notice these examples."

In the same connection, Goldwater and other conservatives pointed to the prevailing double standard employed when Adlai Stevenson was subjected to unceremonious harassment in Texas, and when a few weeks later, during a talk at Harvard, Alabama's Gov. George Wallace was cursed, spat at, and the tires on his auto were slashed. The Stevenson episode was front page news but the Wallace incident wasn't even reported. And Goldwater especially wonders why no one on the left has seen fit to condemn the extremist editorial cartoons of Herblock, who has often depicted non-left political figures as rats crawling out of sewers, drenched with slime. "If anyone is looking for extremists," Goldwater said, "let them look to Herblock. He's probably the worst offender I've ever known. Yet I don't know of any liberal ever apologizing for his deliberate, persistent viciousness." In his biography of Richard Nixon, Earl Mazo said that the Nixons have never subscribed to the *Washington Post* to avoid having their children see the Herblock cartoons which depict Nixon with "a hard criminal face and a stout, sloppy body." When, for variety, he draws Nixon as a sleek, fat cat, Mazo reported, "Herblock says he assures the complaining cat lovers that he intended no offense to them or their cats."

With the growing lack of discrimination in the attacks on conservatives (and on those who advocated positions held to be conservative) Smith Hempstone, African correspondent in the respected *Chicago Daily News*, was moved to write in the opening pages of his influential book, *Rebels, Mercenaries, and Dividends*: "It is a commentary on America today that I should feel compelled to say that I do not belong to the American Committee for Aid to Katanga Freedom Fighters, am not a member of the John Birch Society, am not in the pay of the Katangan government or *Union Miniere*, and really could not care less about the fluoridation of water." Barry Goldwater is similarly dismayed by liberalism's shedding of its traditional ideals in its drive for enforcement of its creed.

Shortly after the inception of the John Birch Society, members were asked to send background information on leftists so that the society could build up "the most complete and most accurate files in America on the leading Comsymps, Socialists and liberals." That notion, happily, died aborning—but not before the *New York Times* observed: "The whole idea of a private group in a democratic, open society such as ours drawing up a 'little list' is—or ought to be—abhorrent. The 'little list' will inevitably turn into a little blacklist, a true symptom of the totalitarian mindlessness that judges individuals by their class, their label, their category, not by what they are, what they say, or what they do."

There was little disagreement with this view in conservative circles, yet six months after the *Times* editorial, an organization calling itself "Group Research" was incorporated in the District of Columbia. Ostensibly, the organization was established to "gather, collate and distribute information concerning organized efforts to affect governmental and economic policies."

As it turned out, however, the organization devoted an admitted 90 per cent of its efforts to establishing a blacklist of conservative individuals and organizations. Already the organization has lumped together more than two thousand persons—including Richard Nixon, J. Edgar Hoover, Clare Boothe Luce, Ludwig Von Mises, William Knowland, Senators Hruska, Dirksen, Douglas, and Byrd, columnist Holmes Alexander, Gov. James Byrnes, James A. Van Fleet, Arthur Godfrey, Norman Vincent Peale, Bishop Sheen, Lewis Strauss, Dr. Edward Teller, and Moise Tshombe.

And it has lumped together organizations as different as the American Farm Bureau, Young Americans for Freedom, the Christian Anti-Communism Crusade, and the Freedom Center in Valley Forge (whose recent misleading "smear" publications, quipped the *Richmond News Leader*, "include the Declaration of Independence and George Washington's Farewell Address").

Group Research is aligned with and financed by the AFL-CIO's Committee on Political Education. It has furnished material to liberal congressmen which they have in turn used in speeches, often verbatim, to denounce various right wing organizations. But the bulk of its efforts are devoted to helping COPE compile a black book on individuals and organizations.

COPE's intentions were spelled out in a COPE bulletin: "When you hear a right wing speaker is coming to town, check him immediately in the [Group Research] Directory and alert friendly groups. Inform your local newspaper by personal visit if possible of the character, background and connections of the speaker. . . . Select particularly interesting items from the material for use in speeches or publications. . . . Armed with the facts about extremist groups, labor union members can take some leadership in combating them, either by heading them off before they really get started or by limiting the damage they do and helping to dry them up. *Preventive* action is best, of course, but it is not easy. . . ."

This, it was apparent, is the very epitome of what the *Times* adjudged to be abhorrent in a democratic, open society—the compiling of lists which are symptomatic of totalitarian mindlessness. (A full-blown exposé of Group Research was contained in a book published in mid-spring of 1964, called *The Democrat's Dilemma*. According to its author, much of the source material for this book came from disgruntled union leaders who had no stomach for such smear attempts.) Group Research is the negation of the canon of ethics, shared by liberals and conservatives alike, that there must be permitted free expression from people of divergent viewpoints. But it is in keeping with the spirit of a memorandum sent to Atty. Gen. Robert Kennedy on December 19, 1961, by Walter and Victor Reuther, advising that the Justice Department list right wing groups as "subversive," that the Internal Revenue Service revoke tax exemptions of conservative organizations, irrespective of whether they are religiously or educationally oriented, and that the power of the Federal Communications Commission be used to harass radio and television stations that give time to conservative broadcasters.

Despite this patent attempt to harass free speech and stifle public dissent, neither the *New York Times* nor any other liberal publication of note has had one word of criticism concerning guilt by association, for Group Research or for COPE's most recent "educational effort."

The attempt to connect Barry Goldwater with the radical right may have had some effect in scaring away some who otherwise might have been attracted to the Goldwater camp, but the effect seems negligible. As Edward Folliard wrote last summer in the *Washington Post*, Democratic professionals "don't accept the view that Goldwater strength is limited to the radical right. Obviously, they say, the Senator must have the backing of a great many orthodox conservatives, middle-of-the-roaders and Southern Democrats. . . ." And the *Wall Street Journal* amplified that opinion by saying, "we can't help being fascinated by the violence of the assault on Barry Goldwater. . . . You hardly ever hear anyone discuss, much less answer, Senator Goldwater's actual views on the current issues of the day. You hear a great deal of discussion about the radical ideas the Senator is alleged to have, and much innuendo about the dangers of his being made captive by the John Birch Society, as if that tiny group were somehow threatening to take over the country. . . . Senator Goldwater does have some controversial views . . . but however controversial, they are hardly radically reactionary or recipes for panic. . . . Unless, perhaps, the panic is on in the camp of the political liberals. Only an overpowering fright would seem to account for the wild arm-flailing at Barry Goldwater."

In fact, most of Goldwater's support has come, not from extremists who are imbued with the conspiratorial view of history, but from those who believe American liberals have too often minimized the dangers of Communism. Goldwater's followers received support from an unexpected quarter when in the spring of 1962 Harvey Schechter, a member of the Anti-Defamation League, made precisely this point in an article in the *New York Times Magazine*.

When Fascism and Nazism were in their infancy, Mr. Schechter noted, liberals responded instinctively through community education programs to alert the world to the approaching storm and all that it implied. Giant rallies were held in all major cities in protest against Nazi brutality and its destruction of culture. Liberal writers loosed an avalanche of meaningful and popular anti-Nazi literature. Hollywood produced substantial numbers of films designed to create a climate of opinion antagonistic to Nazi Germany. Today, however, international Communism has been definitely on the advance for almost two decades, and there is a great thirst among the

American people for information about the enemy. But where, Schechter asks, is the liberal anti-Communist literature? Where are the anti-Communist films?

Liberals, Schechter said, should have been conducting schools of anti-Communism across the country at least since the fall of Czechoslovakia. They should have been conducting community forums and building up a body of understanding about the Communist threat. But this they have not done, so that today there is a notion that liberalism and anti-Communism are somehow inherently incompatible. It is, he says, particularly discouraging to hear young people making the kinds of statements about the Soviet Union and the Communists which were the vogue a generation ago—statements which haunt us in the '60's like voices from the past.

Some liberals are inclined to see Communists nowhere, Schechter wrote. Yet, he wrote, there is a Communist party in this country, and while its ranks are thin, its circle of influence is nevertheless considerably larger than that encompassed by the few thousand dues-paying members. Therefore liberals must be alert to Communist cadres which try to attach themselves to liberal and civil rights movements.

Mr. Schechter scored liberals who demand abolition of the House Committee on Un-American Activities (which Goldwater terms "a very good committee doing a fine job") or demand that HUAC investigate the John Birch Society. And he rapped their abhorrence of the idea that a man should be judged by the organizations to which he belongs, when liberals are guilty of precisely the same thing. "Liberals," he concluded, "have failed their own movement and the whole community by their failure to educate the American public in a sane and sober manner about the true character of the Communist conspiracy."

This, from a different vantage point, reflects Goldwater's concern for the liberal failure in the area of Communism. "Conservatives are always being accused by liberals of being witchhunters and of going off half-cocked," he said. "We've made mistakes, sure, from overzealousness and from faulty perception. But if the liberals had devoted as much time to helping us in the struggle against Communism as in criticizing our efforts, we might have accomplished much more by now than we have."

Through all the hue and cry about extremism, and the concomitant demands that Goldwater repudiate the far right, two factors stand out: As Max Freedman wrote, it makes little sense to ask Goldwater to repudiate these groups. "He can repudiate them and they will vote for him because they dislike all the other candidates much more than they do him." And as *Time* observed, there are indications that their "very enthusiasm is bringing many of the extremists into the regular Republican Party—and in so doing they make the party no more conservative, but rather become more moderate themselves."

"I'm under no illusion that these attacks on the 'radical right' will subside," Goldwater said, "because they aren't aimed just at me; they're aimed at all of conservatism. This is a liberal attempt to destroy conservatism without facing up to the issues conservatism raises. It's the easy way out. It's also the coward's way out. And in the end it will fail."

CHAPTER 11

Why Not Victory?

"The angel of peace will carry a bomb."
—H. G. WELLS
*"A conqueror is always a lover of peace.
He would like to make his entry into
our state unopposed."*
—KARL VON CLAUSEWITZ

THROUGHOUT the long, hot summer of 1963, foreign policy discussion was dominated by talk about the
proposed limited nuclear test-ban treaty. It was a popular proposal, and nowhere more so than in Congress; unofficial
polls taken in advance of the formal vote revealed that it would
be ratified overwhelmingly by the Senate.

Barry Goldwater opposed the treaty. And on two occasions,
in August and in September, he tried unsuccessfully to attach
amendments to the treaty—stipulating that if the Soviets were
as desirous of reducing international tensions as many treaty
supporters claimed, they should demonstrate their sincerity by
removing Russian troops from Cuba and by tearing down the
Berlin Wall. Let Cuba and Berlin be the testing ground rather
than the potentially more dangerous nuclear treaty, Goldwater
asked. Let their actions there be the measure of action on the
treaty, or let us forget the talk we hear of new Soviet sincerity
and of a thaw in the cold war.

The limited test ban treaty was signed by the U.S., Britain,
and Russia early in August (Senate ratification was to follow).

After the signing, while strains of Gershwin's "Love Walked In" filtered through one of the Kremlin's glittering ballrooms, East-West negotiators drank toasts to "peace and friendship." The *New York Times*, reporting on the celebration, said: "One diplomat called it a 'unique day' in East-West relations. 'Peace —it's wonderful,' said another, and meant it."

Goldwater viewed the signing in a different light. The treaty, he claimed, would straightjacket America's military strength while preserving the enemy's advances in big bombs, thus freeing the Soviets to overtake our lead in compact bomb research. The treaty was a political ambush, Goldwater said, dictated by the Soviet need to ease the many internal pressures on its tyranny. What peace we have had, he said, has been made possible through our nuclear strength.

"I do not vote against the hope of peace, but only against the illusion of it," Goldwater told the Senate in explaining his stand against the treaty. "I do not vote for war, but for the strength to prevent it. I have been told, as have others I am sure, that to vote against this treaty is to commit political suicide.

"I will vote against this treaty because in my heart, mind, soul and conscience, I feel it detrimental to the strength of my country.

"If it means political suicide to vote for my country and against this treaty, then I commit it gladly. It is not my future that concerns me. It is my country—and what my conscience tells me is how best I may serve it."

It was an emotional speech, and Goldwater's critics ridiculed what they viewed as histrionics designed to garner political support for his stand. These critics chose to ignore the fact that the speech came one week after the Gallup Poll revealed that 63 per cent of Americans—including 61 per cent in the Far West, a Goldwater stronghold—favored the proposed treaty, while only 17 per cent favored the Goldwater view.

The treaty was ratified overwhelmingly (80-19), as Goldwater knew it would be. But the size of the vote did not begin to reflect the widespread doubts that accompanied ratification—doubts that persist today despite presidential assurances that the U.S. would continue underground tests but otherwise would keep is nuclear powder dry. Nor did it indicate the emotionalism surrounding the test ban issue.*

Some of those who ultimately backed the treaty did so grudgingly, and against their better judgment. Colorado's conservative Sen. Peter Dominick minimized the benefits of the treaty, but said that the U.S. was placed in an untenable position by encouraging other nations to participate before our own ratification. "Rejection at this point," he said, "would have a terrifying impact on our foreign relations, and perhaps irrevocably damage our ability to rally the free world."

Nelson Rockefeller attacked the military and political assumptions upon which the treaty was based, but added that because the treaty "is so identified with the hopes and yearnings for peace, and because the prestige of the United States has already been so solemnly committed to the treaty, I believe that the U.S. Senate should consent to its ratification."

Dr. Harold Brown, director of research and engineering for the Defense Department, and Dr. Norris E. Bradbury, director of the Scientific Laboratory at Los Alamos, strongly endorsed the pact as offering a ray of hope for a slowdown in the nuclear arms race. Dr. John S. Foster, Jr., director of the Lawrence Radiation Laboratory at Livermore, California, said that the treaty would impose severe restrictions on the acquisition of

---

* Undersecretary of State W. Averell Harriman, who negotiated and initialed the treaty for the U.S., was particularly touchy. At a secret briefing for members of the House of Representatives, Harriman became vexed when a congressman asked how the Russians could be trusted in view of their duplicity after signing other treaties. Instead of answering, according to a congressman who attended the briefing, Harriman replied, "I'd just love to run against you in your district in the next election. We'd have all the mothers and children on our side, and we could beat you."

knowledge in the field of nuclear weaponry and missile defense, and added that "from purely technical-military considerations, the proposed treaty appears to be disadvantageous."

The Joint Chiefs of Staff unanimously endorsed the pact, although Gen. Curtis E. LeMay said that political rather than military factors dictated the endorsement. The group, he said, concluded that "there are net disadvantages from the military standpoint, if you consider nothing but that." Gen. Thomas S. Power, chief of the Strategic Air Command, said the threat was "not in the best interests of the United States," and Gen. Bernard L. Schriever, chief of military space development, agreed.

Dr. Willard F. Libby, professor of chemistry at U.C.L.A., summarized his view as one of "worried, reluctant acquiescence." Lewis L. Strauss, former head of the Atomic Energy Commission, predicted that the Soviets would cheat on the agreement. Physicist Edward Teller disputed Secretary of Defense McNamara's claims that the Soviets were no more advanced than the U.S. in development of an anti-ballistic missile defense system. He warned: "To have signed the treaty was a mistake. If it is ratified, you will have given away the future safety of this country, and you will have increased the dangers of war."

Supporters of the treaty, seeking to minimize Teller's testimony, accurately pointed out that the Hungarian-born physicist's beliefs constituted a minority viewpoint within the scientific community. But this seemed an uneasy defense, for Teller earlier had been proved right in his fight, over the opposition of a powerful segment of the scientific community, for development of the hydrogen bomb—a weapon which has kept the Soviet wolf from the American door. And it was that same scientist who persistently, loudly, and almost alone among scientists criticized America's three-year self-imposed moratorium on nuclear testing. He was vindicated when, six months after the Soviets unilaterally shattered the moratorium by resuming tests in the atmosphere, President Kennedy ordered the resumption of atmospheric nuclear tests, saying that a continued moratorium might well invite the destruction of the free world.

Those who supported Goldwater's contention that the test-ban treaty was inimical to the best interests of the free world, pointed, as one example, to Panama. After the flareup in that isthmian republic early this year, demands were renewed in Congress that the U.S. build a modern canal—preferably at sea-level—somewhere in Central America. The House Committee on Merchant Marine and Fisheries had earlier suggested that such a canal be constructed in the Darien Province of eastern Panama. And scientists and engineers later agreed that such a waterway could be dug with nuclear explosives, in one-half the time of conventional construction and at one-seventh the cost of conventional methods.

However, soon after the Panamanian demonstrations subsided, Washington officials reluctantly admitted that the use of nuclear blasts, even for such obviously peaceful purposes, undoubtedly would violate the test-ban treaty. Because permission to circumvent the treaty probably would require each of the many signatory nations to sign a waiver, the prospect of digging a new canal with nuclear energy was felt to be nil. For even if the Soviets did not claim that our above-ground nuclear blasts violated the treaty, signatories from the Latin nations most likely would refuse to sign, either because of fear of fall-out or because of manufactured leftist anti-American agitation.

Goldwater maintains that the frenetic U.S. desire to push the nuclear genie back in the bottle, rather than adapt its awesome energies to national defense and to peacetime use, is a syndrome of which the test-ban treaty—which he terms a "grand delusion"—is perhaps the principal symptom.

There could be no doubt that World Communism in 1964 is different from Communism in 1954—or, for that matter, in

1963. The Sino-Soviet split has deepened. The reign of terror which characterized Soviet Russia under Stalin seems largely to have been lifted. The Communist satellite nations of Eastern Europe have achieved a degree of independence that many in the West would have thought impossible a decade ago.

Some observers have viewed these signs of change as indication that the cold war is drawing to a peaceful close. England's Bertrand Russell wrote in the *New York Times Magazine* last spring that Communism was no longer a menace, and that Khrushchev sincerely wanted peace. A year earlier, two days after being elected secretary general of the United Nations, Burma's U Thant said that Khrushchev was sincere in his calls for peaceful co-existence, even though the Western nations "have refused to recognize this change." Five months later, at a press conference in Geneva, Thant reiterated that Khrushchev was dedicated to the cause of peace. But even less visionary spokesmen than Russell and Thant believed that behind the Iron Curtain the old order was moving toward moderation, and that the fanatical revolutionary zeal had—at some indefinite point and for some unknown reason—burned out of Communism.

Goldwater readily agreed that changes, perhaps significant changes, had taken place behind the Iron Curtain. But these changes, he pointed out, had led to no basic reorientation in Soviet foreign policy—as indicated by the persistent and obvious Soviet attempts to subvert democratic governments around the world. The Sino-Soviet split was undoubtedly real, Goldwater maintained, but it was, as President Kennedy had noted, a disagreement over means, not ends. "A dispute over how best to bury the free world is no grounds for Western rejoicing," the late President noted—and Goldwater agreed. He considered it foolish to suppose that the leaders of China and Russia would find their disagreements so great that either one would prefer to align itself with the hated, capitalistic West.

The effect of the split, Goldwater contended, was not to set the Communist empire adrift in perilous ideological seas. Rather, the rift was working to the advantage of the Communists, as *Time* noted when it said: "The West has almost imperceptibly moved into a new era of softness toward communism. Few any longer talk of defeating communism; coexistence is more or less accepted in the West. This may be only realistic in the nuclear age. But all over the West there is a creeping notion that Khrushchev's kind of Communism can be lived with—that only Peking's is really bad—and this has taken much steam out of the anti-Communist position." Khrushchev's "reasonable approach," *Time* noted, increased the strength of the Italian Reds, revived dreams of a new popular front among once solidly anti-Communist French Socialists, and prompted Belgian Foreign Minister Paul Henri Spaak to say that the removal of U.S. nuclear stockpiles from Western Europe might not be such a bad idea after all.

Goldwater conceded that increased freedom had been granted the satellite nations, which under Stalin's brutal rule had been held in an iron grip. But this loosening up, as Columbia University's Russian expert Philip Mosely observed, was not because Communist goals had changed; it was because Khrushchev sensibly decided that Communist economies could be run more efficiently by substituting the carrot for the stick.

What irked Goldwater, especially during the beginning and middle phases of the new "soft" approach to Communism, was that while Communist subversion was being carried on in every corner of the globe, excuses were continually being made to show that Russia really desired peace. When Moscow began fulminating against the U.S. last year, shortly after the signing of the test-ban treaty, the *New York Times* said, ". . . the Khrushchev of these last few days has behaved very differently from the man who played badminton over an oriental rug in the Crimea with Secretary of State Rusk in August." The *Times* attributed Khrushchev's perfidious behavior to his desire "to mend relations with Peking" or to prepare "the political atmosphere for the meeting of the Soviet Communist party Central Committee," scheduled for later that month. To Goldwater, Khrushchev's action was perfectly understandable if one remembered that he was still every inch a practicing Communist, and that Communist conflict strategy, in 1963 as in 1923, was a firm guide to practice and not a meaningless ritual.

"From the very beginning we've gone out of our way to find excuses for Russia's behavior," Goldwater said. "After the rebellion of the Kronstadt sailors, when widespread dissatisfaction forced a change in Soviet economic policy, many in America hailed it as the beginning of democracy in Russia. When Stalin triumphed over Trotsky we were told the same thing—that he was the great new liberal force, that he was for socialism in one country, that he was a practical man who had abandoned world revolution. And even as Russian ships were delivering nuclear missiles to Cuba, some of our so-called Russian experts were telling us that we should back Khrushchev in his fight with the Red Chinese and with the militarists in his own party because he was our best hope for peace."

Too many non-Communists, Goldwater said, have erroneously attributed Soviet policy to a multitude of irrelevant factors—to fear, insecurity, lack of warm-water ports, and a feeling of diplomatic isolation after World War I. Others claim that the Western powers provoked the Soviets' aggressive behavior. But, Goldwater notes, after World War II Russia was given warm-water ports, a position of power and prestige in the U.N., and spheres of influence in Eastern and Central Europe. And the putative fear of Germany was removed by concessions at Potsdam which led to the death or forced migration of at least 42 million people. Yet despite these concessions, the Soviets arranged the Communist coup in Czechoslovakia, provoked the invasion of South Korea, blockaded Berlin, and imposed Red rule at every opportunity. And now there is no question that the U.S. and its allies are today relatively weaker vis-a-vis the Communist world than they were a decade or two ago—a result attributable in part to our believing that these side-issues were more important to the Communists than ideology. As former ambassador to the Soviet Union William C. Bullitt put it, the U.S. emerged victorious from World War II "like the most powerful creature that ever lived, the carnivorous Tyrannosaurus Rex, who had a body the size of a locomotive, teeth a foot long, and a brain the size of a banana."

All the above excuses were—and those today like them are—nonsensical, Goldwater contends. "Henry Kissinger once said that the cold war is not the result of a misunderstanding between our leaders and those of the Soviet Union, but that it is the result of a deliberate Soviet policy. That's just what it is—a deliberate policy to conquer the world."

Goldwater's Senate colleague, Thomas Dodd, concurred; even though there have been many retreats, deviations and new approaches, the end goal of Communism has never changed. Its object, the Connecticut Democrat said, is still to "reduce man to a mere beast of burden, without a will, without a personality, without a home, without personal property, without knowledge of God, without hope of eternal life." If, by force of circumstance, the Communists were to adopt a policy we view as "right," he observed, it is only a temporary expedient to advance their ultimate ends.

As proof that the Communists remain wholly dedicated to our annihilation, even though their tactics of the moment have changed, Goldwater, in his book on foreign policy, *Why Not Victory?* pointed to the January 6, 1961 Communist policy program, which said in part: "peaceful co-existence of states does not mean renunciation of the class struggle. Peace is a true ally of socialism, for time works for socialism and against capitalism. The policy of peaceful co-existence is a policy of mobilizing the masses and launching vigorous action against the enemies of peace." Stanford's Dr. Stefan Possony, a long-time analyst of Communist strategy and tactics, said that the January 6 manifesto sets forth Red plans for the future in a manner paralleling Hitler's *Mein Kampf*. If one thing clearly emerges from Khrushchev's exhortations, Possony said, it is that if the Western world does not willingly surrender, the Communist world intends to force that surrender. It is unthinkable, he said, that the Communists will abandon their goal of world domination, a goal for which they are willing to pay any price.

The view of those who believe that Communism may purge itself of revolutionary fervor as it matures was eloquently stated by Sen. J. William Fulbright. "Those who attribute to the Soviet leaders a permanent and unalterable determination to destroy the free societies of the West," Fulbright said, "are crediting the Soviet Union with an unshakable constancy of will that, so far as I know, no nation has ever before achieved." The Arkansas Democrat, chairman of the Senate Foreign Relations Committee, said that it was entirely possible that a thaw in Soviet-American relations, even though planned by the Soviet leadership only as a temporary pause, could lead gradually to a new relationship. "Step by step," he said, "their revolutionary zeal may diminish as they find that a peaceful and affluent national existence is not really so tragic."

While this remains the prevailing point of view, a heavy burden of proof rests with those who embrace it. The world situation has changed so drastically since Stalin's 1938 description of the international situation as one of capitalist encirclement of the socialist camp, that eighteen years later, at the Twentieth Congress of the Communist Party of the Soviet Union, Khrushchev described the world situation as the socialist encirclement of the capitalist camp. Lebanon's Charles Malik, U.N. President in 1958-59, noted that "Communism started from zero 43 years ago, and today it rigidly controls one-third of mankind and has penetrated and softened up, in varying degrees, the remaining two-thirds." The simple fact, said Malik, is that the free world has not succeeded in withstanding the tide of Communism at all.

The official U.S. attitude toward the conduct of the cold war, then, continues to amaze Goldwater. "I doubt if any United States Senator or government official, ever before in the history of our Republic, has been called upon to make a case for victory in a conflict where everything that the United States stands for today—or ever stood for in the past—is at stake. . . . I doubt if this nation ever before has found itself in a battle for her very existence where any public official or group of public officials automatically foreclosed the possibility of victory and questioned what we would do with it if it ever were achieved."

Goldwater's remarks were aimed particularly at Senator Fulbright. Over the past few years, their differences as to America's cold war policies have been hashed out in speeches before political groups, on the floor of the Senate, and in the pages of the *New York Times* and other publications.

Fulbright contends, basically, that compromise and negotiation can solve cold war problems as they arise. He believes that the West can do little more than mitigate world problems as best it can and learn to live with them. For example, the U.S. should tolerate a Communist Cuba, rather than risk a vaguely threatened nuclear retaliation from Russia. He has dismissed the concept of victory as a "stirring term with a romantic ring," something that "quickens the blood like a clarion call to arms." He has said that he does not know what is meant by victory in the nuclear age, and has questioned what the U.S. would do with victory if it won it. Would we, he asked, occupy Russia and China and launch a program to re-educate the Russians and the Chinese in the ways of democracy?

Goldwater believes that what he calls "victory" is possible, despite our late start, if America makes use of her entire economic, political, military, and psychological warfare powers. Only in this way, he contends, can we avoid being forced into the rapidly approaching all-or-nothing choice between surrender and nuclear war. "My vociferous critics would like us to believe that there can be no Communist war victory without the destruction of civilization. . . . This is precisely what the Communists would like us to believe. . . . A shooting war can only be *avoided* by *winning* the Communist War. And unless we win this struggle, we will be an easy push-over for the Khrushchevs, the Castros, and the Mao Tse-tungs when they decide the time is ripe to shift their strategy into a shooting phase.

"Senator Fulbright has joined the ranks of those who would paralyze the foreign policy of this nation by advancing the alternatives that either you accommodate the Soviet Union or you fight a nuclear war. . . . My opponents adroitly try to make it appear that I am in favor of nuclear war, that I would make war the prime instrument of our policy. I can't imagine what makes them think that. No one values life more than do I. . . . But that does not mean that I am prepared to *assure* the enemy that under no circumstances will we ever consider war. If we are not prepared, under any circumstances, ever to fight a nuclear war, we might just as well do as the pacifists and the collaborationists propose—dump our entire arsenal into the ocean.

This position was further clarified by Goldwater in *Life* magazine during January of 1964: "The foreign policy of the United States should be the sum of principles and purposes through which we shape our national destiny . . . [and] foreign policy should not be confused with foreign programs. Programs as such stem *from* policy; they do not form it. To debate programs is to beg the issue and avoid the confrontation with our national conscience which a real foreign policy requires."

Goldwater never ceases to stress that we shall certainly have to fight a nuclear war, from whatever beleaguered outpost we are reduced to occupying, "if we continue to yield, piece by piece, all over the world" by refusing to face up to the fact that we have to make a decision, in conscience, whether we ultimately wish to surrender—and face possible genocide on a scale which would dwarf that worked by the Nazis*—or win in the cold war.

To Fulbright's question about what the U.S. would do with victory, Goldwater answers that such doubts become, by extension, an argument against making *any* decision to win or lose. In the eventuality of some form of American victory, however, the Russian and Chinese nations would first of all cease to be an international threat (and could well concentrate once again on domestic issues, as have Germany and Japan—both of which have rejected national socialism, and are enjoying a cultural and economic renaissance). But even if this does not happen, the mere fact that victory would "pose problems" is no reason to stand back and watch the world be devoured—with only an occasional State Department "protest."

Goldwater's call for victory over Communism is admittedly incompatible with the school of thought which sees Russia as slowly evolving toward freedom—the point of view which dominates U.S. foreign policy. Nevertheless, a large number of scholars—some of whom disagree with Goldwater on many other aspects of domestic or foreign policy—also believe that only a U.S. policy aimed at victory, rather than co-existence, can save our country.

"The fundamental decision before us," proclaimed a study of the Foreign Policy Research Institute of the University of Pennsylvania, "is whether we should accept the Communist concept of co-existence. . . . Shorn of all ideological connotations, our policy must be based upon the premise that we cannot tolerate the survival of a political system which has both the growing capability and the ruthless will to destroy us. We have no choice but to accept a Catonic strategy."

* The brother of the Tibetan Dali Llama reported in early January of 1964 that more than 600,000 Tibetans had been sterilized by the Communist Chinese since their conquest of that small country, certainly one of the most subtle—and horrible—variants of the policy of genocide yet devised.

A contributor to that study, Prof. William R. Kintner, amplified his views in a subsequent book, *The New Frontier of War*. In it he argued that the West cannot win, or even survive, without a political counter-offensive whose first condition is a determination to fight eventually to dismantle world Communism. To do that, Kintner said, we must abandon once and for all the notion of lasting compromise, accommodation, or coming to terms with present-day Communism. Such notions are just not realistic, given what we have learned about both the history and ideology of Communism.

America has had opportunities to prove its seriousness of purpose in the cold war, Goldwater says, but, except when Eisenhower dislodged existing Communist power in Guatemala in 1954 and blunted Communist offensives in Lebanon and Taiwan, it has appeared to be transfixed whenever confronted by the Communist menace. It chose the bitterness of stalemate in Korea, it praised and mourned the 1956 Hungarian Revolution when it should and could have acted to save Hungary—and perhaps later all of East Europe—without a war. And now it appears content to ignore Cuba.

U.S. inaction in Cuba particularly disturbs Goldwater. He feels that the presence of a Communist outpost so close to the U.S. is the most important Soviet victory to date. It resulted in the immediate establishment of a "Cuban Soviet Republic" and points to an early establishment of a "Latin American Union of Soviet Socialist Republics." It is a perfect base for launching and sustaining Communist warfare throughout the Americas, as Castro agents proved last year in Venezuela and more recently in Panama. By refusing to apply other than relatively ineffective economic sanctions, Goldwater holds, we have invited the undecided peoples of the world to accept Communist claims of inevitable victory and to line up with that enemy bloc.

Although Goldwater does not advocate a direct invasion of Cuba by U.S. troops, he has suggested that the U.S. invoke an iron-clad blockade and train and equip Cuban refugees. "Then we should give the refugees whatever air support they need so they can go down there and reclaim their country." Furthermore, he believes that while we are training refugee troops we should follow Sen. Gordon Allott's suggestion and establish a provisional Cuban government on the American-leased naval base at Guantanamo Bay, according it full recognition as the legal instrument of Cuban sovereignty.

This move, Goldwater claims, would have an important psychological effect on all captive peoples, and the provisional government would serve as a symbolic rallying point for the forces of anti-Communism (in all Soviet-oppressed countries of the world). "We're always being told that an affirmative action with regard to Cuba would run the risk of nuclear war. Well, here is a proposal that will have enormous effect on the free world without running the slightest risk of any kind" because we wouldn't be directly challenging the Soviets in an all-or-nothing military confrontation.

Many influential Americans share Goldwater's concern over the dangers posed by a Communist Cuba. Last spring a non-partisan group, the Citizens Committee for a Free Cuba, warned of growing Castro-Communist infiltration of Latin America, and asserted that infiltration could demoralize Latin America's democratic forces, which were beginning to pale before the combined power of the Cuban military-police state, the Soviet Union, and Red China. The committee included Joseph Beirne, president of the Communication Workers of America, Dr. Hans J. Morgenthau, Bishop James A. Pike, psychiatrist Bonaro Overstreet, and military analyst Gen. S. L. A. Marshall.

"These people realize that it just is impossible to minimize the spectre of a Communist fortress right under our noses," Goldwater said. He added that the attitude of those who choose to ignore Cuba reminds him of the verse:

"As I was going up the stair
I met a man who wasn't there.
He wasn't there again today.
I wish, I wish he'd stay away."

Barry Goldwater and other critics of America's foreign aid program are, more often than not, accused of jeopardizing America's chances in the Cold War, of being heartlessly unconcerned with the world outside the doors of the American fortress, and with other motives equally execrable.

Goldwater, however, is not opposed to technical and military aid to countries battling the Communist menace, but only to an indiscriminate giveaway to almost all of the world's nations. Increasingly, he claims, our foreign aid goes not to friends but to professed neutrals—and even to professed enemies. (And every one of the neutral countries is committed to a system of state socialism.) By strengthening socialist governments, Goldwater argues, we perpetuate the inefficiency and waste that attends government-controlled economies, and we make it more difficult for free enterprise to take hold. Thus our aid, in the majority of cases, has not made the free world stronger; it has only made America weaker, and has created an image the world over of a nation that puts prime reliance not on spiritual and human values, but on the material things that are the stock-in-trade of anti-American Communist propaganda.

Goldwater further notes that by trying to keep freedom alive in Communist satellite nations we have bestowed more than a billion dollars upon Communist Poland and Yugoslavia— money which has not aided the oppressed, but has made it easier for Red governments to keep their subjects enslaved. A study prepared three years ago for the Senate Internal Security Subcommittee by a former Yugoslav diplomat, Dr. Charles Zalar, now with the Library of Congress, revealed that Yugoslav dictator Tito has distributed more than $100 million in economic aid and credits to neutral nations in an effort to export his brand of Communism. At the same time Yugoslavia was receiving aid from the U.S., Dr. Zalar noted, free-world assistance to Yugoslavia during this period amounted to one-half to two-thirds of Yugoslavia's annual budget.

Last year's bitter fight over the foreign aid bill revealed the growing congressional opposition to the program. This opposition clearly indicated congressional disapproval of $3 million in U.S. aid funds being spent on a luxury yacht, complete with air conditioning and gold wallpaper, for Ethiopian Emperor Haile Selassie; of aid money being used to construct an expensive highway through Cambodia—a highway which began to crumble shortly after it was built; of powdered milk, given to Indonesia by the U.S., being sold by vendors on the sidewalks of Jakarta; of U.S. foodstuffs earmarked for Leopoldville commanding high prices in markets across the Congo River in Brazzaville; of U.S. aid officials working side by side with the Chinese Communists in Cambodia, sanctioning the use of U.S. materials in a Russian-built hospital there. (When Jerry Jackis, an investigator for the foreign aid agency, protested the use of U.S. aid for the Communist hospital project, he was told by his superiors that this was none of his business. Soon afterwards he was fired. Then, after months of unemployment, the foreign aid agency finally rehired him at its Washington office—but only after congressmen and the press kicked up a storm of protest.)

It is true, as proponents claim, that no large-scale aid program can ever be free of mismanagement and corruption. It is also true that the amount of waste involved in the U.S. program is comparatively low—at least when weighed against a $50 billion annual defense budget. But critics claim that far more than monetary waste is involved. They point to a comptroller general's report to Congress two years ago which charged that some $1.2 billion in aid to Korea between 1957 and 1961 was more money than the economy could absorb productively, and more than the government could administer efficiently. Thus, the report said, "it weakened the moral fabric of business practice and stultified the growth of the country's economy."

Paul Hoffman, managing director of the U.N. special fund, charged that hundreds of millions of dollars had been wasted in foreign aid projects designed to buy friends. And three University of Chicago professors wrote in *Revolution in World Politics* that America is faced with the dilemma of increasing hostility from the new and under-developed nations it has helped with considerable outlays of financial aid and technological advice.

Supreme Court Justice William O. Douglas told a college commencement group in 1961 that the under-developed nations which received U.S. aid were, for the most part, worse off as a result. The main impact of that aid, he said, "was to widen the gulf between rich and poor, helping to create the vacuum into which the Communists easily move." The billions we sent to Asia, the Middle East, and Africa did not build schools or hospitals, but only military bases, army barracks, and a few factories. "It launched them on military projects that gave them such an amount of armament that they crushed all dissident elements," Douglas declared, "and the result was the liquidation of democratic influences and the entrenchment of feudal overlords."

"We've been too ready to offer another spending proposal as a substitute for resolute leadership," Goldwater has said. "We're too ready to listen to those who claim that foreign aid is humanitarian, or that it is the only thing that can bring the neutralist countries to our side. I disagree. I think that one important cold war victory—in Cuba, or Laos, or Viet Nam— would do far more for the U.S. position than all the billions we've spent so far." The Arizonan contends that the backward countries are usually more interested in being on the winning side—the side that will determine their future—than in mere charity-of-the-moment.

Goldwater contends that the entire concept of the foreign aid program has been misconstrued. He points out that every country is in a position to accumulate capital if its people have the incentive, drive, and desire to make some part of it available. And he notes that poor nations can always obtain interest-bearing loans, as America obtained capital in the course of its development. He recalls Prof. Milton Friedman's observation that there is hardly an underdeveloped country in the world today that does not have an overdeveloped airline company, all of whose planes fly half full and cost much more than they are bringing in. But like the modern giant steel mills which grace the landscape of so many underdeveloped nations, these airplanes are status symbols. It is a sign of a modern nation to have an airline, said Professor Friedman; therefore, every nation is determined to have an airline.

Goldwater further points to an article by Columbia University economist Norman A. Bailey, who noted in the Columbia University Forum that the bureaucrats of recipient nations look upon foreign aid loans and grants as substitutes for internal effort and initiative. In that way, then, our aid harms rather than helps. Instead of welcoming private foreign investment, which is most helpful because it is intended to make a profit and generate its own capital without taxing it from workers' pay checks, most underdeveloped nations do their best to drive it out or to prevent it from entering at all. Excessive taxes, bureaucratic red tape, chauvinistic antipathy—all work to discourage outside investment.

The only things that can bolster the economies of backward nations are work and profit, wrote Dr. Bailey. But these countries want the best of all worlds. They want to have high wages, costly programs of social welfare, and rapid industrial development—all at the same time. This cannot be, any more than it could in the past. Yet even with illiteracy, poverty, and squalor, Bailey maintains that all underdeveloped countries can raise their living standards. Some can even become wealthy and powerful. They must, however, reject the Communist way, adopting policies better suited to men than beasts and working within a framework of political freedom—by dint of hard work, low wages, honesty, efficiency, free enterprise, high profits regularly reinvested, the proper political climate, and inducements to foreign private investment. Although this is not intended to be a prescription for social justice but for economic development, those countries which today have the highest degree of social justice are precisely those which in the past have followed this prescription.

Goldwater has been a long-time supporter of NATO, SEATO, and CENTO, as *Life* recognized when it said that he "is a firm supporter of . . . our alliances generally." But Goldwater is not an uncritical supporter. While it is likely that the existence of these alliances has helped discourage military adventurism by the Communists, "we should not overestimate the value of the alliances. Though they play a significant role in safeguarding American freedom, there are a number of reasons why it is a limited role."

Those reasons include the fact that there are vast areas of the non-Communist world that remain untouched by the alliances, that the alliance system is incapable of coping with political penetration and internal subversion, the most prevalent kind of Communist aggression, and that it is completely defensive in nature and outlook. "This fact, in the light of the Communists' dynamic, offensive strategy, ultimately dooms it to failure. . . . No nation at war, employing an exclusively defensive strategy, can hope to survive for long."

It is clear that Goldwater strongly believes that the U.S. is at war, just as he believes that U.S. participation in the United Nations has thus far tended to hamper our cold war effort. Communism will not be beaten by a policy that is a synthesis of the foreign policies of the many nations of the U.N., some of which are our enemies, and nearly all of which are less determined than we to save the world from Communist domination.

This does not mean that the U.S. should withdraw from the United Nations, however. Although Goldwater stated in late 1961—when United Nations troops in the Congo had launched an attack against Katanga and Indian troops had annexed Goa while the U.N. looked on without comment—that he had reached the "reluctant conclusion that the U.S. no longer has a place in the U.N.," he has since adopted the position that the U.S. should withdraw only if Red China is admitted. He would insist, however that a condition of America's continued participation in the U.N. be its determination to oppose the atrocities of Communism. "Let the U.N.-firsters, of whom there are many in this country, put their enthusiasm for 'international cooperation' in proper perspective. . . . Let them understand that victory over Communism must come before the achievement of lasting peace."

There is no mistaking Goldwater's disillusionment with what he considers to be the hypocrisy of the U.N.—epitomized by the declaration of one of its staunch supporters during the opening session of the U.N. two years ago that "the U.N. has no more important task than adding colonial areas to self-determination." This hypocrisy, Goldwater explains, is the major reason why the U.N. has been a failure: it has never come to grips with the central problem confronting civilization—the threat of Communism. Colonialism may be an important problem, and understandably so to the African nations. But it is ridiculous for anyone to assert that the organization has no more important task than this, when a large portion of the world is suffering under Communist tyranny.

Goldwater agrees with Democratic Sen. Henry Jackson that the U.N. "passes all sorts of intellectually dishonest resolutions," such as U Thant's call for a two-week moratorium on the U.S. blockade during the height of the 1962 Cuban missile crisis. He also cites its initial inaction in Hungary in 1956, followed by its resolution just last year to abolish the special U.N. Committee on Hungary. This committee, headed by Sir Leslie Munro of New Zealand, was virtually powerless, except that in each of its annual reports it pressed for free elections and the withdrawal of Soviet troops in Hungary, thus keeping alive an issue which the Soviets wanted forgotten.

The U.S. voted with other General Assembly members to abolish the committee, substituting a resolution requesting Secretary General U Thant to "take any initiative that he deems helpful in relation to the Hungarian question." A few days later the U.N.'s weekly 15-minute news broadcasts in Hungarian—broadcasts which were begun shortly after the revolution and which had been under continuous attack by the Soviet Union—were ended. Several months after, the U.N. accepted the credentials of the Hungarian delegation to the General Assembly. (Earlier the Assembly, at U.S. insistence, refused to rule on the Hungarian credentials one way or the other—a move of no practical value except that it at least symbolized U.N. disapproval of Soviet action.) This was done, the *New York Times* reported, because the U.S. felt that Khrushchev, "in view of his climactic struggle with the Chinese over control of the world Communist movement, needs a tangible demonstration of the United States' desire for improving relations with Moscow."

Goldwater felt that other U.N. moves were equally cynical and hypocritical: Its resolution condemning Portugal in Angola (a resolution which the *New York Times*' Arthur Krock called "a kind of lynch law"); its resolution favoring Indonesia in the West New Guinea settlement, a settlement which the *Times*' U.N. correspondent said violated the U.N. Charter's basic principle of self-determination; its resolution granting U.N. membership as an independent nation to Soviet acolyte Outer Mongolia, the world's first Red satellite, which sent 5,000 Communist troops to fight against the U.N. in Korea; and its resolution in 1960, piously signed by Soviet Russia and other Communist states, calling for the immediate end to colonialism everywhere, regardless of the area's capacity for self-government—a policy that caused so much terror, death, and destruction in the Congo and Africa generally, and which failed to take note of Soviet colonialism in Europe, Cuba, and Africa.

What particularly provoked Goldwater and galvanized considerable American public opinion against the U.N. was its naked aggression in the Congo—which many believed to mark the nadir of this organization's existence. When the Congo received its independence from Belgium in the early summer of 1960—largely at the insistence of both the U.S. and Soviet Russia—native soldiers immediately sparked a nation-wide orgy of murder, rape, and pillage. The Belgian government sent units of paratroopers back to the Congo to protect the lives and property of its citizens, and when pro-Communist Prime Minister Patrice Lumumba (who has since been immortalized by the establishment of the Patrice Lumumba University of Friendship of the Peoples in Moscow) requested U.N. troops to protect the Congo against the Belgians, the U.N. Security Council adopted a resolution demanding that Belgium withdraw its troops, and it authorized the Secretary General to provide whatever military assistance might be needed until the Congolese army could be brought under control.

Meanwhile, President Moise Tshombe of the Congo's Katanga province, saying "I am seceding from chaos," proclaimed Katanga an independent country. This secession was deemed legal because the provisional constitution had not been ratified by the Congolese House of Representatives and Senate. But the U.N. paradoxically refused to recognize Katanga's secession, while concomitantly refusing Lumumba's demand that it intervene in Katanga. In a 4,000-word summary of its stand, U.N. Secretary General Dag Hammarskjold noted that Katanga's secession *"is an internal political problem to which the United Nations as an organization obviously cannot* be a party" (italics added).

Internal political problem or not, the U.N. changed its mind when it became apparent that Tshombe had no intention of rejoining the lawless, disorganized central Congolese government. At the urging of extremist African nations—notably Ghana and Guinea—the U.N. launched a surprise attack against Katanga in what it claimed was an effort to capture and expel "white mercenaries," ignoring the fact that many of these mercenaries were Europeans who had lived in Katanga all their lives, and that their "mercenary interest" was in protecting their families and homes.*

While U.N. officials in Leopoldville claimed that their troops attacked in self-defense, the badly outnumbered Katangese denied the charge. In a book published a year later, Dr. Conor Cruise O'Brien, Irish U.N. official who served as representative in Elisabethville at the time of the fighting, admitted that the fighting was not the result of resistance by U.N. troops to Katangese aggression but the result of Katangese resistance to a planned U.N. action. O'Brien (to the chargrin of U.N. officials who later tried to discredit him) said that the attack was politically inspired and even was given the code name "Morthor," a Hindi word meaning "Smash."

When the secretive U.N. offensive was thwarted, the Security Council then passed a resolution (November 24, 1961) to send U.N. troops to Katanga, violating its own charter and international law. U.S. Ambassador Stevenson originally op-

* When a *New York Times* report implied that the most celebrated mercenary—"Lieutenant Deulin," a pilot who had scored considerable successes against the U.N. in his antiquated airplane—was a "rightist," an objection was raised by an assistant professor of anthropology and art at the University of California. In a letter to the *Times*, he pointed out that Lieutenant Deulin was a friend of his—a fifty-year-old ex-shopkeeper who, with a proletarian socialist background, was "moderately left." "While some of Tshombe's European officers are undoubtedly mercenaries looking for gold and glory," he wrote, "[the pilot and his wife] sincerely believe in the viability of an African-ruled Katanga where they hope to live out their lives. With the whole world against them, their gallantry at least deserves note."

posed the resolution because it was directed exclusively against Katanga and exempted the remainder of the Congo, which was by then totally lawless. When an amendment proposed by Stevenson was vetoed by the Soviets, the U.S. Ambassador then voted for the original resolution, explaining his action by saying he could not send the Congolese Foreign Minister home empty-handed.

In the end, the U.N. subdued Katanga, but not before it managed to cast serious, perhaps irreparable doubt upon its claim to be a freedom-loving organization. On the day the U.N. launched a third and final attack on Katanga—every day disclaiming any intention to invade, and all the while preparing its attack to coincide with the New Year—Goldwater teamed up with Sen. Tom Dodd to castigate the U.N. "I hope Tshombe beats the hell out of the United Nations," he said. "I have never seen such a sickening display in my life. This is a terrible way for the U.S. and free people to start 1963, by browbeating a government that is a friend of ours and submitting to the demands of weaklings who are in the U.N. Yet ninety miles off our shores is a nation which has joined hands with the forces that have openly admitted their desire to destroy us. It will be to the everlasting shame of the U.S. that we allowed ourselves for the first time to succumb to the desire of destroying the government of other people."

Goldwater claimed that the U.S. never went farther out of its way to placate the vocal Afro-Asian bloc than it did in committing itself to support of the U.N. war against Katanga. Three times the State Department refused President Tshombe a visa to visit the U.S., claiming his visit would not be in the best interests of American foreign policy. And, after harassing New York-based Katanga Information Service director Michel Struelens for months, it denied his request for permanent residence and began deportation procedures (a move that the *New York Times,* which supported the U.N. invasion of Katanga, said was "contrary to American ideals of free speech").

Yet it was subsequently revealed that the same State Department which considered it risky for Tshombe and Struelens to be in the U.S., requested a special waiver to admit to the U.S. Mario de Andrade, leader of the openly pro-Communist faction of the Angolan rebel movement.

State Department officials, said Goldwater, went out of their way to slander not only the Katangese but also the many Americans who expressed bewilderment at the U.N. aggression. They claimed—falsely—that Struelens was retained on Belgian civil service rolls. State Department spokesman Lincoln White falsely accused Struelens of trying to bribe officials of an unnamed Latin American government—later identified as Costa Rica—to persuade them to recognize Katanga's independence. Assistant Secretary of State G. Mennen Williams and then Deputy Assistant Secretary of State Carl Rowan charged—falsely—that there was "a clever, big-money campaign" on behalf of Katanga. Other State Department officials falsely labeled all their opponents "right wing extremists," hinting that they had a financial stake in Katanga. In the end, they even sought to discredit Dr. Albert Schweitzer, who in a letter to a Brussels newspaper from his jungle hospital outpost in Lambarene, Gabon Republic, said that in the interest of reason and justice the U.N. should withdraw its troops from Katanga and the U.S. should keep its hands off.

Seldom before in U.S. diplomatic history had officials lied to so many so often.* Woodrow Wilson's "self-determination" principle, embodied so conspicuously in the U.N. charter, had been trampled underfoot.

No wonder, Goldwater commented, that many long-time U.N. advocates—among them Dean Acheson and James

---

* Anyone believing this to be an exaggeration can read the 76-page report to the Senate Committee on the Judiciary, "Visa Procedures of Department of State: The Struelens Case" (August 6, 1962), for corroboration.

Byrnes—called for an agonizing reappraisal of U.S. participation in the organization. Even Senator Fulbright admitted that the U.N. had failed, adding, "we must look elsewhere for a system that can unify the forces of freedom effectively." What Goldwater feared more than anything else, however, was the attitude typified by *New York Post* columnist Max Lerner, who wrote: "There is plenty of room for doubt about the wisdom of the U.N.'s action [in Katanga], but no room for hesitancy about backing it up in an open-eyed way, doubts and all. *Once the U.N. has decided wrongly or rightly, that a certain political solution is necessary for peace, it seems to me it must be imposed*" (italics added). This was the attitude Goldwater warned against when he said that U.N.-firsters were leading the U.S. down a dangerous path, along which—in order to satisfy an ephemeral concept known as "world opinion"—it was steadily abandoning principles of morality and justice.

"When we talk about world opinion," Goldwater said, "we are not talking about a consensus of two billion human beings, most of whose opinions we know nothing about. We are talking about that tiny segment of the world's population that can make itself heard: intellectuals, journalists, the organizers of street mobs." Goldwater agrees with Lewis Strauss that even if world opinion should exist one may still doubt whether it is fundamentally concerned with justice and fairness, or merely an amalgam of considerations, most of which are temporary, self-servingly political, and basically uninformed.

Goldwater believes that many of the technical functions of the U.N.—assembling statistics, formulating air and space navigation rules, disease control, allocation of international radio and TV channels—are both desirable and necessary. But he believes that the political functions of the U.N. are often fraudulent and potentially dangerous, and that they are unlikely to change until most of the U.N.'s energy is directed toward winning the cold war. "The plain fact is—and we either fear or are ashamed to acknowledge it—that if we go

down, the whole free world goes down with us. . . . If we survive, all other nations can have a reasonable hope for their
own survival."

Unlike some of his more vocal critics, Goldwater does not
suggest that he has the ready-made answers to every particular
ailment of American foreign policy. "I don't know all the
answers and I have very little patience with those who pretend
they do," he wrote in the final chapter of *Why Not Victory?*
But he does believe that if the U.S. is to withstand the Communist challenge it can no longer merely react to it. The free
world, he believes, must go on the offensive.

One of the first steps in this offensive, Goldwater contends,
would be for the U.S. to renounce disarmament as a national
goal. History teaches us that armament races are no more than
symptoms of international friction, and not the causes of it,
he says, echoing the late E. B. White's contention that blaming
armaments for war is like blaming fever for disease. He insists
that the only real disarmament will come when the reason for
arms is removed. In our case that reason is Communism; for
the Soviets it is the free world. "Does anyone believe that the
Communists will voluntarily give up their gains and their objectives?" he asks. "Does anyone believe that we will give up
our way of life and settle for peace under slavery?"

Goldwater simply doesn't believe that the Communists will
disarm in good faith.* He quotes a fable related in 1932 by

* Goldwater engaged in a running feud with the U.S. Arms Control
and Disarmament Agency during spring of 1962. In a speech at North
Aurora, Illinois, he asked whether there was any truth to reports that a
plan was being considered to burn thirty U.S. B-47 bombers along with
thirty Russian Badger bombers. Disarmament Agency officials denied the
report, and one official said that Goldwater apparently confused it with
provisions of a proposed general disarmament treaty, suggested by the
U.S. at Geneva the previous summer. Three weeks later the *New York
Times* reported that such a plan was "still in the study stage." Secretary
of State Rusk then admitted, in congressional testimony, that the plan

Salvatore de Madariaga, then the chief Spanish delegate to the Disarmament Section of the League of Nations. Sr. de Madariaga attributed the fable to Winston Churchill:

"The animals decided to disarm, and held a conference for that purpose. The eagle, with an eye on the bull, suggested that all horns be razed off. The bull, with a squint at the tiger, thought that all claws should be cut short. The tiger, glaring at the elephant, was of the opinion that tusks should be pulled out or at any rate shortened. The elephant, staring at the eagle, thought it indispensable that all wings be clipped. Whereupon the bear, with a circular glance at all his brethren, cried out: 'Why all those half-way measures? Let all weapons be done away with, so that nothing remains in the way of a fraternal, all-embracing hug.'"

Goldwater has said that he would have the U.S. refrain from joining the Soviets in coalition governments imposed on strife-torn countries (especially where the strife is fomented by Communist-led mobs). This, he said, amounts to "making book" with the enemy, for such coalitions are at best merely way-stations on the road to Communist domination. Every time we insist on a coalition government with a Communist and a neutral, we automatically set up a two-to-one balance against freedom.

He is not impressed with the notion that it is better to "jaw, jaw, jaw than war, war, war," for this presupposes there are no alternative solutions. He would put away the alpenstock and eschew trips to the Summit with the Communists as long as they remain attached to their deceitful code and their global ambitions. The Communists, he says, look upon negotiation as an instrument of political warfare. For them, a summit meeting is just another battle in the struggle to win the world, and a

"had been discussed inside the disarmament agency and with other departments." And the public affairs spokesman for the disarmament agency told the *Times* that "It seemed like a good idea."

diplomatic conference just a propaganda forum from which to speak to the masses over the heads of their leaders. Fruitful negotiations, then, must await the day when a meaningful change has occurred in the Soviet system.

Goldwater often quotes de Madariaga's observation that the slogan "Let's talk to the Russians" ignores the fact that we can only talk to the Red bosses, which is quite different from talking to the people themselves. This slogan is used to cash in on all the diffuse sentiment for Old Mother Russia, the Volga Boatmen, the Russian ballet, and our Russian comrades-in-arms who defended Stalingrad. It is used to make us forget that we are dealing not with the Russians or the Ukrainians, but with the tiny minority who hold them in the immense concentration camp of the Soviet Empire.

Goldwater has said that the U.S. might withdraw diplomatic recognition of Russia, in order to give heart to the Communist-enslaved peoples when they realized that the U.S. did not regard Khrushchev's "murderous clique as the legitimate ruler of the Russian people or of any other people." And it would be in keeping with Secretary of State Bainbridge Colby's assertion in 1920, when the U.S. declined to recognize the U.S.S.R.'s Red government: "The existing regime in Russia is based upon the negation of every principle of honor and good faith."

Goldwater believes that we must always seek to keep alive the hope for freedom of the captive nations of Eastern Europe. "We must realize that the captive peoples are our friends and potential allies—not their rulers. . . . A truly offensive-minded strategy would recognize that the captive peoples are our strongest weapon in the war against Communism, and would encourage them to overthrow their captors. A policy of strengthening their captors can only postpone that upheaval within the Communist Empire which is our best hope of defeating Communism without resorting to nuclear war."

The major objective, then, of his "can-win" victory-oriented foreign policy is, as Goldwater put it in a *Life* magazine article in January of 1964: "The reduction of Communist power to a level from which it cannot threaten the security of our nation or the peace of the world. This will require full mobilization of the free world's resolve and its resources to undermine the power now held by Communists and to encourage their eviction from positions of control.

"This does not mean war. It means the alternative to war; a way to win peace—to end threats to the nation—without war. Together the advanced free nations hold the balance of world power. . . . Psychologically, too, we have the advantage. Freedom is our century's most inspiring cry. . . . Communism demonstrably has been freedom's archenemy. But we have tended to hide freedom's light under the bushel of our own reticence. We must remove the bushel so the light that is there will shine—brilliantly."

Goldwater realizes that this is hard counsel because it acknowledges that the price of freedom is active and aggressive (not a defensive and isolationist) vigilance, which intrudes on our national complacency. Nevertheless he knows that bold measures must be taken. For, as Reinhold Niebuhr said, "If the democratic nations fail, their failure must be partly attributed to the faulty strategy of idealists who have too many illusions when they face realists who have too little conscience."

CHAPTER 12

Goldwater for President?

"If a man does not keep pace with his companions, perhaps it is because he hears a different drummer. Let him step to the music which he hears, however measured or far away."

—HENRY DAVID THOREAU

IT was a typical warm Phoenix day when some 300 newsmen from across the land gathered on the patio of Goldwater's house on the morning of Jan. 3, 1964. The sun was shining brightly through cloudless skies. The temperature at 11 a.m. stood at 56°. The desert flowers on the patio were decked out in their raiment of red and yellow.

Well-dressed Young Republicans, equipped with walkie-talkies, directed the human and vehicular traffic. Well-scrubbed Young Republican women checked credentials before allowing visitors to proceed up the long, steep drive to the Goldwater residence. This was the day the Arizona conservative had scheduled a press conference to announce his decision whether or not to seek the GOP presidential nomination.

At precisely 11:33 the draperies parted in the living room and Goldwater appeared at the sliding doors. He paused momentarily, waiting for the signal that the network television cameras were operative. An Arizona political reporter quipped, "Come on in, Barry, the water's fine." Goldwater smiled amid scattered laughter. Then, trailed by two aides and his wife and two daughters, he hobbled on crutches (necessitated by a minor operation for removal of a bone spur on his right foot) to a lectern.

"Ever since the last Republican convention thousands of Americans have asked me to seek the Republican presidential nomination in 1964," he said. "I have withheld a decision until now, not because of any attempt to be politically coy, but because I have been giving every aspect of such a decision the most serious consideration.

"Today, here at our home, in the state I love, with my family and with the people whose friendship and political interest have placed me where I am, I want to tell you . . . that I will seek the Republican presidential nomination.

"I have decided to do this because of the principles in which I believe and because I am convinced that millions of Americans share my belief in those principles. I have decided to do this also because I have not heard from any announced Republican candidate a declaration of conscience or of political position that could possibly offer to the American people a clear choice in the next presidential election."

There was no mistaking this last reference, inasmuch as Nelson Rockefeller was at that time the only announced Republican candidate. Nor was there any mistaking Goldwater's determination to seek the nomination as an avowed conservative. "I will not change my beliefs to win votes," he said. "I will offer a choice, not an echo. . . . I have always stood for government that is limited and balanced and against the ever increasing concentrations of authority in Washington. I have always stood for individual responsibility and against regimentation. I believe we must now make a choice in this land and not continue drifting endlessly down and down toward a time when all of us, our lives, our property, our hopes, and even our prayers will become just cogs in a vast government machine.

"I believe that we can win victory for freedom both at home and abroad. I believe that we can be strong enough and determined enough to win those victories without war. I believe that appeasement and weakness can only bring war. I have asked and will continue to ask: Why not victory—why not victory for sound, constitutional principles in government—why not victory over the evils of Communism?

"I am convinced that in this year 1964 we must face up to our conscience and make a definite choice. We must decide what sort of people we are and what sort of a world we want—now and for our children.

"My candidacy is pledged to a victory for principle and to presenting an opportunity for the American people to choose. Let there be a choice—right now and in clear, understandable terms. And I ask all those who feel and believe as I do to join with me in assuring both the choice and the victory."

It was the announcement conservatives long had been hoping to hear, but were beginning to feel would eternally be denied them—the chance to vote for someone who truly *believed* that the best government is one which governs least, and who—if nominated and elected—could be depended upon to translate his promises into performance, insofar as it was within his power. It was a consummation conservatives had wished for devoutly. For, regardless of whatever else it would prove, Goldwater's candidacy, in the words of the *Wall Street Journal*, "already performed a political service of no small dimensions. He has demonstrated to the politicians that a man of what are called conservative views can exert a powerful voter appeal. . . . [when] most politicians have been acting for years, even decades, as though only an advocate or imitator of Democratic 'liberalism' could hope to win the White House."

Among these imitators of Democratic liberalism was Nelson Rockefeller, who, together with Senators Jacob Javits, Clifford Case, and Thomas Kuchel, comprised the backbone of the GOP's left wing. Goldwater long had been anathema to this quartet, especially when it became clear that "Goldwater Republicanism" was supplanting the Modern Republicanism among rank-and-file GOP voters. Javits earlier spearheaded an unsuccessful internecine effort to dump Goldwater as chairman of the GOP Senatorial Campaign Committee, even though Goldwater had personally raised campaign funds for Javits and publicly supported the New York liberal's candidacy. Javits' and Case's carping over the years moved the Arizonan to remark that the two of them "spend more time fighting me than fighting Democrats."

But it was Rockefeller who stooped lowest in his attacks on Goldwater. The New York Governor sought to tie Goldwater to right wing extremists, then indicated that he would not support the Arizonan if Goldwater became the 1964 GOP presidential nominee, and then said he would support Goldwater, if nominated, only under conditions which *New York Times* correspondent Arthur Krock noted would require Goldwater "to run as a moral political bankrupt."

Russell Kirk described Rockefeller's attack as "a deliberate wrecking operation." Columnist Raymond Moley labeled it "unfair." The *Wall Street Journal*, in an editorial entitled "Politics by Epithet," commented, "This is always a shoddy way to carry on the public debate." Indiana Congressman Donald Bruce accused Rockefeller of stooping to "gutter tactics," adding: "In one breath he calls for 'love and understanding' and then in the next breath mouths hatred and bitterness against all those who have indicated that Rockefeller is not their personal hero." Obviously alarmed that he has not captured the enthusiasm of the millions of young people who have swung over to the Republican Party, Bruce said, Rockefeller launched a "personal assault aimed at destroying the reputation and integrity of those who stand in the way of his personal path to power."

Sen. Carl Curtis was equally disturbed at what he termed "self-serving tactics by a man desperately trying to retrieve his declining political fortunes." And other observers wondered how it was possible to reconcile Rockefeller's claim that Goldwater is "not in tune with the mainstream of Republican thinking" when in fact Goldwater was far ahead of Rockefeller and all other Republicans in every political poll or survey.

Goldwater refused to retaliate, other than to question Rockefeller's committment to the principles of Republicanism, "It's time for Republicans to stop chewing on each other and start chewing on the Democrats," he said. "The Democrats are better fed now that they are in power and they are getting soft. We ought to get our teeth into them."

Despite Goldwater's refusal to trade name-calling with Rockefeller, or to engage Rockefeller in debate and thereby give the New Yorker extra exposure (a political ploy Rockefeller used when in 1962 he refused to debate his gubernatorial opponent for identical reasons), there is no question that Goldwater was annoyed by the viciousness of Rockefeller's assault. For even when the polls had, briefly, showed Rockefeller the GOP front runner in early 1963, Goldwater refused to attack him personally or to talk to anyone about Rockefeller's much-publicized divorce and remarriage. Goldwater contended candidly that Rockefeller's private life was his own business, that it had no bearing on politics and therefore should not be dragged through the political mud. Furthermore, Rockefeller and Goldwater had occasionally met for breakfast in New York every six weeks or so, before either announced his candidacy, and Rockefeller during those informal meetings tried to talk Goldwater into accepting the second spot on the Republican ticket. And although Goldwater avoided that importunity, he had no reason to suspect that the New Yorker had taken his political decline so much to heart that he would be willing to risk rending the Republican Party—a risk against which Goldwater counseled his followers in the first week of his own campaign.

Nevertheless, Goldwater now feels that some members of the Eastern liberal wing of the Republican Party—the faction that Everett Dirksen once charged had "a habit of winning conventions and losing elections"— intend to fight his candidacy just as vigorously as will the Democrats if he wins the nomination. And he doesn't discount the ability of these "king-makers" to turn a seemingly nondescript political figure into a formidable contender for the nomination. When, during the press conference at his home, a reporter asked if he considered Henry Cabot Lodge a potential candidate, Goldwater responded: "Yes. I consider anybody who has visited with Mr. Eisenhower in the last two weeks a potential candidate."

This riposte was in reference to Ike's expressed view that he hoped to see a GOP convention dogfight so that Republicans could have a wider choice of ideologies, and to the ex-President's benediction upon a swarm of nominal and actual Republicans. Goldwater realizes the difficulties he faces, not just from Ike, but from anti-conservatives who would seek to promote practically anyone in order to deprive a genuine conservative of the nomination. And he is guided by Morrie Ryskind's warning that: "Suddenly liberal columnists who wouldn't vote for Barry if he were running against Al Capone are slapping him on the back, telling him he's not such a bad fellow after all and even advising him just what he must do in order to win. This is like having seconds in your corner who have bet their wad that your opponent will win by a knockout in the third round."

Goldwater is aware that the opposition of GOP liberals will continue until the convention. But he is certain that the liberal stranglehold on his party, the party for which he has worked so tirelessly, can and will be broken by the enthusiastic conservative revival. For it was, as he said during his press conference, the young people who had the greatest influence on his decision to run. And they are as determined as he to offer the voters an alternative to liberalism, of both the Democratic and Modern Republican variety.

On the wall behind the desk of Goldwater's Washington office, just above his book case, is a framed inscription, lettered in black ink, which says: *Noli Permittere Illegitimi Carborundum.* "Sometimes Catholic priests or nuns will be in paying me a visit and they'll see the sign and they'll start to grin or chuckle without saying anything," Goldwater said. "Then I'll realize what they're chuckling about so I'll turn to it and pretty soon we'll all be chuckling."

For that Latin phrase is, simply stated, Goldwater's working motto: "Don't let the bastards grind you down"—advice he has followed since long before his entry into politics. Certainly, Goldwater's political opponents have seldom tired of trying to grind him down. No sooner had word been flashed that President Kennedy had been assassinated than liberal analysts, in the plentitude of their wisdom, were gleefully writing off the Arizonan, saying the political scene had shifted its center of gravity closer toward the center . . . and Walter Lippmann was once again depicting Goldwater as a "radical reactionary" whose philosophy is "not of the conservators of the social order but of the newly rich on the make."

"There is some reason for thinking that this shift is not altogether fair to Senator Goldwater and his supporters," said the *Christian Science Monitor* in a candid editorial. "The leading commentators and analysts of press, radio, and TV incline to be internationalist and liberal and had developed a considerable opposition to the Goldwater brand of more belligerently conservative and nationalist policies. They seized on the collapse of the Goldwater 'southern strategy' to erase him from the blackboard with almost indecent haste."

Undoubtedly Lyndon Johnson's acsendency to the White House altered Goldwater's strategy for capturing the nomination and the presidency. Goldwater himself said that any honest assessment would have to admit that his chances in the South had been hurt, largely because the chairmen of congressional committees are mostly Southerners who understandably would be reluctant to support a Republican—especially when the Democratic ticket is headed by the first Southern President in more than a century. But he also felt that it was foolish to suggest that the South would once again blindly deliver her votes to the Democratic Party without weighing the issues. The South will not be won on the old segregationist issues, Goldwater said. "It will be won on economic issues and on conservative economic issues more than anything else." And, he told a Michigan audience during his first formal campaign speech, "The Democrats are still the party of high taxes, unbalanced budgets, and disregard of property rights."

The South is undeniably turning away from blind obedience to the Democratic Party. Until 1952, Dixie had never delivered so much as one electoral vote to a Republican presidential candidate. That year Eisenhower, running as a conservative, picked up 57 and increased this to 77 the next time around. But the total declined to 43 in 1960 when Nixon narrowly lost Texas' 24 electoral votes. In the four years from 1958 to 1962, Republicans impressively increased their share of the popular vote in Southern congressional races from 606,000 to 2,084,000.

In the wake of Lyndon Johnson's ascendency, it is next to impossible to gauge what will happen in the South in the 1964 election. But Goldwater supporters contend that Dixie will no more rally 'round Johnson that it would 'round a carpetbagger if the President pushes for a strong civil rights bill or for those many spending measures Democratic liberals—whose support Johnson needs in the big city machine states—have insisted he adopt as a sign of his fealty to liberalism. Moreover, these supporters argue that the Arizonan is still the frontrunner—against Johnson or against any other GOP challenger—in the Midwest, the Far West, and the Mountain States, and that, because of the zeal of his followers, he stands a better chance against Johnson in the large industrial states than does any other Republican (especially since Johnson lacks the charisma necessary to make the city machines work at top efficiency, while *Goldwater* charisma can be expected to tip the balance by bringing in a large suburban and rural vote).

Goldwater realizes that President Johnson's election strategy will depend, to a large extent, on his ability to resurrect Franklin Delano Roosevelt's successful wedding of the solid South to the big city machines. And whereas political commentators, particularly liberal political commentators, have been quick to write off Goldwater's appeal in the large cities of the industrialized North, Goldwater himself is unwilling to cede these areas to the Democrats because he doesn't feel that Johnson can make the city machines work well enough.

Goldwater has long campaigned against what he believes to be "a cynical, dinosaur alliance of welfare state liberals and big city bosses." Fifty years ago, Goldwater said, liberals were inspired reformers who won the vote for women. They wrote fiery polemics and popular books exposing evil and corruption. They led admirable fights to destroy the vice-ridden city political machines which lived off graft. They led a genuine fight to break the power of these corrupt political machines, whose power had become so great they could dominate whole state and national party organizations.

But now, Goldwater maintains, the alliance between liberal Democrats and the big city machines—Tammany Hall in New York, the Green machine in Philadelphia, the Daley machine in Chicago—means that "no Democrat candidate for office at the national level can be nominated or elected without the support of big city political bosses and their corruption-ridden machines. This puts the hammerlock of boss rule squarely on the necks of every American . . ."

Goldwater charges that the politicians who have inherited the tradition of liberalism in the U.S. today are not liberals at all, but merely ambitious men who have become the captives of these machines. These ambitious men, he says, know that the tradition of liberalism in this country demands that they carry on an appearance of righteous crusades. But as captives, "they can now carry on only those few token crusades that actually tend to strengthen the big city machines. It is a fact that they dare not attack in any way the evil forces that generate the power of these city machines of the North—least of all the profound and spreading evil of the corrupt machine itself."

Goldwater senses a public reaction to the raw power politics of the machines and says only the Republican Party, "providing a focus of principled energy for decent men and women of both parties," will break this cynical alliance.

The tendency to indulge in statistical speculation has become an indispensable part of the game of politics. Yet it obscures, necessarily, the acute issues which will confront the American electorate in 1964—issues of how best to meet the Communist challenge, of the proper role of government in the economy and in our daily lives. Shortly after the assassination, conservative columnist Frank S. Meyer asked whether the issue between liberalism and conservatism was any less or any more acute: "Is there any reason why Goldwater's principles of limited government, personal freedom, and firm resistance to Communism have a different significance than they had a few weeks ago, or why the American people should now be deprived of normal political debate and of the right to vote upon the issues, why they should be given again another of the meaningless choices of the past thirty years?"

Meyer reminded those who were anxious to write off Goldwater that he remained the only candidate with a powerful independent following, for himself and his principles; that he remained the overwhelming choice of the great majority of Republican professionals, politicians, workers; that his appeal to the American people as a whole is the singular appeal of a man as distinct from a field of Madison Avenue constructs and second-raters. Goldwater, in this view, remains the leader of the veterans of what *Fortune* described as a Thirty Years' War that began with the New Deal.

Liberals often attribute Goldwater's popularity to what they term his "simple views." "Goldwater, the Great Simplifier," wrote Emmet John Hughes. "It is as though a child were speaking on the problems of the times, with a child's directness and lack of complexity," wrote a Washington reporter of the *New York Times*. The charge has become virtually an article of faith with Goldwater enemies.

In part, this charge is an attempt to vindicate the many mistakes and misjudgments of the past, and the expected failures of the present, by making it appear as though they were and are too complex to be solved by anyone, especially conservatives. Goldwater counters by charging that the simplifiers are those who for three decades have counseled that all we need to insure peace and freedom is merely to vote appropriations for increased foreign aid, increased public works programs, more and larger unemployment doles, grander Alliances for Progress, and expanded trade and aid with the Soviet Union.

But the charge also represents an attempt to call Goldwater's intelligence into question.* As *Newsweek* columnist Raymond Moley noted, it is a "snooty appraisal based upon the rather

* An example of this approach occurred late last December when Goldwater, recuperating in Phoenix from his foot operation, fired off a telegram to the Secretary to Republican Senators, charging LBJ with trying to stampede Congress into voting for foreign aid. Furthermore, he described the underwriting of the wheat sales to Russia as "an action which flies directly in the face of all practical experience in dealing with Communists." Anyone who has ever received a telegram knows that words often become garbled in transmission. Yet when the AP reported the story, it quoted Goldwater thus: ". . . an action which flied [sic] directly in the face, etc. . . ." Goldwater, who had the original, grammatical draft to prove his correct usage, was left powerless to counter the obvious effect on the countless millions who read the AP story.

limited contribution to Goldwater's equipment provided by formal education and 'deep' reading. These critics are mostly sitting proudly upon an A.B. or sporting a Phi Beta Kappa Key. . . ." In fact, Moley said, "academic credentials are a minor qualification in grappling with public issues and national policies. The indispensable ingredients are a resourceful mind and an abundance of common sense."

William Buckley observed: "The more complicated and powerful the job, the more rudimentary the preparation for it. You cultivate virtues: High purpose, intelligence, decency, humility, fear of the Lord, and the passion for freedom. And these are qualities Barry Goldwater appears to have. . . ."

Shortly before the assassination Russell Kirk also analyzed Goldwater, saying: "Intellectually considered, Mr. Goldwater is more farsighted than Mr. Kennedy; more quick-witted than Mr. Rockefeller; more self-reliant than Mr. Stevenson; more reflective than Mr. Eisenhower. He is not Disraeli (despite a similar flair), nor is he John Adams (notwithstanding a certain similar hardheadedness). He is no master of theoretical politics, and no glowing rhetorician. Yet he possesses, in his easygoing way, what Kent discerned in Lear: authority. His words carry conviction, because men perceive that they come from a sound head." No politician of our time is less of a rabid ideologue than Barry Goldwater, says Kirk.

It is true that Goldwater is not an intellectual. Nor is he a scholar, in the limited sense of that word. The chances are that he knows little about the Theory of the Multiplier or the Consumption Function. The Arizonan was well aware of his own limitations when he confessed, "I'm not even sure that I've got the brains to be President of the United States"—a candid and self-effacing assessment that moved the liberal *Chicago Daily News* to comment: "There is something almost Lincolnesque in this modest outburst. We would be far more gravely concerned about the abilities of a man who was positive he had what it takes."

As Goldwater's detractors well understand, voters holding for a specific approach to matters of government policy support those candidates whose promises and previous conduct indicate they will come closest to adopting that approach. And there can be no doubt but what Goldwater, if elected, will work to implement the conservative approach—at least the *political* policy of conservatism, which is committed to rolling back omnipotent government. (As Frank S. Meyer has noted, the political problem is only one of many facing conservatives. The conservative movement looks towards nothing less than a deepgoing renewal of American life in the spirit of the Western and American tradition—a renewal at every level of existence: social, intellectual, philosophical, as well as political. Its ends cannot be attained by a political victory alone, Meyer warns, important though such a victory is.)

Like many adults who lack formal education, Goldwater has a great respect for education. And—although critics who have devoted the better part of a lifetime to denegating the conservative position would disagree—his political and economic beliefs are also held by *bona fide* scholars—men of intellectual excellence who, though they be in the minority on the nation's college campuses, are nonetheless scholars. Goldwater has successfully enlisted many of these men as advisors, to aid in drafting position papers on important topics. They include:

The University of Chicago's Milton Friedman (Money and General Economic Policy); Notre Dame's Gerhart Neimeyer (Communism); Harvard's Gottfried Haberler (Fiscal Policy); University of Virginia's Warren Nutter (Soviet Economy); Stanford's Stefan Possony (National Strategy); NYU's William Peterson (Agriculture); Harvard's Edward H. Chamberlain (Labor); Yale Law School's Robert H. Bork (Antitrust and Civil Rights); Notre Dame's Stanley Parry (Political Theory); the University of Pennsylvania's Robert Strausz-Hupé (Foreign Policy); Stanford's Karl Brandt (Economic and Farm Policy); Claremont's William Stokes (Latin America); and Virgil Salera of California State College at Hayward (International Trade).

Even before these men began preparing position papers for Goldwater, the charge was raised by critics that Goldwater had modified his views. He has "begun his Great Mutation," said the *New Republic*: "It is as much a part of Nature's wonderful plan for politicians to absorb their worn out opinions as it is for tadpoles to absorb their tail."* And so it is.

Goldwater's Great Mutation amounted solely to changing his mind on the question of applying anti-trust laws to unions, and on the question of the federal government's right to force school integration. Neither of these is an example of tergiversation; rather, both represent genuine changes based on the advice of scholars who share Goldwater's philosophical beliefs, and who are unconcerned with pandering to the voters or the opinion influencers.

Goldwater realizes that changing one's mind is cited as proof of wisdom and broadmindedness in a philosophical ally, while in an ideological foe it is considered a sure sign of rank opportunism. But he disdains talk that he will ever alter or retreat from a condition merely for political reasons.

Where Goldwater did change his mind for strictly political reasons was his decision to file for re-election to the Senate while simultaneously seeking the presidential nomination. When a reporter asked whether he hadn't criticized Lyndon

* The magazine quotes the *Wall Street Journal* as saying that Goldwater today "wouldn't call Chief Justice Warren a 'Socialist,' as he did in Jackson, Miss., in 1959. . . ." Goldwater denies ever having done so. "What happened," he explained, "was that when I learned that Ike had appointed Warren to the bench I opposed it because of what I characterized as his socialist thinking on some issues. I told Eisenhower of my objection. A year or two later I was asked at a press conference in Jackson if I still thought Earl Warren was a socialist, and I again stated that I thought he entertained socialist beliefs on some issues. I didn't then and don't now consider Warren a socialist. But he does take an egalitarian position most of the time."

Johnson for virtually the same thing, when the Texan in 1960 ran for both the Vice-Presidency and Senate, Goldwater quipped, "When the teacher is running, I'd rather be a good student." Later he explained that he would not have filed for the Senate had he been running against President Kennedy. But now, he said, it seemed unlikely that Johnson could criticize him for insuring himself with "policare"—the care of politicians who are too young to quit politics and too old to return to work. It should be noted, however, that Arizona election laws have at no time forbidden politicians to file for or seek dual offices. This differs from Lyndon Johnson's situation in that the Texas Legislature, in April 1959, passed a special bill permitting LBJ to run for both offices.

National Review noted that the obsessive anxiety on the part of liberals ("who truly hope and believe that Senator Goldwater will move over in the direction they have arbitrarily hallowed as 'moderate'") to make it appear as though Goldwater is shifting his position, arises from the fear of contemplating a nation presided over by the author of *The Conscience of a Conservative*. And it arises from those deeply opposed to Goldwater who are "anxious to portray him as an opportunist, as a hypocrite who will gladly relinquish the principles that brought him to public attention [on] his way to the White House."

In reply, Goldwater merely points to his record: he alone voted against the supposed labor reform bill . . . he criticized TVA at a time when he knew his criticism would hurt him politically . . . true to his conservative principles, he criticized President Eisenhower despite Ike's popularity in Arizona and across the U.S. . . . and he voted against the test-ban treaty even though he had been told that to do so was to commit political suicide.

While there are those who believe that the granting of the presidential nomination to Barry Goldwater would defy all the rules of politics, and cause a wholesale alteration in the Political Handbook, Goldwater strategists point out that such was the practical result of the FDR campaign in 1932, which wedded the city machines to the Democratic South. As Arthur Krock noted shortly after Goldwater announced his decision to seek the presidential nomination, the Arizonan's candidacy offers voters the first clear choice between political philosophies since 1936. Thus, a new coalition of voters is obviously in the cards.

Goldwater believes that liberals, well-intentioned though they may be, have ignored Justice Brandeis' dictum, "Experience should teach us to be most on our guard to protect liberty when the government's purposes are beneficent. Men born to freedom are naturally alert to repel invasion of their liberty by evil-minded rulers. The greatest dangers to liberty lurk in insidious encroachment by men of zeal, well meaning but without understanding."

"Conservatives know that the future is perilous," Goldwater admits. "But we also know that we are the only ones resolute enough to face that peril with even a chance of succeeding. We don't want to repeal history—we merely want to keep from repeating it!"

Index